The Last Pastor

The Last Pastor

Faithfully Steering a Closing Church

Gail Cafferata

WESTMINSTER
JOHN KNOX PRESS
LOUISVILLE • KENTUCKY

© 2020 Gail Cafferata

First edition
Published by Westminster John Knox Press
Louisville, Kentucky

20 21 22 23 24 25 26 27 28 29—10 9 8 7 6 5 4 3 2 1

Scripture quotations are from the New Revised Standard Version of the Bible, copyright © 1989 by the Division of Christian Education of the National Council of the Churches of Christ in the U.S.A., and are used by permission.

Book design by Drew Stevens
Cover design by Barbara LeVan Fisher,
www.levanfisherdesign.com

Library of Congress Cataloging-in-Publication Data

Names: Cafferata, Gail, author.
Title: The last pastor : faithfully steering a closing church / Gail
  Cafferata.
Description: First edition. | Louisville, Kentucky : WJK, Westminster John
  Knox Press, 2020. | Includes bibliographical references. | Summary:
  "Gail Cafferata was heartbroken when the church she pastored voted to
  close its doors. It may have been the right decision, but it led to a
  million questions in her mind about her call, leadership, and future.
  She began to think that other pastors who close churches perhaps go
  through this same experience. This led her to obtain a grant from the
  Louisville Institute to conduct a sociological study of over 130 pastors
  in five historically established denominations (Episcopal, Lutheran,
  United Methodist, Presbyterian, and United Church of Christ) who were
  called to serve churches that closed. This book tells the results of
  that study, which consisted of many interviews, and the hard-won lessons
  learned by these courageous pastors"— Provided by publisher.
Identifiers: LCCN 2019041278 (print) | LCCN 2019041279 (ebook) | ISBN
  9780664264987 (paperback) | ISBN 9781611649758 (ebook)
Subjects: LCSH: Church closures. | Pastoral theology. |
  Clergy—Appointment, call, and election. | Vocation, Ecclesiastical.
Classification: LCC BV652.9 .C34 2020 (print) | LCC BV652.9 (ebook) | DDC
  254—dc23
LC record available at https://lccn.loc.gov/2019041278
LC ebook record available at https://lccn.loc.gov/2019041279

Most Westminster John Knox Press books are available at special quantity discounts when purchased in bulk by corporations, organizations, and special-interest groups. For more information, please e-mail SpecialSales@wjkbooks.com.

Contents

Introduction

Closing a church was my worst nightmare. I fought it with all my being. We hoped we might survive as a congregation, yet our church died. Through the process, we struggled with many forms of grief—anger, sadness, confusion. Darkness hovered, like Good Friday or Holy Saturday. Afterward, I wondered how other pastors and congregations who experienced the closing of a church felt and, particularly, how it affected pastors who, like me, had accepted their call with starry-eyed hopes for renewal.[1]

This book is informed by my experience as an Episcopal priest and, prior to that, as a sociologist. My theological perspective is Trinitarian with a focus on the ways God calls the church to make God's compassion and truth incarnate in the church and world. Here, I report the results of a sociological study of over 130 pastors in five historically established denominations who were called to serve churches that closed. I draw on their completion of written surveys and semi-structured, in-depth interviews.[2] I contacted clergy first by letter and found most of them eager to share their stories, even though it meant revisiting what was surely a painful time. Many (42 percent of those invited) completed the written questionnaire, and of these, most participated in semi-structured in-depth interviews. The rich stories that over eighty pastors shared were a great gift, which is why I chose to quote them liberally in the pages that follow. To maintain confidentiality, I have changed some identifying details, and I tell no one story completely, but much of what I share here is in the pastors' own words.[3]

This book evolved with prayer and guidance from the pastors who dared to answer my invitation, "Tell me the story of how your church closed." Some of what I learned might seem surprising. One pastor told me he would do it again "in a heartbeat," and another spoke about how his faith had grown as a result of the experience:

> I would close another church in a heartbeat if that's what I felt God was calling them to do. I once met an elderly pastor, long retired,

and asked him, "So how was your ministry?" He replied, "Well, if you count closing five churches as a good thing, I had a good run." I think God does at times move on to other things.

I can bring with it the assurance that we serve a God who's a God of the living and use that imagery from Scripture to remind congregants that it is all about resurrection. We are an Easter people, and so death is part of life. And it is not the end of life. And we go on.

All the pastors I interviewed were changed by the pilgrimage journey to and through closure.[4] Many moved smoothly into new churches. Some have scars. A few were grief-stricken longer than they had hoped to be. Others retired or left congregational ministry for another vocation. Yet nearly all shared wondrous stories of God's compassion and presence in the midst of grief, and of hope and joy in new lives and ministries at journey's end. Many have not only survived but thrived.

As practical theology, this study explores pastoral leadership, suffering, and healing.[5] It is organized around the theme of God's love for the church, and that of the sacred, yet flawed, human relationships between pastors, congregations, and judicatories. It explores how pastors accessed faith and leadership skills to lead their congregations. It also describes how the journey affected pastors' lives and identities while they served and after the church doors closed. It concludes with the reflections and recommendations of these pastors, whose voices of wisdom and hope cry out to be heard.

Although the literature on pastoral leadership is rich with metaphors like "servant leader," "potter," "pastoral director," "shepherd," "spiritual interpreter," "artist," "gardener," "administrator," and more, one practical theologian explicates a biblical model of leadership from Paul's First Letter to the Corinthians: it is called *kybernesis* (1 Cor. 12:28), the Greek root evoking the use of a tiller to steer a ship.[6] Although leadership in a church requires the collective effort of all of God's people, the pastor is called by God to hold the tiller of the ship.

Holding the tiller involves engaging in actions that embody the Christian values of justice, righteousness, and reconciliation. In closing a church, pastoral leadership becomes centered in resurrection faith, awareness of the pastor's own pilgrim journey with the congregation, and an understanding that a church is not a building but a sacred community of God's people journeying together. Minding the tiller means bearing hope when the journey seems hopeless.

Indeed, sailing as a metaphor for a church moving toward the mission of closure is a useful hermeneutic, or interpretive tool. The gifts of all the baptized are needed to keep the ship working and safe on its journey. When the congregation confronts strong winds or crosscurrents, the company of the faithful moves their ship ahead by loving God and one another. They gather in prayer and community to discern God's call, what route to take, and how to organize themselves and care for one another. On this journey in response to God's call, the denomination and its midlevel administrative representative, the judicatory, are in the background, like the coast guard, to clarify values, norms, and roles and to intervene when a church calls out in distress.[7]

For some sailboat enthusiasts—like me—racing adds another exciting dimension to the sport. Racing a sailboat is all about discernment. Choices begin at the start line and don't end until you cross the finish. Although some decisions leave you behind the pack for the duration, others are life-giving, moving you steadily ahead of the field. It's often a gamble. When a group of us raced recently on San Francisco Bay, the choice was whether to sail to port, far into the fierce, steady wind blowing through the Golden Gate, or to starboard, into an unpredictable wind closer to the mark, and about half the distance of the other option. As the fog rolled in, we thought maybe we'd pick up a header or two to lift our sails on the short course. The crew was divided. I argued for the shorter course. It cost us the race. I should have known better. It's always about the wind. That's all that matters.

As in a sailboat, the wind of the Holy Spirit lifts the sails of a congregation and propels it forward. Wind fills our faces with hope and expectations for a good future. When the wind shifts, a good skipper follows it. The best way isn't always the shortest. There is no easy way. It's all about discernment—choices—throughout the life of a congregation. Sometimes they are the most difficult choices we could ever make. To ask, "What is God calling us to do?" or "What kind of people is God calling us to be?" is to make a brave choice. It is to let go of preconceived assumptions about our destination and to invite God into the conversation.

What does it mean for a congregation and their pastor to follow the wind? It means to be and become a sacred community intentionally seeking God's guidance, God's call. What made closing our church so difficult was that I wouldn't let go—we wouldn't let go—of our vision to relocate to another church building. Like many mainline churches, we took the short course with unpredictable winds, hoping against hope there would be a header to save us.

When we took the shorter course in that San Francisco race, we didn't have enough wind to overcome the swift tidal flood entering the bay. Sailboats that had chosen to reach into fierce winds could do so. With 25-knot winds in their sails, they overcame the longer distance to beat us to the mark. Likewise, the church and I mistook the course of relocating to another building for being faithful to God. We missed the mark. God's "mark" isn't the survival of a congregation. It's being and becoming more and more the people God is creating us to be, even if that means leaving the ship that carried us with peace, joy, and hope for so long and so far.

By the grace of God, Christian faith yields a harvest of healthy grieving: the recognition that loss, while painful, is also transitory; that God is present in the darkness; that resurrection is happening and will continue to happen; and that we are blessed with a community of sojourners to share our burdens. It means that no pastor has to go through this alone. If it is a slow, slow death, it may seem that grief will never end. Yet faithful pastors who served their congregations to the end have experienced grace and hope and light splitting through their darkness. This book tells their stories in hopes of offering insight to others who may face similar sailing conditions someday and need encouragement as they mind the tiller.

PART I

*The Pastor, the Sacred Community,
and the Judicatory*

1

The Pastor

Minding the Tiller

From my journal, four years before our church closed:

> Precious Lord, I am incomplete without you. I am like my boat
> without a wind direction indicator. The wind was there, but I didn't
> perceive it. Where is the wind to carry Holy Family Church for-
> ward? I feel that I'm not perceiving it. I have to look around and see
> and feel where the wind is coming from. Help! I feel like our boat is
> stalled. I feel stupid. Help us, Lord. Amen.

As a pastor, you're at the start line of a race on a glorious sunny
day. You hear the sound of the mainsail flapping and fluttering overhead, but the boat doesn't leap forward. The wind blows from bow to
stern, and your hat would fly off if it weren't tied under your chin. Yet
you remain still: the boat doesn't move; it may even drift backward.
The first leg of a sailboat race is straight into the wind, but a sailboat
can't fight that force—if you try, the wind whips past the sail on both
sides, teasing you but not filling the sail with the power that would lift
your boat like wings and launch you on the journey. You are stuck "in
irons," to use a term from the days of square rigging when leg irons
secured prisoners to the deck.

The day I wrote the journal entry above, I felt like our church was
in irons. The wind of the Holy Spirit was blowing, but somehow we
couldn't catch it. Even so, much was going well. Our leadership team's

annual mutual ministry review affirmed our congregation's increasing engagement with the community: a growing food bank we had cofounded, a consortium of community gardens we had newly joined, and a winter overnight shelter program for families. We shared our majority Anglo congregation's worship space with Latino and Antiochian Orthodox congregations and multiple 12-step groups. And our community garden, "The Neighborhood Farm," would be a reality in the spring.

However, during that summer, our leadership team had weathered a painful interpersonal conflict ending in several people leaving the church. Our expenses had exceeded our income, which would soon diminish further when one of our sister congregations moved away; in the new year, subsidized congregations like ours would be fully responsible for the payment of clergy health insurance. We were vital in mission but weakening in our capacity to sustain our ministry.

I had faith that God would lead us forward—if only we found the wind to empower us. If it weren't money, which we always hoped for, it would be the movement of the Holy Spirit in our hearts that would open us to a new life. I longed for the fulfillment of the Celtic hope "May the wind be always at your back," yet the church doesn't often sail with that blessing. More often, we must search for the wind in trees upon the shore or feel it on our cheeks as it dances around us. Once we recognize it, we must harness that wind and move the tiller to embrace its freshening power, the surge of new life in Christ. We have to pray, study, worship, and open our hearts and minds to the new thing God calls us to do and to be, even if that means ending ministries and dissolving the church.

Nonetheless, I couldn't imagine abandoning our pilgrimage and closing the church. No one could. Just one year before our church went onto the real estate market, our senior lay leader wrote, "If you looked at last year's annual report like I did, you would have seen the amazing rebirth [that] happened at Holy Family." The lay leader responsible for property wrote, "This has been a very productive year for Holy Family Church." He noted the painting of the church, a new sound system, and landscape improvements including a new church sign. Hope for the future of our congregation dwelled deep in my heart as well. I had faith in the unseen spiritual gift that steadies the ship of the church and transforms the power of the wind into forward movement.

However, something I said a year earlier at the annual meeting presaged our church's failing roof: "Yes, the skylight still leaks, but what is that in the midst of such blessings!" Just two years later, the dissolution of the church felt precipitous and devastating, like St. Paul's ship crashing on the rocks. Leading a church in the best of circumstances, let alone in crisis, requires a strong and sturdy faith, imagined here as the ship's rudder. When the Holy Spirit blows into the sails, the rudder transforms its energy into forward motion. The tiller controls the movement of the rudder, especially when the winds are not at our back but flowing across the ship and threatening to push the church sideways. With the guidance of the rudder, the power of the Holy Spirit pulls and lifts the church forward on its journey—even a journey to closure.

Reflecting on surveys and interviews with pastors in five historically established Protestant denominations who have had the experience of closing their churches, this chapter describes the faith of the pastor, the ship's skipper, as the church journeys toward closure. I sought to understand the aspects of faith that strengthen pastors' rudders so they will hold their congregation's course steady on its passage in the presence of unexpected storms, hidden currents, or tidal waves. These pastors differ from one another in many ways—age, gender, years of experience, vocational and avocational backgrounds, urban/rural living, census region, and especially denomination. Unfortunately, people of color were less likely to respond to the survey than whites.

In the narratives of over eighty pastors who were interviewed, I identified three essential commitments to God's hidden spiritual reality. What strengthens pastors for ministry wherever they serve is, first, their call to preach the gospel of hope in the resurrection; second, God's call to each congregation and pastor to journey with God into a new future; and third, the belief that the church is the people of God serving the world in Christ's name. I found that pastors called to serve a fragile church employed these three elements of faith to help guide their sacred community safely through grief and the letting-go process that allows church members to begin their journey to a new future. One pastor said, "The good news of Christ is not going to be an easy thing to bring. Belief can be upsetting, but without it, nothing really matters."

First, pastors receive the call from God to proclaim the good news of Jesus Christ, with the sacrament (or rite) of ordination setting them apart for a ministry of leadership. When ordained clergy and members of

Characteristics of the Clergy Sample ($N = 132$)

Demographic	Distribution* (%)
Gender	
Male	60
Female	40
Age (M = 59 years)	
< 45 years	12
45–64 years	62
65+ years	26
Denomination	
Lutheran (ELCA)	14
Presbyterian (PC(USA))	13
Episcopal (TEC)	30
United Church of Christ (UCC)	12
Methodist (UMC)	30
Race/ethnicity	
White	91
Nonwhite	9
Ordained experience (M = 14 years)	
0 to 5 years	30
6 to 10 years	18
11+ years	52
Multipoint charge (yes)	44
Bivocational (yes)	31
Years serving congregation (M = 6 years)	
1 to 3 years	41
4 to 6 years	22
7+ years	37
Location of church (2010 census categories)	
Rural area	28
Small town or city (pop. 2,500 to 50,000)	30
Urbanized area (pop. 50,000 or more)	42

Some totals may not reach 100% because of rounding error.

a church hover in prayer over someone in a service of ordination, the Holy Spirit transforms that baptized person into a servant committed to and gifted for serving God's people as their pastor, spiritual leader, and teacher.

God's call is often mysterious, unexpected, and gripping, blessing pastors with charisms such as spiritual wisdom, faith in the resurrection and hope for new life, and the gift of faithfulness or perseverance. One pastor, a guest preacher in a congregation, observed about his first service with them, "As I was distributing Communion to people, I just felt this really tremendous sense of being drawn towards the people and felt like 'Oh my God, I feel called to serve this church.'" He applied that day and was chosen. "I was the only candidate that they didn't know. The congregation knew the other two candidates, yet something in them wanted to choose the unknown. The Spirit was always present in them and in me." Another pastor noted his surprise: "When I interviewed, it felt like it was a calling." A different pastor noted how difficult it was to find a position when one is older than fifty, but was determined that "where God wanted me, I was going to go."

A call to lead blesses a pastor's faith and natural gifts and recognizes that "God doesn't call the equipped; God equips the called," as one pastor put it. One's gifts may include spiritual wisdom such as "seeing other people's gifts, enabling them to do ministry in ways that are good for the kingdom of God."

God bestows spiritual gifts on called pastors inexplicably, as needed. For example, one minister had tried multiple strategies to renew the church. When she thought the end was near, the church resisted and wanted to keep on working. She went home from a leadership team meeting in tears. "The whole weight of trying to save this church for three years just poured out of me," she said. She then had a dream that she was preaching:

> My co-pastor in the dream, a black man, tapped me on the shoulder and said, "You need to go sit down." He was right, so I went to the front of the church and knelt down. He came over, put his hands on me, and prayed over me. I started to cry. He said, "When this pastor kneels, cries, and prays, the Holy Spirit will come to this church." And I turned around, and in my sanctuary, there were a diversity of people: black, white, brown, young, old, [from] all over the world, and the Holy Spirit was there. And I woke up from this dream and thought, "OK, I've been visited. What is this?" I told the

congregation this dream, and they thought I was crazy. [But three months later] I got a knock on the door of the church. An African pastor from down the road needed a place for his refugee church. He was Kenyan. The church had been Sudanese. They didn't speak the same language, so they started meetings in English. Buffalo is one of the places where refugees are resettled; this particular set of apartment buildings is like the United Nations. He was passing out flyers saying, "Come learn about Jesus. Come learn English. We're starting this refugee church of people from all over the world."

The refugee church came to the historic congregation for a while before moving on; the older, dying congregation eventually dissolved. The pastor's spiritual discernment and faithfulness blessed her congregation as they offered hospitality to another congregation and then closed with dignity.

Besides prophetic visions such as this, God blesses called pastors with other spiritual assets. As the above story reveals, a call to a church on the precipice of a transformation or death can be difficult and frightening. It may mean a pastor's exhaustion from powerful emotions of loss, being seen by colleagues or by oneself as a failure, or anticipating a hard time finding another position. Nonetheless, by the grace of God, pastors called to this challenging ministry may find their rudders full of hope in resurrection. This allows pastors to let go of what cannot be changed, to believe that their call commands faithfulness, and to trust their congregation's own call and spiritual gifts.

For one pastor, a call to serve a fragile church meant having faith that "God was my strong rock, in a Psalms kind of way." He continued: "I realized that this is not my fight. It's not my decision. It's like any other death in a way. We can die with hope, or we can die in bitterness, but we all have to die." For him, every liturgy is

like a resurrection occurrence of the Lord. This is where hope is. Hope can be found here. If the organization falls apart, the hope doesn't go away. The hope is still there because the true God who loves us remains. God was my hope and my present foundation while going through the emotional upheaval. God helped me sort out what is my stuff as a human being, what is my stuff as a priest— as opposed to what is my call and what God is calling me to do. It helped me, that faith, that certainty, as in the resurrection itself. Good Friday looks like a disaster, and Holy Saturday is not much better, but who knew what God had in store?

A pastor's call to serve a weakened church may be blessed with the freedom to let go of what he or she cannot change. For example, church founders may have made overwhelming sacrifices in building new congregations, yet God asks even their called pastors to let their churches die.

"When do you know when to quit?" one pastor pondered. Yet he had "God moments" that helped him with his decision. After an out-of-town funeral, the judicatory executive and a retired pastor who was "kind of like the godfather of our judicatory" invited the young pastor out to lunch. Having had experience with church starts, the retiree "just talked about the time when he wanted to go, and then he decided it was time. It just gave me permission in my own mind. It's hard to do that." The pastor valued having "my judicatory executive there. It was kind of another God moment, a great liberating thing that helped me to say, 'OK, I can let go of this.'"

God often blesses pastors serving in struggling congregations with the certitude of resurrection with its blessings of resilience and perseverance. Despite the red ink in our church budget, I believed God had called me to be faithful in my ministry—to keep preaching, teaching, working with the community, and caring for those in need. I would not let fear or despair chase me away. A British study of clergy speaks of "sacrificial" faithfulness.[1] In this study, one pastor who had decided not to leave his congregation until the death said, "I'm not here for my own success." Another said, "I would say you just do what you're called to do and work faithfully and work hard, and so when you walk away, you can hold your head up and say 'I did my best; I did what God called me to do.'"

Faithful is a word used often by pastors who close their churches. "If I'm going to get nailed to that cross," said one, "I'm going to get nailed to the cross because I figured someone else has been down this path; this is nothing compared to what he did. I had to be faithful to Christ [even when it was clear that the church would not be faithful]. The ministry and the leadership I was trying to provide them could not happen."

To commit to perseverance in a call to ministry means for one pastor "I'm doing what God wants me to be doing. This isn't an occupation. This is a call. If I didn't have a strong sense of call, then a lot of things would be a lot more difficult—like, why am I not getting as rich as fraternity brothers that were goof-offs and, you know, now are retired and living in Hawaii [laughing]?" The pastor continued: "I'm called to ministry. This is where I should be, I'm doing what I'm supposed to be doing, and I've got all kinds of satisfactions they'll never know . . . like the discipline of understanding that this is where God wants me." Another pastor concluded, "I also recognize that my call was very real. And I hear God when I'm thinking in that direction. God just says, 'No.'"

In the midst of the "little deaths" that accompany closing a church, God blesses the called with affirmation of their identity. For one pastor, her first appointment in a church "was a big affirmation." For another pastor, his first church appointment "meant finally doing what God called me to do." A pastor battling cancer felt strengthened by God to continue to serve despite illness: "He was with me all the way. I never questioned his love for me or his concern." Her cancer journey went from Ash Wednesday through her last surgery on Good Friday: "That was my Lenten journey; that was my wandering in the wilderness and being on holy ground with God. My strength and my faith didn't question it at that point." God blessed her with grace to heal and a loving congregation, which confirmed her continuing call to serve.

Even when the church dies, a pastor's call persists: "Our call to ministry is bigger than the congregation that we serve. Likewise, the congregation that we serve is bigger than us. At times, I have to remind myself of this." That thought helps pastors sustain hope for the church and for themselves: "I remind myself that the ministry will continue after I leave, as it did for ninety years before I got here. My ministry will continue too, regarding what God has called me to do, my divine call beyond the congregational call."

Besides this commitment to discerning and living out their own call to ministry, *a second spiritual commitment that empowers pastors in closing churches is that God calls congregations and their pastors to share a journey or pilgrimage with Jesus Christ.* "I am about the complete engagement and renewal of the people in the church so they can sense what God has called them to continue to do in the life of the church," said one pastor. In a parish that was discerning what to do, another pastor recalled, "I just try to embody that gospel of hopefulness and promise, and that we're called to be faithful, not necessarily successful. They claimed that, and they were OK with that. And sometimes that means you have to allow some things to die—yourself and [the church]. That's the gospel." While teaching, the pastor would "recall Scripture stories of Jesus, of Moses, Jacob, Esther, Deborah—all the heartache and the battles and how they kept on going because they knew that this was God's call to do that." She encouraged her dying church to "stand strong and take whatever comes at you and make sure you get somewhere where you can really get angry and get healing."

A pastor may inspire a congregation to sacrificial faithfulness as well: "Keeping our eye on the right thing. It's not money. It's not that. It's about how do you conduct ministry as you're dying or when you die." This pastor noted, "I think that it's important to tell anybody not to give up, because it's easy at this point just to say, 'I'm done.' I think I never said, 'I'm done.' Even the day after I turned the key in." He added, "Ministry doesn't stop." God's call to witness to a gospel of resurrection hope is a reason pastors can bear the burden of grief, engage their congregations on a pilgrimage to discern a future, and eventually sacrifice their building and their life together for a higher purpose.

One grace of a call is to trust that God will be present in the chaos of the journey no matter where it ends. Let me explain with a personal story: Before I was a pastor, I was a professor of sociology. The university where I worked had offered my husband an appointment too, but it never materialized. What's more, it was unclear whether I would be granted tenure. My anxiety grew. With our finances, the capacity to remain in our home, and an academic career now all uncertain, I sought the guidance of my priest. He invited me to join a women's retreat focused on the spiritual journey that was scheduled to take place at a nearby Trappist monastery. Until then, my faith in God was in my head but not my heart. Through prayers with the monks, Bible study, and being in community with women like myself, I suddenly grasped God's presence with me, as with "the birds of the air; they neither sow nor reap nor gather into barns, and yet your heavenly Father feeds them. Are you not of more value than they?" (Matt. 6:26).

Now spiritually well fed, I came away from the retreat with hope that God would be with my husband and me even if I did not receive tenure. My priest had understood my need to trust God no matter where I was called. When I didn't get tenure soon after, I believed God would provide for us, and God did. Just as my last year at the university ended, I was called to serve as a sociologist at the National Center for Health Services in Washington, D.C. My husband joined an industry where he is still employed. Our family grew as I enjoyed my new colleagues and our work to understand American health care. And it was there I first felt called to the priesthood—though the bishop gently told me, "Not yet." I did become a priest sixteen years later, but even now, I must keep learning this lesson: trust God no matter what.

So it is with diminishing churches. Pastors called to this challenging ministry know it will be a journey on which, as with the birds of the air, God is always present. Yet many anxious and grieving people in a declining congregation can't imagine leaving their church home, or that God has a need for them elsewhere, or that by God's grace, a new faith community will welcome and love them. So with a pastor's call to serve as a leader comes this other needed gift—to teach or remind congregations that God is with them wherever they go.

One pastor observed, "The clergy really operate out of a theology of journey. Abraham journeyed from one place to another. The laity operate more out of a theology of place." The pastor continued, "That's why the promised land for the Israelites was so important. [People] attach themselves to these things a lot more. The people that you're ministering to are not focused on this journey; they're focused on place. They go through a much deeper sorrow when the church closes."

A theology of place comes from experiencing the transcendent God within a church building.[2] In one congregation, named St. Andrew's, when a youth in the church died tragically, "the first place that members needed to go was St. Andrew's," reported the former pastor. "When they got that call, and they got that news, where they went was the church." In the building, people experience God holding them and their pain in love. Although "the church is the people, that sacred space is where the Word is proclaimed, where the sacraments are administered, where a word of hope has been preached. In our difficult times, there's something about being in that space [where] we can still find hope."

One pastor invoked Isaiah to call his congregation to trust God on their journey into a new future: "Isaiah is trying to help the people understand that God isn't just the God of Palestine. God can also work with them while they're in exile, there in Babylon as well, so God doesn't have boundaries." Jesus was not "a settled person," said another. "His ministry was not a settled ministry. It didn't exist within four walls, set on a place. [His] ministry was in motion. We're not called as Christians to settle in. We're called on a journey. Our journey included one another for a while. Now it includes other people in other ways."

Pastors called to the tiller continually encourage church members to participate in their church's spiritual journey. One diminishing congregation in a cathedral-sized building on the brink of death "still [had] this image of a 1,600-member congregation in their heads" when their pastor led them on a pilgrimage through weekly Bible study on seasonal readings. "Easter, Lent, and the resurrection story were critical," the pastor said. The pastor then asked the congregation to reflect on "what resurrection means and what it means to us, what it means to me and our baptism." When they realized that the new congregation assuming their building would be African American, the pastor recalled, "We had a manger with a black baby Jesus. It was a Christmas. It was a birthing of a new congregation within that building. The gospel was critical throughout."

A third spiritual commitment or gift that pastors may draw out from their rudder is what it means to be church in the world. A pastor and a congregation are called by God to journey together for a reason—to serve the world in Christ's name. For example, God called members of my church and me to join a group of clergy and community organizers intent on identifying the specific needs of our city. Out of that collaboration grew NOAH (Neighbors Organized against Hunger) Food Pantry, which our congregation served faithfully for over six years. For eight to twelve weeks a year, they attended to the needs of over two hundred families and worked with its board of directors to plan a sustainable future. As they embraced and celebrated this servant ministry, I joined them in being church.

Among those called to proclaim what it means to be a church was a pastor who reflected, "When I would preach and then do the benediction, I would encourage [the congregation] to let the light of Christ shine through them into the world and into the community." He added, "I really want to be the pastor of a church that listens to their call in the ministry, and I want to help them do that." Another said, "I'm always on the lookout; I'm always looking for God at work in people's lives and how we could use that in building the kingdom." By grace and faith, a congregation coming together to build the kingdom, with or without a building, is blessed with a resurrection hope even as they face the challenges of closure.

A pastor's gift for teaching that the church is the people of God on Christ's mission is salient within a congregation's process of discernment for its future. For example, one town had three churches of the same denomination within a three-mile radius. The dwindling congregations agreed to hold only one service each Sunday, rotating among the three. The people liked the increased attendance at any given worship service, as well as the greater sense of fellowship. Yet after three months, recalled the pastor, "what broke down in negotiations is, everybody wanted it to be their church that would house this new reality, and nobody was willing to give up their building." The pastor concluded, "They loved the building more than the idea of being a productive, mission-minded church. The building was almost like an idol. People were literally worshiping their building."

When another church decided to close, the pastor said to those who opposed the decision, "You see the church in this building. You have grown up coming to this place to find God. I have been to lots of churches. For me, church is the gathered body of people." The pastor named a difficult truth: "Unless we come to the point where we agree on the definition of what church is, we won't agree on the right answer for the church." The church, the pastor knows from his call from God, is the body of Christ.

Some ministers called to a diminishing congregation may perceive in its spiritual community an inward-looking "family gathering" without commitment to serve the world in Christ's name. For example, one pastor determined he was serving what he called a "family chapel": "It wasn't a congregation. It wasn't a group of people striving to meet the purpose and mission of what Christ calls us to do as a church. If it's not a church, then really there's no purpose in calling it a church." He added, "That sounds more negative than I mean it." It wasn't their fault, but the rural community was simply disappearing, and no one lived near the church anymore. During the week, there was no local connection, no local outreach. The pastor felt called to help them see what they had become.

One pastor, seeing the church as the hands and feet of Christ in the world, taught what it meant to love your neighbor as yourself. When his parishioners participated in a community food pantry, he encouraged them to "engage the people, sit down and talk to them. Find out their story." He also encouraged them to "find a child who can serve as an interpreter to help you to understand the Hispanic person who's immigrated here." But that did not happen. "They would not step out of their comfort zone and do that. They would hand [out] the food [and say,] 'Thank you for coming,' but the relationship piece was not there." He tried to teach what it means to be a "church," but "they wouldn't do it."

Having a gospel understanding of church is a pastor's spiritual gift, but when pastors take a mirror and invite their congregations to look at their ministry through this lens, the congregation may feel defensive, as if being judged. When one pastor remarked that "the church has a different purpose and mission" than the Rotary Club, she had to explain herself: "[I had to] assure them I wasn't trying to change them, and I wasn't trying to change anything. I was just trying to reflect and be what we're called to be." Another lamented that teaching the gospel meaning of *church* may be "difficult to do because of your judging what they have. [It's like saying,] 'Your church isn't enough.' But it wasn't," she said. "If you're reading Jesus in the New Testament, it really doesn't look a lot like us sitting around loving each other inside a building. It looks a lot more like us getting out into the streets and bringing transformation to what we find there. If we're not doing that, what are we doing? I think that's part of the gospel too, just that challenge of, 'Does our church look anything like the New Testament?'"

By the grace of God, I finally found these words to preach before our church closed:

> The church is not a building, but God's people gathered with a common purpose of reconciling humanity to God and us to one another. "Love the Lord your God with all your heart, and with all your soul, and with all your mind, and with all your strength. Love your neighbor as yourself" (Mark 12:30–31). This is how Jesus put it. Those are his commandments, and they are [for us] too.

CHAPTER SUMMARY

This chapter has illustrated how pastors describe three spiritual gifts with which God blessed them: (1) a commitment to their call to pastoral leadership, with charisms of spiritual wisdom—resurrection hope and faithfulness; (2) a commitment to recognize God's call of the baptized to their own spiritual journey or pilgrimage; and (3) a commitment to be the church as the people of God on a mission in Christ's name. These three commitments provide a sturdy rudder to guide the spiritual lives of pastors and the lives of those they serve.

God grants pastors these charisms because church communities who face possible closure may be fraught. Unexpectedly, powerful tides or currents such as economic recessions, community transitions and attrition, disagreements, or alterations in leadership within the church may unbalance a congregation and challenge a pastor's ability to stay the course. Although not always visible, a pastor's rudder of faith can keep the boat firmly on course and responsive to the wind of the Holy Spirit. The church or the sacred community is the pastor's partner in this mission. Together they journey with faith in God to weather the storm even when the trip is perilous. To that community, we now turn.

2

The Sacred Community

Sailing in the Groove

Every sailor yearns to achieve "sailing in the groove"—when the wind pulls the boat forward effortlessly, the weight of the crew and the centerboard perfectly balancing the gust sweeping steadily over the sails. Sailing in the groove is hard to achieve on a bay where nearby hills and buildings can cause the wind to swirl. Airstreams shift; the tide comes in; currents push silently against the centerboard. Yet when it happens, the helmsperson has no need to fuss with the tiller, as the way is clear and all is well. Just so, pastors at the tiller and congregations in the vessel of the church cherish journeys sailing gracefully in the groove.

From my experience in the church and as a sailor, being part of a sacred community committed to a pilgrimage of loving God and loving their neighbors as themselves feels like sailing in the groove. As the Holy Spirit's wind fills the billowing sail, the pastor's alert tending of the tiller and the congregation's centerboard of lively faith and loving relationships balance and leverage the power of the wind and bear the church forward as curious about God and willing to take risks for the sake of the gospel—even to die, if it should come to that. The church remains upright despite unexpected currents or waves. Although management theorists might call this feat a "holding environment" that is "infused with meaning,"[1] I call it "sailing in the groove."

While considering the content of this chapter, I remembered the gifts that allowed our church to sail in the groove, even when it felt like huge waves were pounding on the hull and spilling over the bow, pushing us far from our hoped-for course. Although it's been seven years since the church I served closed, several congregational leaders spoke recently about what made for peace and hope amid the storm. Their comments point to their love of God and their love for one another. "The Old Testament readings were from Exodus," said one former lay leader, "and for me and for others, that was a great comfort. [The Israelites] were without a home, but God was still there." She noted that the sermons "went deep within each of us. You could tell by the silence that people were deeply focused." Another noted, "[Worship] was a place [where] I definitely felt called to get on my knees. That was not the only time I could talk to the Lord, but that was an especially close way of talking to the Lord. Sometimes it was in a pew; sometimes if nobody else was around, I would go to the altar rail and I was just that much closer." Bible study among these church members, which continues today in a bagel store they dubbed St. Bagels, is described by one participant as "probably as close as I can think of to what it must have been like to be Jewish in the Old Testament, because we would kind of discuss and argue over certain things, and try to figure out what they meant and look up the words."

As Holy Family Church faced dissolution, and as rain outside often mirrored the tears within, these six to nine church members would gather around a table, in the middle of which lay Scriptures appointed for the following Sunday, a Bible dictionary, and various commentaries. "I like to play with those kinds of things, so I really liked that," said one participant. "I learned so much at Holy Family. Jesus was pretty much a revolutionary, and I learned from Holy Family [that] St. Francis said, 'Preach the gospel; use words when necessary.'" Though they lamented the judicatory's lack of concern for their spiritual lives ("People in the judicatory didn't have to use words because their actions spoke way louder than words"), the sacred community that was Holy Family was consoled by their lively faith in God. Their love for one another was especially revealed in one spiritual leader's memory:

> The people that went to Holy Family regularly were very, very, very welcoming. They were a small congregation and everybody there did not necessarily agree on everything, but you never heard that disagreement anywhere. Everybody there contributed to everything. They participated in everything. When we had potlucks, everybody came. Everybody brought things. [When I joined the church,] I'm pretty shy and I didn't know most of these people, but I remember Bob walking up to me one time and saying, "Why do you always sit

in that same pew?" [I said,] "I don't know, Bob. It seems like home now. That's my pew." So, I mean, everybody in their own way made you feel a part of the community.

In the church's final months, the judicatory asked my spiritual community to perform an inventory of church goods to be posted on the judicatory website so other churches could choose what items to receive. This tangible reminder of their loss was made bearable because members did this painful work side by side while the senior warden (the lay leader of the congregation), in honesty and love, admonished the grieving to abstain from emotionally overtaxing work: "Don't do anything you don't want to do." Nonetheless, with patient steadfastness, the children's choir still gathered for weekly rehearsals, the bills were paid, and the grounds were kept neat. No one left the church early when they knew it would close. With faithful endurance, the sacred community for whom I held the tiller managed to sail in the groove, remaining steadily on course even in the midst of seeming crisis.

This chapter describes, through the eyes of their pastors, how closing congregations maintained a lively faith; loving, honest relationships; curiosity about God's call; and a willingness to take risks, which, like a centerboard, held them on a steady course in the face of death. A church budget in the red, a leaky roof, a broken furnace—all mean someone will have to speak the uncomfortable truth in love. As in families at home, no one wants to be a messenger of bad news. Yet any congregation must name, resolve, and overcome waves of unexpected challenges to fulfill their mission in the world, even to ask and answer together questions about their pilgrimage as a sacred community: Why are we here? Who are we? What are our gifts? What is God calling us to be and to do?

Through waves of conflict and grief, the love of God and one another sustains the sacred community in its sailing in the groove to the destination of closure. As every pastor and congregation is unique, no one way is best to guide a church to closure.[2] However, in the face of dissolution, a congregation with a lively faith will seek to strengthen their relationship with God by way of spiritual disciplines such as faithful attendance at worship, Bible study, or book study; curiosity about God's call to the congregation and themselves; and conceding that God's call includes a willingness to try something new. For example, one pastor honored her congregation's lively participation in worship, especially when they were called to the front of the church to profess their faith:

"People started coming up for the altar call and telling stories about healing, but really any 'God sighting' became part of worship as we got closer and closer to closing, as we talked more and more about closing." Another pastor saw that "God was continuing to bless [the church members], even in their struggles and in who they were. God's not left them behind or anything and God's not abandoned them, but in fact God is truly in their midst. It was God present in struggle and closure."

Some pastors in closing churches speak with joy about their members' pursuit of Scripture and spiritual books. One pastor in a congregation of six to eight was a spiritual director, so they participated in spiritual formation every Sunday: "We talked about where we saw the activity of God. The prayers were so fervent. Instead of preaching, I finally figured out after a couple of months that preaching was ridiculous, so we did Bible study." Another pastor admired the eagerness of the faithful adult Sunday school class who read *What's So Amazing about Grace?* by Philip Yancey: "The people loved it so much they wanted to study it twice. We read it together, . . . took our time going through it. They didn't want just a Bible study; they wanted something like a book study."

Besides spiritual disciplines like these that strengthen faith in watershed circumstances, curiosity about God's call for a new future is another sign of a lively faith. A willingness to try something new was apparent in churches that had formed visions of a new mission before their last pastor arrived. For example, one church had researched the surrounding city, which was transforming from a predominantly European-immigrant community to a Middle Eastern–immigrant community. They decided to find a pastor in the new community who could build a congregation that would eventually assume responsibility for the building. They told the incoming pastor, "We only have this much money. We've got about two or three years left. We could hire you. It would have to be part-time. This is all we can offer. Our mission is basically to create this [cultural] mission." The two cultural groups worshiped together and apart as the Middle Eastern congregation grew and the European congregation supported them before eventually closing. Both congregations maintained an enlightening, hope-filled experience in the groove until the end of their shared journey.

In another church, whose members were reluctant to absorb others in their rapidly changing community, a young Nigerian man joined; he was a new immigrant and very poor. Despite the ethnic and economic-class gap, the majority white, affluent congregation welcomed him. The pastor recounted:

> After his dad died unexpectedly back in Nigeria—how crushing is that?—Amahl invited me to a wake at his apartment. I invited the church, and amazingly, some of these elderly white people went with me, and they did really well in an environment very different than their usual one. They talked about it for months after, what it was like to be at this Nigerian wake. They were all a Christian community; they all came from these different churches, and they got to see that the gospel was so much bigger than this white, mainline thing.

These openhearted, open-minded church members had a lively faith that empowered them to embark courageously on a spiritual journey on a mission to an unknown destination in the midst of threatening seas.

In churches disbanding with peace and hope—that is, sailing in the groove (unlike those described in chapter 6 that are wracked by conflict)—the pastors I interviewed witnessed to their congregations' loving and honest relationships. They recounted how members of the sacred community shared burdens of ministry even when complicated by loss and grief. They testified that members of the congregation accepted responsibility for their emotions and actions. Finally, they were grateful when laity showed respect for one another and the pastor in other ways.

For the pastors in this study, loving one's neighbor often means, first, that the congregation and pastor collaborate in the work of ministry. One pastor founded a new church alongside an old one, focusing on youth ministry with all its challenges, such as "policing" young people after concerts broke up and dealing with financial deficits, even as he coped with resentment by the traditionally organized congregation. In the midst of turmoil in his new church and tension with the established congregation, the pastor valued the church's laypeople: "Those of us who worked together in this ministry, while at times it felt like we were carrying enormous burdens, we carried each other's burdens, through that whole process of being vulnerable, you know, and being dependent on each other." He noted, "The model of sharing the burdens and the blessings of ministry becomes a dynamic that deepens your relationships. I mean, I still have wonderful relationships with those I worked with. We shared a history that was the best of times and the worst of times."

Another mark of loving relationships in these churches studied was that often they took on the burden of responsibility for bringing everyone to the table and made an extra effort to keep them there. For example, one pastor in a closing congregation noted the congregation's commitment to good communication: "We tried to be aboveboard by inviting people to be a part of the conversation. We were intentional about being good communicators." The congregation sought "a process of being on top of what was happening and maintaining that transparency."

Loving one's neighbor in crisis can be difficult when the neighbor is of a different culture. In the church with a mission to create a Middle Eastern congregation, the Middle Eastern and European communities brought to the church different cultural norms about women in leadership, respect for people in the LGBT community, and food and other lifestyle preferences. Many women in the European comunity were church leaders. By means of an amplified grace present among church members anxious about dissolution, they came to accept one another. "The way we got around it, we said, 'If we're really going to be hospitable and this is their culture, we have to allow this. This is also their church. We don't have to participate, but we have to allow it.' That was hard, but we did it." They were able to find the groove.

Finally, uniting a lively faith in God with love of one's neighbor, one rural congregation whose town died in a series of floods decided to close and gift their building to another town to be used for the threshing bee every year. The pastor described this step:

> I guess it's just the faithfulness in which they did it. They knew it was going to take $10,000 plus to move this church. We had five thousand. I said, "Let's try to have some fund-raisers." They weren't worrying about it. They weren't obsessing about it. I mean, the money just came. They just trusted that it would happen, and it did. There was no wringing of hands and gnashing of teeth. Well, that's the way I was brought up in Scandinavia and Germany. You do things quietly and things get done. It'll happen. God will provide. You don't even say "God will provide"—it's understood. All of a sudden it was done, and then I'm like, "What? It's done? It's there? OK!" [laughter].

This resurrection story describes a sacred community in crisis closing its church and then making Christ's love present to the wider community by moving its spiritual home to a new site for a new use. It was like Advent, anticipating the miracle of Christ's incarnational birth. It was a Pentecost story about the church, inspired by the Holy Spirit to be faithful people of God, about the church's not being a building. It was an Epiphany story about bearing the light of Christ to others. In whatever "season" a church closes, and whatever sort of pilgrimage of discernment takes place, a sacred community with a lively faith comes alive when Christ's love is boldly and courageously shared in love for one's neighbor. The church's vessel catches the wind in its sails and moves in a groove forward into new life.

Another charism of congregations to which pastors testified was emotional competence that fosters reconciliation and forward movement.[3] We've seen that loving God and others even while experiencing restless anxiety often ensures that a congregation's ship sails in the groove. However, amid the tensions of their loss, a sacred community's emotions may flare as people grieve differently. In my study's survey, pastors were asked, "How skillful were members [of your closing congregation] in communicating fear, anger, sadness, tenderness, acceptance, and gladness?" About four in five clergy judged their congregation's facility in expressing sadness, anger, and fear as "adequate," "good," or "excellent." Members' ability to convey tenderness and acceptance was "adequate" or better in about three-fourths of congregations. As one might expect in the midst of grievous loss, expression of gladness was more elusive (56 percent "adequate" or better).

Congregations more adept in expressing their emotions were more likely to move through denial to seize the initiative in the discernment process for closure rather than depend on the pastor's or judicatory's lead. Significantly, they were more likely to have a closing experience akin to a festival season like Christmas, Epiphany, Easter, or Pentecost. As well, the higher a pastor judged a congregation's emotional competence, the more respectful the congregation seemed to the pastor, and the less stressful the pastor found it to serve the church.

Congregations in crisis can ebb, but also grow, in their emotional dexterity. When trust is broken, as with boundary violations, for example, it is to be expected that people will withdraw from meaningful relationships and honest, loving communication. One congregation had a history of sexual misconduct with a former pastor—a matter that had never been fully resolved. In their faith-filled pilgrimage, the final pastor shared, "There was a growing trust. I think they learned to trust in a new way. It was a time of healing and continued spiritual nurture and growth on all of our parts." This study confirms that having the capacity to share difficult emotions with respect and compassion facilitates a congregation's pilgrimage.[4] Especially in a community facing its church's shutdown, healthy communication of emotions born out of lively faith facilitates honest conversation about the state of the church. One pastor noted how her "spiritually grounded" congregation had the capacity to share and to listen to difficult, as well as positive, emotions:

> Members of this church were so spiritually grounded as a congregation, and so prayerful about the whole process, [such as] when they realized, "Our money, where we thought we had five or six [years' worth], we really now have two, two and a half. What do we do? This is the moment; we're not going to just play out the clock. We're going to make a prayerful and thoughtful decision." They came up with an initial plan [that they] called the Pathfinding Process. We had six people called the trail guides: me and five members of the congregation, whose sole role for several months was to research options, listen to the congregation, pray, reflect back, pray some more, research some more options, and think, think, think. They talked about the identity of the congregation and the love of worship, and the care for the congregation.

As the congregation demonstrated honest, loving communication centered in respect for each member of the church, the pastor affirmed the presence of sacred community: "[They had] the knowledge that the energy was waning, and they felt called to figure this out."

A lively faith and emotional maturity in their relationships helped these closing congregations find the freedom to break through denial. One congregation grew to understand the difference between miracles and magical thinking: miracles are of God; magical thinking is, for example, believing that wishing for the church to grow will cause it to grow. The pastor noted that in their discernment process, the congregation listed over forty things they had done over ten years to try to grow and save the church:

> They recognized that not a single activity they did grew the church. They had that kind of capacity to say that "We had a ball, we wouldn't change anything, everything was great." . . . They planned stained-glass windows, beautiful stained-glass windows, [and] so many other things, but they also were able to say, "And we did not grow." . . . In the middle of meetings they would say, "That's magical thinking." It really just took on a life of its own. The leadership team started to talk that way; the congregation started to talk that

way. It would put brakes on the notion that if we try harder, we'll get ten new people. . . . There was a constant speaking the truth in love throughout those eighteen months. More and more people came on board as they saw senior members of the community and long-time members of the community begin to ask questions.

The congregation was able to move steadily and safely in the groove to their Easter-like decision to close.

Another congregation was willing to own their feelings of weariness, led by a matriarch of the congregation who, one pastor reported, in a meeting "basically said, 'I just think we should close.'" From then on, that was the decision. "Other people said, 'Yeah, this is the way we could be doing this, but we don't have the energy. We just need to go elsewhere and give our time and our talents to another church that maybe is going to thrive.'"

Taking responsibility for one's own emotions leads to respect for others with different emotions, including feelings of denial. I found in the study that courageous lay leaders respecting the fact that people grieve differently often ease the burden on the pastor and allow the community to stay focused. One pastor whose church was moved said, "It was probably the middle-agers or the fifty-year-olds that were the leaders. They admitted they didn't want to lose the building but realized, 'There's just not enough of us.'" The pastor observed the leaders of the church talking with the seventy- and eighty-year-olds to decide: "We could wait a few more years and we still have people, enough people to come to church. [But] if we wait five years, then we won't have any money in the bank." With lay leaders' support in insisting on taking time to respect the different paces with which members would accept the truth and grieve, the church held steadily to its course—in the groove.

Another pastor valued the blessing of "the strength of the people on the leadership team at the time, even though they were in despair—were watching a parish pretty much all of them had been a part of most of their adult lives just really blow up in their faces." People whom they had known and trusted and loved for years threatened them. Yet "despite all of that, they really were very clear about what was acceptable to hear and what was not. They were very clear about what was, you know, this is how a godly community acts; this is how it does not." They protected vulnerable and distressed members of the congregation from disrespect. The pastor said, "That was really a blessing to see that there was no, almost to a person, there was no 'Gee, I have known this person my whole life, so I'll just look the other way.'" Taking responsibility in crisis, lay leaders took on the burden of insisting on norms of respect.

Finally, I observed in my study that *a sacred community's ability to sustain itself in what may feel like a crisis was also marked by honest and loving relationships with the church's ordained leader.* Sailing in the groove requires openhearted respect for the pastor. In this study, most pastors who served their congregations until the end felt their congregations respected them. Fully two-thirds of clergy in this study were "very satisfied" with their congregation's inclusion of them in decision-making, fairness with them, gratitude for their ministry, acceptance of their pastoral identity, and placement of trust in them. In addition, 50 to 60 percent of pastors were similarly satisfied with their congregations' promise-keeping, compassion, understanding, and "safety" when they expressed their truth and didn't fear negative repercussions. However, one pastor in five was "somewhat" or "completely dissatisfied" with their congregation's level of honesty or accountability toward them.

Congregational respect gives pastors the freedom to be who they are and who they are becoming. When the people of God trust a pastor, the pastor can take more risks for the sake of God and the church. Respect means extending the benefit of the doubt and forgiveness when pastors err and things don't go as expected or hoped for. Statistical analysis confirms that congregational respect for the pastor is associated with a festival-season closing; it eases the challenges of pastoral leadership and reduces clergy stress.[5]

CHAPTER SUMMARY

When congregations love God and honor God's image in one another and their pastor, their pilgrimage toward dissolution is more likely to be like sailing in the groove. The wind of the Holy Spirit will fill their sails with transforming power, creativity, and compassion. Although gusts of God's holy power may be unexpected or unsettling, the spiritual community's centerboard of lively faith, made incarnate in loving, honest relationships and the pastor's skilled hand at the tiller, will sustain both balance and momentum on their journey into a new future.

Adaptive work is difficult. Maneuvering a vessel on high seas may raise hairs on one's head and provoke knots in one's stomach—anxiety that can stall a church's capacity to make clear decisions and may threaten bonds of friendship. Nonetheless, congregations that regularly participate in worship and other spiritual disciplines, share the work of managing the vessel, take responsibility for their emotions and actions, and respect the dignity of each other and their pastor can sail in the groove and journey safely to their destination, even if that is the death of the church. Healthy congregations can die with dignity. Unhealthy ones will also die, but it will be more painful for everyone. Although congregations I've cited vary in their praxes of faith and building trusting relationships with one another and their pastor, it's clear that these actions support the transformational work needed for closure that is consoling, healing, and covered in resurrection hope.

3

The Judicatory

The "Coast Guard"

We've seen that churches can be likened to ships with centerboards of faith, and pastors to skippers at the tiller. In the same way, judicatories such as conferences, dioceses, presbyteries, and synods are sacred communities, like ships, guided by the Holy Spirit. They are also analogous to the coast guard, which helps make sea travel as safe as possible by ensuring that passages are navigable, bridges are operational, ships are seaworthy, and pilots are trained and licensed. Like the coast guard, judicatories "provide the environment and the support for [mission] to be happening in the local church," as one Methodist bishop put it. They come to the aid of the spiritual community of the congregation and the pastor by rescuing all souls on board from impending crisis.

Soon after I was ordained and called as priest-in-charge of my first congregation, the judicatory informed the church that it owed nearly $9,000 in clergy health insurance payments and nearly $30,000 in money earmarked for support of the judicatory and national church. With support from judicatory consultants, we sorted out the financial obligations and conducted the first audit in over five years. At our leadership team's first meeting with the bishop, however, a representative of the team, disgruntled over the church's obligation to pay my health insurance and retirement contributions, in an aside asked the bishop to replace me with temporary supply clergy, for which there would be neither of these obligations. The bishop firmly told the leader he would not do that. I was deeply grateful for the judicatory's expertise and moral support. The bishop exercised his authority with compassion, coming to the aid of the congregation, and me, in rough seas.

Judicatories, like their member churches, have a centerboard of lively faith in our Savior Jesus Christ. Through prayer, worship, and sacred community involving honest, loving relationships, judicatories seek to discern God's will in their duty to support member churches and the world around them. In addition to being a sacred community, though, judicatories, like the coast guard, have elements of contemporary bureaucracy, with authority embedded in canon law or constitutions and bylaws. So they balance budgets, have administrative personnel, and use formal rules for decision-making when member churches become unsustainable or less vital in their capacity to be the church in the world.

This chapter identifies the complex character of judicatories, as well as ways in which a judicatory with a lively faith; loving, honest relationships; and organizational resources such as moral authority may aid distressed pastors and their congregations. A sturdy centerboard of faith promises a sound journey when the denomination comes together in prayer, worship, and fellowship "to see what God has done in the past and where God is leading, what are the goals for the future," in the words of one Methodist bishop. This chapter also demonstrates the tensions in—as well as the opportunities for the transformation of—denominational relationships in the context of closing a congregation.

The diversity within judicatories may create underlying tensions in sacred community. For one thing, a judicatory is composed of member churches that may be historically, culturally, and theologically diverse, some dating back to the American Revolution and others that are newborn church plants. A cathedral or megachurch with multiple clergy may serve a community across town from a congregation with fewer than fifty members, no staff, and one part-time clergy. Mainline congregations also span these divides: urban, suburban, rural; Anglo, ethnic minority; white collar, blue collar; theologically conservative, theologically progressive; wealthy, poor; and so forth. Declining membership and scarce resources may increase competition for those resources. For example, one judicatory official said, "I hear grumbling, of course, from the larger churches: 'Why should we care about these other [smaller] churches?'"

Tensions also may arise about the exercise of authority, particularly by bishops, in what is a hierarchical authority structure in some denominations. Authority means that the exercise of power is considered legitimate, or morally justified. Bishops have canonical authority, or the legitimate right to use power, by virtue of biblical and historic traditions embodied in canon law. Because of this, bishops may be considered like admirals in the coast guard making authoritative decisions about clergy deployment or church openings and dissolutions. Bishops and other judicatory executives may also act out of what I call here the "authority of compassion," or moral authority centered in a gospel of justice, mercy, and reconciliation. Thus can judicatories be considered like sailboats with motors, running by the wind of the Holy Spirit that empowers transformation by compassion, and by marine fuel (the power of traditional or bureaucratic authority) that sustains the momentum otherwise.

Denominations are diverse not only in their authority structures but also in the way church property is held. In the Episcopal, United Methodist, and Presbyterian traditions, local church property is usually held in trust for the denomination; a closing church and its property revert to the wider church. Bishops or canonically authorized commissions such as presbyteries have the authority to "plant" (in secular terms, to open) and to close churches, usually—but not always—requiring congregational consent. On the other hand, most ELCA and all UCC congregations own their own property and must make their own decision to close, sell, and dispose of all property before they can dissolve. In congregational polities such as the UCC, members of the judicatory maintain moral, if not bureaucratic, authority over property decisions; commissions of colleagues and laity may offer prayer and consultation about opening or dissolving a church.

Like the coast guard, judicatories may bring the power of sacred community, organizational authority, and denominational resources to closing churches. They may remind people of God's love, mediate disputes, publicly back a pastor when he or she is in potential or actual conflict with the congregation, or remove a pastor threatened by emotional or physical abuse in the church. They can provide churches in distress with resources of various kinds such as consultations, financial or material assistance, and spiritual and emotional support.

Faithful judicatories may bring their authority to turbulent situations. For example, when one church was about to have a vote about whether to close, leaders notified members by mail. One dissenter, who had left the congregation and did not get a letter, protested to the judicatory executive, who later affirmed the pastor's decision that "she shouldn't have a letter." Another minister reported that as the congregation was exploring a possible sale, one of the "strong leaders" of the church decided it was time not to renew the pastor's interim ministry contract and to call in a new pastor. "The [judicatory executive] came in and facilitated the discussion and supported the direction we were going," said the pastor. The pastor was grateful that the judicatory recognized "that there was just anxiety at some point" and that they encouraged the process to continue.

A judicatory executive or representative may attend a meeting, send a letter, or in other ways back up a besieged leadership team and pastor. For example, when one congregation decided to close but a dissenting group—actually just two members—begged, "Can't we explore just a few options?" the leadership team reluctantly agreed to "start a group and just explore." The pastor recounted:

> Next thing I knew, they were calling it the [renewal] group, and there were sixteen people on it. You know, they were fooling themselves. When they came with their final report, it was sad. The judicatory consultant had showed up, and we had to tell them, "You're not meeting anymore because you're not coming up with anything. This is not a good use of time."

The intervention may have been uncomfortable, but both the pastor and the congregation who made the decision to dissolve had the backing of the judicatory.

Another judicatory executive stepped in to affirm a congregation's decision to merge with a neighboring church of the same denomination. Even though the vote was short by 8 percent, the pastor and the leadership team decided to go ahead. "We acted as a unit . . . probably twelve people who were very clear about the vision and united and strong," recalled the pastor. A dissident group "was so aggressive and confrontational that the judicatory executive facilitated a quick shutdown and a move. We just did it." The pastor added, "They tried to get the judicatory executive to meet them and support them, and the executive wouldn't do it. 'The leadership of your church has spoken,'" the judicatory member emphasized, "and he helped us close it down really fast."

Judicatories can also address potentially dangerous situations for a pastor. One congregation secretly planned to fire their pastor, close the church, and use the assets to begin a new, nondenominational church. Once the pastor uncovered their intentions, she explained, "the judicatory pulled me out because they just said, 'You don't need any more of this.'" She recounted the care with which they removed her:

> The judicatory official said, "You've got about a week. Get everything out. Get everything you own out of there." I went in for a couple of days and on a weekend and pulled out books and stuff, because I had so much in there. I did it in small trips. I just kept doing it until I got out of there. When we had that last meeting, I got up to walk out. The lay leader said, "Leila's going to step out now while we vote." The judicatory leader said that if I did go back in, they'd just be abusing me more. He just said, "Go ahead and go. You've got everything?" I said, "Yep," and then I left. Those in the meeting were asking, "Where is she?" The lay leader said, "She's not here. She's gone." Someone said, "She doesn't have everything out of her office yet." But the judicatory leader said, "Yes, she does." The meeting members asked to go in and see my office, and it was bare. I guess that really blew their minds away. That was good. At least I didn't have to face them again.

A bishop's exercise of canonical authority to summarily close a congregation also may save that congregation from harm. In one conflicted congregation, said the pastor, "this small group had decided that if they got me to leave as a pastor—that is, to resign—then they could take the church away from the judicatory." Most leaders and members in the church were supportive of a process ensuring the future of the historic congregation. In the midst of their revitalization effort, however, one unsettled member of the congregation threatened another. The pastor notified the judicatory executive immediately. The church had Sunday services, but, remembered the pastor, "the judicatory executive had given me a letter to read. So after the service I read the letter, which said the church is now closed. The locksmith came and changed the locks. That was the end of that."

As we've seen, one of the charisms of a judicatory is the exercise of leadership with authority. Yet another blessing of a wider church body that acts like a coast guard is its capacity to provide resources such as consultation or financial aid. One pastor in a congregational polity who realized the church was "losing leadership" asked judicatory colleagues, "Listen to us while we're wondering what to do, and see what you think." The representative "listened, spent a number of sessions with us, with me personally, and with the leadership team." The pastor was grateful:

Here were people volunteering from their regular jobs, their regular church activities, to spend time solving the problem that was little Community Church. The body of Christ was bigger than our little congregation. It was a judicatory. It was a blessing. There is no way I could have done it by myself or I would have messed it up.

Another pastor, after informing the judicatory about a rapid decline in the willingness of church members to revitalize the church, reported, "Anytime I called, a bishop or staff member would show up, or whoever needed to come down. They would make time to come down as soon as possible. Go over the finances? Absolutely." Another pastor was grateful for the judicatory executive who helped develop a set of guidelines for closure: "[The guidelines] felt good to everybody at our church, knowing we're helping to create a pace and an orderly way that did us well and to the glory of God. There's not confusion in the midst of this painful process."

One congregation had help wading through a title search required for the church's sale. In this case, a less resourced judicatory didn't have staff available, so they told the pastor to talk to the pastor of another church that had closed earlier, who provided an outline of that church's process. Another church received help with "the selling of the pews and what needed to go to the thrift shop and who got what. That was done by a representative from the judicatory's office, who was a big, big help."

Another pastor assigned to two failing churches proposed to the judicatory that he and a neighboring pastor take on the task of gathering their five nearby churches together so that they could discern a future together. When the neighboring pastor left his posts, he assumed responsibility for them as well. The work resulted in closures that would have affected the pastor's salary. He said, "It wouldn't have been possible without the judicatory. They paid me when the congregation couldn't anymore."

Drawing on commitments to justice and mercy, judicatories may allow churches in impoverished rural communities to leave property to the community rather than the national church. Although the UMC may hold proceeds of sold church property in trust for the denomination, under some conditions the congregation may also donate them. One rural UMC congregation wanted to donate their building to a community nonprofit to become a community center. The pastor was grateful when "the denomination just didn't want to fool with it, and nobody would buy it because it was next to the school, so the cemetery association was given the property." On behalf of another small, rural church, clergy said, "the judicatory trustees said that they would deed the property over either to a group of them or to the community to allow it to continue to be used as a worship space and a community gathering location."

Besides exercising moral authority or contributing resources such as consultation, money, or property to churches in troubled waters, *judicatories may play a crucial role by offering compassion and respect to their pastors.* One pastor, who was caring for a dying former pastor who was a member of his congregation and was also caring for members grieving the impending closure of the church, shared that his judicatory executive "took me to lunch probably every week for six weeks before this ended. He was on the phone with me often." The pastor also said that the judicatory "believed that some churches need to close so that others can be [healthier]. So they were very supportive, very encouraging."[1]

One of the most important blessings clergy can receive from a judicatory is respect for their ministry; the presence of judicatory respect relieves the stress of a pastor serving a closing church.[2] As one pastor said, "I never felt from anybody in the judicatory like 'Oh, Sally killed that church.' I mean, they were very much aware that it was dead before I walked into the room and that closing this church was an act of faithfulness and courage . . . [and] important work that not everybody is willing to do."

Although a written survey of pastors who have experienced the closing of their churches shows that most experienced respectful relationships with bishops and judicatory colleagues, about one-third of pastors responding were "very dissatisfied" or "somewhat dissatisfied" with their judicatory. Particular concerns involved judicatory officials' level of compassion for the pastor, accountability to the pastor, and communication with the pastor, including failure to acknowledge the pastor's concerns, understand the pastor, and speak honestly. As well, one in four respondents lamented the judicatory's lack of fairness, promise keeping, and concern for the pastor's safety when the pastor spoke the truth to the congregation.[3] In some judicatories, pastors failed to experience God's creative, redeeming, and sustaining Spirit moving through the wider church.

Just as, for sailors, mountains or hills can block the wind and create "wind shadows" that slow their progress, judicatories may have historic hills, cultural mountains, or other systems that block the Holy Spirit's power to heal, console, and redeem difficult circumstances like church closures. In a time of religious decline, bureaucratic imperatives such as balancing a diminishing judicatory budget or needing to take swift action may displace the inclusive, prayerful, and slow work of discerning God's call and showing compassion for pastors and God's grieving people.

Interviews with pastors reveal that they feel dissatisfied, or even betrayed, when judicatories fail to engage in honest, respectful, and difficult conversations about what it means to be a church in the twenty-first century. Pastors who close churches may perceive the following "hills" blocking the Holy Spirit's movement in their sacred community: denial of religious realities, unilateral exercise of legal or canonical authority, hierarchical decision-making that lacks compassion, a lack of empathy for congregations and pastors (especially first-call pastors, who have unique needs) throughout the ordeal, and a lack of cultural sensitivity.

Reflecting the prevalent denial of death throughout American culture, one of the most prominent wind shadows judicatories may sustain is denial.[4] One pastor noted that his judicatory had clergy workshops on revitalization but didn't facilitate dialogue among pastors for whom closure might be a future reality: "Who's moving toward closure? . . . Close your eyes." Another pastor's executive offered no support, saying, "We are in the business of creating churches, not closing churches." One minister was disappointed that judicatory staff was "not in any way prepared to say to me, 'I think it's time that we named the fact that this isn't going to work and started working together to find a graceful way of closing the church.'" The pastor wondered whether they didn't want to name it because if word got out that they had named it, anger toward them would have resulted. "The executive actually said, 'I would feel like a murderer.' In retrospect, I find myself thinking that taking that position for himself and being reluctant to help a church die put me in the position of being the killer."

Similarly, denial was apparent when one pastor of a dying church reported that the judicatory executive advised him to ask the congregation for more money. Then the judicatory leader came to the meeting where the congregation had already arranged the vote to close and said, "Well, there's one other congregation in our judicatory that has taken all their reserve funds, and they've hired a full-time pastor." Often centered in care, the fear of death can flow like a fierce current throughout the church—members, pastors, and judicatory executives at times pushing against the transforming wind of the Holy Spirit.

Denial may result in the disrespectful absence of a denominational leader at the final worship service. One parish with two denominational affiliations voted to leave one denomination and then planned a worship service in which the lay leader of the closing congregation would symbolically hand off "a notebook for membership" to the other congregational leader. The closing church's judicatory chose not to publicize it; moreover, they didn't attend and blamed the pastor for the loss. The pastor said, "They weren't real thrilled. But I said, 'I'm sorry, but this was their choice.'"

Another complexity is that the comfortable exercise of legal or canonical authority may block compassion for pastors. Said one pastor:

> Particularly for bishops, there's something different between exercising canonical authority and influencing through moral leadership—moral, ethical, theological, spiritual leadership. The issue is how to be in companionship with the closing church. I've not seen too many bishops who know how to be present without the anxiety or the desire to make a decision. "If I can't make a decision, then clearly there's no place for me" seems to be the knee-jerk response.

However, a judicatory executive can exercise the authority of compassion by being present and accountable for the well-being of the people and for assisting with a "good enough" death. A "good enough" death is one that honors grief by evoking God's consoling presence and remembering the church's ministries, while promising the hope of new life through legacy gifting and assistance to church members in finding new spiritual homes. Without this, the bonds of sacred community may be broken, but with such compassionate help, members can move forward in spiritual resurrection.

The Spirit can seem absent when a judicatory's lawful decision to acquire church property and assets by bureaucratic fiat blocks compassion for the spiritual community. One pastor said the judicatory wasn't involved in their congregation until "the assets were threatened." Another closed a rural church only a few months before the congregation's fiftieth anniversary because a "commission wanted the assets by the end of the calendar year." The pastor said, "All the churches in the judicatory wanted that money. It's enough to make a person leave the church." Judicatories by their very nature are demographically, culturally, and theologically diverse. Without caring efforts for reconciliation of differences, open conflict among churches, pastors, and judicatory officals can lead to executive decisions to close a congregation without involving the pastor or the membership.

Judicatory decisions like this can create an experience of isolation for church members and pastors who hope to work with the wider church "firm in one spirit, striving side by side with one mind for the faith of the gospel" (Phil 1:27). For example, one Midwest judicatory placed a church building on the real estate market a few weeks before their denomination's annual conference. Members of the congregation attending the conference were dismayed to hear no mention of their circumstance or grief in the prayers or any other venue; no one approached them with empathy. Nonetheless, they maintained hope that neighboring churches in their denomination would attend a special celebration of praise and thanksgiving for the church a few weeks later, notice of which was sent to the judicatory e-newsletter. Although the notice appeared, the statement noting the reason for the celebration—the church's impending sale—was excised from the listing and no one came.[5] Three months later at a clergy conference, many did not know the church was being sold until the pastor told them. Caught in a current of solitary grief, the congregation, the lay minister who organized the thanksgiving service, and the pastor felt alone on the sea, shunned and shamed by their denomination.

Whereas the exercise of canonical, or legal, authority by a judicatory executive such as a bishop (reflected in the obedient response, "Yes, Bishop") may block the healing wind of the Holy Spirit, some bishops secure moral authority, or the authority of compassion, by their commitments to pastors and the sacred mission of the church. As one ELCA bishop put it,

> My authority really came out of my pastoral care, for the most part, and I worked very hard. When I first started, I did a lot of things to ask myself what kind of leadership I wanted to provide. It came from that, it came from a spiritual base, and it came from my portraying myself as a pastor. One person said to me, "I really appreciated your time as a bishop because you weren't a transactional bishop; you were a transformative bishop." What I was seeking, and what I was trying to encourage people toward, was transformation, both individual and parish.

Hierarchical decision-making without inclusion of affected pastors or churches functions like a "wind shadow" blocking the Holy Spirit's consoling movement. For example, when one congregation chose a different path for redevelopment than its judicatory expected (but never shared with the church), its executive dissolved the church, leaving the pastor to share the bad news. The pastor took his time to process the judicatory's decision before disclosing it to the congregation with an empathy that the congregation needed from the wider church. He recounted:

> The lack of agency that we had in the process of the closure in terms of the decision to close was very disturbing, but I vowed that I was not going to handle it in a way that blames the judicatory. I did not want to get into an "anger at the judicatory" kind of thing. I knew that people might well have [that anger] themselves, but I wanted to be able to do pastoral care without joining them in that. I had my own reactions that I felt I needed to take care of as much as I could, and then be present to them and really encourage them to claim their agency in the closure process.

This pastor had strong boundaries and a good support system. Wanting a safe and healthy grieving process and a peaceful end, he sacrificed authenticity to prevent roiling the congregation, though not without personal cost.

Judicatories and their executives may need to learn how to conduct difficult conversations with congregations and pastors with respect and empathy. For example, one pastor was informed of the building's sale by a judicatory staff member's phone call, another by a neighboring pastor, and one more by a judicatory email. When one pastor broke the news to the congregation,

> the people were like, "Whoa . . ." because they realized they had had no face-to-face human contact about the decision, and so to me, that's disrespectful. If you're going to make that decision, at least come talk to people, get to know them, and explain the reasoning in what's going on and why it's going on. But there was no face-to-face.

Frayed relationships among pastors, congregations, colleagues, and judicatory leaders particularly affect first-call pastors because of their lack of experience and weaker clergy support systems.[6] If judicatories are like the coast guard, they need to prepare newly ordained pastors for challenging voyages, keep them on "a locator," remain in communication with them, and assist when they call out an SOS. Too often this doesn't happen, according to the answers to this study's questionnaire. Stress among pastors who close churches is significantly higher for first-call pastors and those with difficult relationships with their judicatory.[7]

Lacking communications, colleagues in a judicatory may seem to fail pastors. For example, one young pastor beginning a new church was promised that a "mother church" would support him by sharing resources. Unbeknownst to the pastor, the sponsoring congregation reneged on its promise. The pastor "hit the ground not knowing this." When he asked the pastor of the mother church to print some flyers, he was rebuffed, not knowing what had happened.

Pastors are disappointed when judicatories don't act like a sacred community of loving, honest relationships. For example, another "wind shadow" is not sharing vital information when succeeding pastors begin ministry, as noted by one pastor: "When the judicatory executive said, 'This is a church, this is the information on it,' I took it at face value, and it wasn't true." Poor communication may have an unintended consequence that churches feel marginalized. For example, one pastor averred the judicatory's main concern was "whatever it takes to get these distractions off our plate so we can concentrate on helping the people who are doing something."

Yet another first-call pastor was disappointed when the judicatory executive failed to establish an authentic, compassionate relationship at his final meeting with the struggling urban church:

> The bishop and all the rest of us went around the table and talked about what the future of the congregation could be, etc. The bishop got up and said, "OK, thank you," walked out, and I never heard from him again. He didn't call and say, you know, "They had valid points," or "This is what you guys could be working on," or "I think you should do this, or maybe you should do that." . . . He didn't even say good-bye! All of a sudden, I turned around and the bishop was gone. Never once after that did I hear any criticism—constructive, helpful, or otherwise—from the bishop. And that was my first call.

One young pastor related, "My impression was that the judicatory staff person knew that this church was going to have to close, and that's what he wanted me to do. But he didn't tell me that." The judicatory executive "just acted oblivious," and the judicatory committee responsible for oversight and support to the pastor was disinterested. "Nobody reached out to me," one pastor disclosed. "I was supposed to have some mentorship with some older pastors in the judicatory. I didn't receive that. I felt like I was swimming in a pool all by myself. It was emotionally draining." Similarly, another first-call pastor spoke of being ignored by her judicatory executive, contrary to the respect one hopes for in a sacred community: "It just was horrible and just got worse and worse. The judicatory executive didn't communicate very much. I would keep him apprised of what was going on and many times wouldn't receive a response at all."

Nonetheless, judicatories are increasingly aware that journeys or outcomes that feel like Good Friday rather than Easter, or even Lent, are preventable. Many denominations and their judicatories are striving to strengthen the bonds of sacred community among pastors and congregations and to remove the wind shadows that block the Spirit's healing, consoling, and reconciling movement over churches that close. The Episcopal Church's baptismal covenant's promise is to "strive for justice and peace among all people and respect the dignity of every human being," calling the judicatory, like all other expressions of the church, to seek the Holy Spirit in all its work.[8]

One impediment blocking the wind of the Holy Spirit is cultural insensitivity. For example, one judicatory once had placed an immigrant congregation in the same building as a majority Anglo congregation. "There was suspicion that that judicatory had planned this and that's why they wanted to close them, to give the property to this immigrant congregation," the pastor said. "I don't think [the judicatory committees] had training that helped them see the dynamics of what was going on." The pastor paused to consider what could have happened. She felt there was never any "reflective work" or "any level of saying, 'Why did we do that historically?'" Unable to resolve its intercultural conflict, the church closed.

Another cultural reality underlying the complicated dynamics internal to judicatories is the changing social and cultural context of religion in America. It is hard to be nimble when centuries-old images of "congregation" continue to have impact, according to one UMC consultant. She went on to outline some of the strains:

We have this mentality that every town should have everything. We also have the mentality that every church should be able to stand alone. In our denomination, we had at one time more churches than post offices. A church was built in a village, then it was built in the city, and then it was built on the outskirts. And [each one] stood alone and [each] had a single pastor. We're dealing with an ethos that really is no longer existing, on top of the whole Christendom paradigm.

One UCC conference minister spoke of the need not only to merge small congregations but also, especially in rural areas and small cities, "to give birth to the progressive trans-denominational church." He continued: "Denominations are a thing of the past, but they are still the defining currency in which American Protestantism deals." He sees a "generative future that awaits us, that we just have to live our way into."

But another perspective is that we should not look to end denominations altogether, but to unfold transformation at the grassroots level as well as through ecumenical dialogue.[9] The diversity among Protestant denominations can be seen as a strength, as the reality of declining identification with Christianity across our society calls us to seek God's will through dialogue with other branches of the faith that are also doing God's work.

CHAPTER SUMMARY

When the wind of the Holy Spirit fills the sails of sacred communities we call judicatories, congregations and their pastors move forward together with the love of God and the love of their neighbors under an alert and compassionate eye. Like the coast guard, the wider church may bring the charisms of sacred community, moral authority, and material and spiritual resources to vulnerable closing churches and their pastors. However, when systemic hills of denial, a hierarchical culture, historic and cultural rifts, or the absence of accountability create "wind shadows" that block the Spirit, judicatories may run on the marine fuel of canonical authority alone. When they do, God may seem absent to closing congregations and the clergy who serve them. By the grace of God and holy intentions, many judicatories now are seeking to overcome these barriers and provide churches and their pastors the protection, order, and guidance needed on perilous seas. How they navigate their journeys in the context of these dynamics is the subject of part 2.

PART II

Leading the Pilgrimage

4
Leadership Gifts
of a Transformational Pastor

One afternoon our sailing crew crossed San Francisco Bay to begin a key race, one that would decide our standings in competition. As a 20-knot breeze beat against the sail, the skipper shouted commands over the roar of the wind: "I need one of you to point out where the mark is! My eyes are on the instruments and the sail! I'm looking up, not out." And "I need someone to yell when we're 90 degrees to the mark so I don't turn too early, like we did in the last race!" And "I need someone to look out for boats that aren't paying attention!" Quickly, the rest of us all knew our jobs. We would be a team working together as best we could to be safe, have fun, and, hopefully, win the race. We knew our skipper would provide protection, order, and guidance. He respected every member of the team and let us know we were all needed.

This particular skipper is very good—even outstanding—at leading. However, he is not what I would call a "transformational" leader because that's not what sailing calls for. Interviews with pastors reveal that when a church is on the brink of closure, a transformational leader has the capacity to lead the church on a pilgrimage with God—whether toward merger, dissolution for the sake of new life, or something else. On this pilgrimage, a pastor empowers others to take responsibility for their own actions, sustains a culture of transparency, values others' contributions, and encourages the church to listen for God's calling. Unlike a sailboat race, the pilgrimage of a sacred community has the potential to transform the hearts, minds, and souls of the people of God and the world they serve.

This chapter describes transformational leadership skills that facilitate a church's movement with grace into a new future, as opposed to stasis or a precipitous death; it also relates pastors' life experiences that may create or strengthen those skills for service in a diminishing church. A pastor's capacity to lead adaptive change in the church depends on what family-systems theorists such as Edwin Friedman call "differentiation"—that is, the "capacity to become oneself out of one's self, with minimum reactivity to the positions or reactivity of others . . . charting one's own way."[1]

This emotional differentiation, along with a clear sense of call, allows a pastor to stand apart as an "I"—ordained to preach, teach, and pastor—as well as to lead among the "we," the spiritual community, in guiding a fragile congregation on its journey to closure. As one pastor puts it, even as members of the church respect the pastor's authority, "our ears matter too, that we listen to our parishioners." Loving one's neighbor as oneself means a pastor as "I" respects others—"they"—who speak. Inasmuch as a church is the body of Christ, the authority of all voices—"I," "we," and "they"—is needed to sail in the groove as the church moves forward; authority is power that is exercised "rightly" or "legitimately" in the eyes of the ruler and the ruled.[2]

Interviews in this study confirm that *pastoral differentiation facilitates the leadership tasks required for a church's healthy dissolution.* Congregations are organizational systems and, as such, have unique histories, values, norms, and roles (the church's "DNA"), which any shifts will challenge.[3] To understand a church's history as well as its current context, pastors may go "to the balcony"—that is, to stand as a differentiated "I" apart from the congregational "they" in order to listen to members of the sacred community—and then return to help them understand their historical roles or norms and even allow healthy conflict to emerge.

When I heard other pastors tell their leadership stories with respect to closing churches, I realized I could count myself as one of the less differentiated pastors. One way to identify the differentiation of pastors is to listen to their pronouns as they tell stories about their churches. I can hear myself telling the story of how "we" spent more than a year opening "our" new organic community garden. "We" were hoping that neighborhood farmers would feel welcomed by "our" congregation. "We" planned a garden blessing after church one Sunday, followed by a potluck lunch to which "we" invited the neighbors. When church members sat completely apart from new gardeners at the luncheon, I was disappointed but so emotionally fused with "we" that I noticed it but never named it. I didn't want to hurt members' feelings because I valued my emotional attachment to others in the congregation over the truth telling of a prophetic "I" voice.

As in most organizations, pastors have to earn authority from others in order to lead as an "I." Although pastors may have official authority grounded in denominational codes, not everyone may respect or trust a pastor's leadership. For example, canon law gave me formal authority to oversee church leadership meetings, but when I, a newly called pastor, tried to lead my first vestry meeting with Bible study, people strenuously objected: "We're too busy!" "We don't have enough time!" I persisted in explaining why it was important to pray for God's will. Joining her voice with mine, a new church member (also new to the leadership team) added that vestry meetings in her former church always began with Bible study. As both of us, women new to the church, stared at the others in puzzlement and frustration, the treasurer suddenly picked up his things and stormed out, saying something like "Not on my watch." I had no idea how angry people were at the diocese that had removed their long-term pastor and replaced him with me, a newly ordained woman, an academic, an outsider from the East Coast, and someone who warmly welcomed new church members to the leadership team. I expect that my introducing Bible study was as unwelcome as the bishop's decision to appoint me there. My authority depended on trust, and without listening with compassion and respect, I hadn't earned the right to speak as a differentiated "I" to the congregational "they." I had formal authority but had not yet earned their trust as a spiritual leader, that is, moral authority.

The respect a pastor shows a congregation embodies, in essence, loving one's neighbor as oneself.[4] It requires curiosity about members' hopes and dreams, as well as about who they are and the gifts they bring to relationships. Respect means creating a safe space for difficult conversations through inclusion, honesty, and transparency, as well as giving the benefit of the doubt and striving to remain in relationship through the course of disagreements. It also means holding people, including oneself, accountable for their actions. In the words of one pastor I interviewed, it means "fighting fair." Also, respect means showing reverence for the life of another human being, keeping promises, avoiding harm, and seeking reconciliation, such as by offering amends, when harm has occurred. Respect does not mean that the pastor loses his or her "I" identity in emotionally enmeshed "we-ness," but rather that he or she can act autonomously as well as collaboratively with members of a congregation to frame problematic issues, ministry goals, and ways to reach those goals.

Pastors in my study shared many examples of differentiated, respectful leadership in the course of closing their churches. For example, one minister clarified Christian values to challenge his congregation. His church had received a quote of $50,000 for repairs of the sanctuary ceiling. Although they had $250,000 in reserve funds, he said, "This is not good stewardship for us to continue the way we are and put this kind of money into *us*. If we see that this is something that is part of a bigger plan for revitalization, that's great. I want to know that it is before we commit to this." In considering the expenditure, the pastor as "I" emphasized to the congregation the value of conserving resources and the hope of resurrection, or new life, when a dream of immortality is threatened.

Another clergy member named dysfunctional communication in her church's system and insisted on a norm for respectful relationships. As she reported, in the midst of a difficult meeting, one member of this closing church rose and spewed out "how angry he was, that it was my fault, it was the ethnic folks in the congregation who were bringing it to an end." The pastor stood next to him and said, "OK, you had your say; you heard what they said. Now there is no more of this. If you want to talk, you have to dialogue in a proper and respectful manner." She reflected, "You know it's funny, being an introverted person, how much energy [it took] making sure that it wasn't going to be a free-for-all and that we still had respect. I couldn't believe myself standing there saying those things!" Standing as a differentiated "I" with someone who has been victimized models the love of Christ for the oppressed. Standing as a differentiated "I" with a person who has been verbally abusive is also a form of modeling respect. These stances also exemplify forgiveness and the anticipation of new life.

Differentiated pastors promote thinking about the church as a family system or social system. In John Donne's words, no one can be an island, but all are part of the "main."[5] In this vein, one pastor always tried to be a leader "who cares about process, that the process is more important than the outcome." Process is about sustaining mutually respectful and loving relationships in the sacred community: "I try to practice good family systems, respecting your 'I' and calling people [collectively] to do that together."

A differentiated pastor is able to recognize one sign of frayed sacred community—emotional triangles.[6] An emotional triangle develops when a relationship between two people becomes unstable and one seeks emotional support from a third party to shore up one's identity rather than dealing directly with the anxiety or conflict in the dual relationship. Relationship instability can arise from conflicts about values, such as tradition; about norms, or generally accepted ways of behaving; or about roles, such as what one expects or doesn't expect of someone in a particular position. For example, Sally tells Cathy that Carol (a teenager) is eating the bread before worship, and Cathy tells Jennifer that Sally isn't doing anything about this. Complaining about someone to a third party creates an emotional triangle. Triangles may even be created with outsiders, such as a ghost of the past ("Alice always did it that way") or a ghost from a previous church.

When I asked one pastor what she did in situations where there were triangles, she had a differentiated response:

> I strived to not take part in them. I strived to trust that the person who was telling the story was hurting and to stick to my sympathy being around the hurt and not around the actual item. I strived not to hit anyone [laughter]. Some days I was really good and some days I was really bad, but overall, I strived not to take things personally.

A differentiated leader understands that anger is an emotion that belongs to a given person, who has the responsibility to deal with it in a respectful manner.

Thinking systematically facilitates peace and reconciliation. One pastor was called the "church killer" and "all sorts of names." He said, "I know, myself, that I internalize, so I know I took it to heart; I tried to not let it bother me. I kept saying, 'It's not about you; it's all about him,' so I wasn't feeling like I was a failure." This signifies emotional differentiation from the other; the pastor is not expressively dependent on others liking her but is secure in her own being.

It is important for a differentiated and compassionate pastor to remain in contact with everyone. For example, when a judicatory decided to close a declining church, the pastor met with those who opposed it. "It was a cordial conversation. I mean . . . we came out in different places. We thought differently about what the church was. But we respected each other's faith." In another unsustainable church, where denial was thick like fog, the pastor modeled transparency and truth telling at a regular leadership team luncheon meeting. He invited people to read Scripture and discuss what they heard. "I would say . . . take a moment to visualize [our church]." As well as standing "above" them as a teacher, he nurtured sacred community by standing along-side them: "We would talk about what we saw [in our church], and [our church] became a place where I could speak my truth with abso-lute candor. And they spoke their truths with absolute candor, and it was profound trust." Having earned authority as a spiritual leader by inviting spiritual reflection with personal honesty and curiosity about what others thought, as well as easily holding the authority granted him by church bylaws, this pastor spoke comfortably about this experience as "I" amid "we."

Many differentiated pastors in the study respected the authority of the congregation to make the decision to close. One said, "They kept asking me privately, 'What do you think we should do?' [and] I would say, 'I don't know what you should do; this is your discernment pro-cess.'" The pastor then led a six-week sermon series on discernment; she said that she "used a bunch of Ignatian stuff on [the] discernment process"—that is, that Christian discernment is beyond the head or reason but is about the heart, where Jesus lives.[7] She said, "And when they'd ask me privately [whether to close], I'd say, 'I don't know; it's your discernment process.' I kept saying, 'You guys, this decision you're making—it's like you're a woman having a baby, and I'm your midwife, helping you birth this baby with this decision.'" This pastor took a year and a half as a differentiated "I" to create a congregational process in which "they" could reach a decision on their own.

One differentiated pastor in a church that needed prodding judi-ciously brought about a sense of crisis to hold the "you" accountable. He sensed the congregation was postponing closure for three months until the end of the program year because it was too painful. When the pastor held firm, "No, I'm done," they agreed, "Your last Sunday will be our last Sunday." As a differentiated "I," this pastor spoke his truth and escalated the conflict to help the congregational "you" to face the truth.

A differentiated pastor in a crisis strives to maintain a peaceable presence, like Jesus' serenity when waves threatened the disciples' boat. One differentiated pastor I spoke with drew on his experience as a parent to model an easy presence within a storm. He recalled, "When [our] toddler was learning to walk and she'd fall down, my wife and I made a point of trying not to get all concerned, but we'd go, 'Oh, fall down and go boom.' If we had been all alarmed that she had fallen down, she would have picked up all that trauma and nervousness." The pastor continued, "That's the type of thing we were trying to do at the church. You know, don't overtraumatize it. After all, this church has been part of the life of a lot of them for forty, fifty, sixty years. But let us be as adult about this [closing] as we can."

Differentiation meant setting clear boundaries between "I" and "they" that allowed one pastor to be clear about what she sensed. She recounted how she felt like "it was God's desire at that point that we close the building. I was at peace with that." She felt "called to comfort the afflicted and afflict the comfortable" and explained, "At that point, that was my job. I had to afflict their comfort zone and get them out of it, because it wasn't healthy for them either." The pastor sacrificed her desire to be liked for the sake of the church's setting of well-defined limits for her role and the role of laity.

Many pastors spoke about the differentiation theme of taking responsibility for self-care. One cautioned, "I'm not one to preach it, but find a way to take care of yourself. Don't wait to see your daughter's [bridal] shower going on and you miss it because you're sick." This pastor continued: "For me it's always helpful to know where the hope is, to really be able to see [it]—in your own life and in the life of the people and in the life of what's going to be happening—and to hold on to that." Jesus was an example of differentiation when he went off to pray and just be by himself, as well as when he surrounded himself with trusted friends.

We've seen expressions of differentiation from my interviews with pastors, but I also discerned in this study some *roots and supports for a pastor's capacity for differentiated, transformational leadership: first, personal life experiences before ministry*, such as being a PK ("preacher's kid" or "preacher's kin"), participation in 12-step groups or therapy, and working previously in a field that requires differentiation, such as social work, human resources, counseling, or chaplaincy; *second, training and experience in systems thinking or differentiation; third, certain types of church calls*, such as multichurch appointments; and *finally, the prior experience of serving a diminishing church with all its tensions.*

Growing up in a clergy family is among the personal life experiences that prepare a pastor for differentiated leadership. For example,

one pastor found distance from her congregation by remembering her
father as a pastor:

> There were times when I did not want to go to church. I didn't want
> to show up on a Sunday morning because I knew people were angry.
> I would show up and I would preach and I would talk to them even
> if they were mad. It's probably something I learned from my dad.
> He had a difficult ministry and he too would show up, still show
> up. I'm not going to take my marbles and go home. I'm going to
> show up.

Another pastor credited his own "personal spirituality," part of which
was "gained through 12-step programs." As he recalled, "It wasn't hard
to trust, even though I wasn't particularly happy about what was coming forth." He concluded, "It would just mean [to] work as best I could
and 'Thy will be done,' which is one of the hardest things to do. You
want to hop in there and control it."

One pastor, who had a master's degree in counseling and had worked
as a counselor for ten years before seminary, narrated many stories with
"they," referring to the congregation, as in "They tried to figure out a
bunch of options, and they actually started trying to engage the local
congregation to figure out who was even interested in having a conversation." Another pastor, who worked as a chaplain, relayed, "What I
was doing was helping them with grieving the past and transitioning
to the future. Also, using my training in spiritual direction, I really did
a lot to try to reframe things in terms of hope and in terms of legacy."
These pastors' life experiences as 12-step participants, counselors, or
spiritual directors prepared them to honor the agency of "they" in the
congregation.

Formal training in systems thinking gives clergy the courage to lead.[8]
For example, one minister with a doctor of ministry degree recalled
that in her program, "all we looked at was, How do you make changes
in churches?" After speaking privately with key stakeholders, the pastor
"realized that some people were thinking about 'Should we close?'"
She said, "At that point, it was not something that anybody would talk
about publicly or in a meeting, or with anybody else present. It was just
me and a lot of hushed conversations." Systems thinking encouraged
the pastor to introduce respectful, transparent communication into the
discernment process.

Certain church contexts support a pastor's capacity to engage a congregation both as an "I" and as "we." These include being bivocational

(working as a pastor and in another line of work at the same time), having closed a previous church, having served many churches as a pastor, or serving multiple congregations at the same time. For example, a bivocational pastor simultaneously working in health care easily distinguished between "I" the pastor and "they" the congregation: "I was trying to help them discern where they were, where they felt God was leading them . . . [in] grieving the loss and then being able to see that there is resurrection and hope in new ways, even if they are in a new place."

Many pastors in rural areas and inner-city neighborhoods have multichurch appointments; the burden of serving more than one congregation encourages clear pastoral boundaries, or differentiation. For example, one pastor had a two-point charge, including a small church that "could not support a pastor on its own." Although using the pronoun "we," he was also clear about his own differentiated role:

> We realized that after we had cut budgets and done everything else, about three months in my role was, I guess, sort of twofold: My role was, from the [judicatory] side, to bring a closure to the church as far as it being an active congregation. Secondly, it was to shepherd those individuals into other congregations that were nearby, to try to take care of the people.

A pastor's call to lead with grace may be eased when the pastor serves several churches, as seen in this pastor's conclusion: "It wasn't a lot of trouble. I didn't have a lot invested in it emotionally or spiritually." He found that "the members, the ones who wanted to, landed in other churches, and one of the families is a very active part of my [other] church now."

Finally, pastors may grow as self-differentiated leaders through serving a diminishing congregation. A "bad surprise" may jerk them into awareness of their "otherness." First-call pastors (as I was) tend to be more stressed by their ministries in closing churches.[9] One of the stresses is realizing that the "I" needs to differentiate from the "we." This happened to one first-call clergyperson:

> Early in the process we had developed a revitalization plan. Part of it was hosting booths [at community events] and being present. One of the significant things that happened for me is, I was away and there was a booth we were supposed to be staffing. The parishioners didn't go staff it, [supposedly] because it was raining. [But]

the booth was inside. That was the breakthrough moment for me to realize that "I" was revitalizing the church. It wasn't that "we" were revitalizing the church: nothing happened unless I was there. That wasn't feasible for the long haul.

Pastors may find themselves catapulted into differentiation as "I" by standing apart from skirmishes in the congregation. One pastor made sure she kept saying "we" as she entered her congregation. In recounting how she realized the congregation had only hired her to pastor the older members and was holding secret meetings to leave the denomination, she shifted into "they" in narrating the closure story. For example, when she wanted to look over the church's failing finances, she said with exasperation, "They wouldn't give me the books."

Another pastor said, "I had to be honest with them. I showed up at one all-church meeting wearing a referee shirt. I said, 'I'm not trying to be silly.'" The pastor felt he "had to do something symbolically." He explained: "I had talked to the judicatory executive about it. I'm in leadership here to say, 'This is the role that I was asked to play here.'" Conflict can create the initiative for vocational maturity and differentiated, transformational leadership.

Although most pastors rise to the many challenges of leading through dissolution, others may be reluctant or may lack the skills for graceful intervention. *Some contexts that might limit a pastor's capacity to recognize and respond to dysfunctional appeals or attacks include a personal history of abuse or trauma, being a first-call pastor, or personal commitments the pastor will not let go of in order to fully embrace a congregational pilgrimage to dissolution.*

A pastor's memories of personal and church experiences of trauma, such as being treated disrespectfully by a judicatory or another congregation, as had happened to me in another part of the country, can "push the buttons" that set off fear, anger, or confusion and limit anyone's access to faith or reason. Even the most differentiated ministers can have moments when a powerful current of "they" or "we" overwhelms. Later, they may regret either their failure to do an intervention or the reactive way they responded to resistance or personal attacks. Every pastor can slip unintentionally into enmeshed codependency and undifferentiated behavior, which often comes with not knowing the triggers that lead to surrendering one's identity to the needs of others.[10]

For example, one pastor still in grief from a difficult appointment fell in love with her spiritually alive yet dying congregation, becoming emotionally attached to their vision for survival. Although she understood that "it was not good stewardship to use $100,000 a year so six people could have a good worship experience once a week," she saw herself as "their advocate." When her advocacy failed to forestall closure, she felt she had failed. When the judicatory forbade her from seeing them for one year after the closing, she said, "That helped me a lot. It made me feel less guilty."

Even without a history of trauma, idealistic clergy in their first appointment may easily "fall in love" with their new congregation, finding it difficult to "go to the balcony" to see what is happening.[11] For example, one pastor fresh out of seminary closely identified with the vulnerable new congregation he had planted with sacrificial faithfulness, working eighty-hour weeks. He narrated his story with mostly "we," as in "we were able," "we ran into," "we were growing," and "we ultimately closed." He grieved deeply at the church's sudden closure, before taking time off to heal and accept a new call from God.

Pastors also may have personal commitments they are hesitant to "let die" for the sake of the congregation's dissolution—for example, a pastor's passion to maintain a community ministry or to keep a job. "Well, for me I knew it would be, just in terms of my age, this would be my last church," said one pastor serving a rural cluster of churches. If one closed, it was not clear that the others would be able to maintain his full-time salary. "We were slowly dwindling," he recalled, and a rumor had circulated that one church was going to close. "I assured the people that I've not gotten any directive from the [judicatory] that that's happening. It's not part of my agenda. Not part of my make-up. I didn't sign on to do this kind of thing." Lay leaders came to him saying, "There's no future. This is not going to work." The pastor asked for a moratorium on such discussions, but they decided to close. The pastor admitted, "I was disappointed, but I realized I didn't have a better alternative other than my own stubbornness. It's not exactly an alternative." He faithfully helped them say goodbye with joy rather than with recrimination or sadness, seizing the tiller.

Pastoral differentiation carries the risk that the pastor may disengage from the sacred community altogether, becoming an indifferent or autocratic "I." Philosophers such as Immanuel Kant and Martin Buber criticize ethics in which "I" treats "you" as "it"—that is, as a means to an end rather than as an end in itself.[12] In conflict, pastors may be unable to see the Christ in each person, as a "you" worthy of respect. Conversely, faithful pastors will see all members of their congregation

as created in the image of God or, with the cover of canonical authority, as those to whom they have a duty to attend.[13]

CHAPTER SUMMARY

In a sacred community, a pastor is not a lone ranger "I" yet is healthiest
as a differentiated "I"—one who refrains from enmeshment with the
congregation while respecting everyone's dignity as "we," the people
of God on a pilgrimage together. In his Corinthian letters, St. Paul
called the church to be the "body of Christ," recognizing, sometimes
with frustration, that being the body of Christ in the world is not easy.
Nonetheless, differentiated pastors and laity alike may draw on well-
springs of faith and authenticity to lead their churches safely to a "good
enough" death. Clarifying the sacred community's values, such as
respectful relationships; using systems thinking to recognize and name
disrespectful norms, such as emotional triangles; respecting the authority of the congregation; maintaining a peaceable presence; setting clear
boundaries; and practicing pastoral self-care are life-giving and transformational leadership skills.

In the midst of profound sadness, anger, or confusion, the Holy
Spirit will empower a pastor, lay leaders, or an entire congregation to
name the coming shoals and "go below deck" to discern a new destination, recalibrate a course with the GPS of faith, and sail beyond "this
place"—to rebuild, to transform, or to set sail for the fog-covered shore
to begin a new life elsewhere. The next chapter describes how differentiated, transformational leadership gifts may be used to lead a dying
church into resurrection.

5

The Pilgrimage
to a Grace-Filled Closure

It was a beautiful sunny and gusty evening on the bay. We had sailed two long races and were headed back to the berth. Suddenly I realized our skipper was having trouble starting the outboard motor that would drive us safely to our slip in the marina. He tried vainly for the next twenty minutes as the sky darkened. My anxiety rose. Then he stopped. He asked someone to put on the running lights. I had a pit in my stomach: we were going to sail in the dark. (We couldn't simply call AAA for a tow!) Going in by the power of our 40-foot mainsail could be tricky and dangerous. We'd be going too fast to turn into the marina's channel without hitting a pier or another boat. Everyone looked at everyone else. I said to the skipper quietly, "What's Plan B?" He was silent. Then he said, "We'll sail in." I asked, "Have you ever done that before?" "No." Suddenly everyone was alert: "What should we do?" He gave us our orders. We neared the marina, we passed it, and then we did a 180-degree turn to slow our entry. As we sailed in, he shouted to a friend on the pier to run down to our berth to meet us. Our skipper ordered the sails to be dropped quickly. That slowed us down, just enough to make the turn safely into the slip, where the sailor on land caught our rigging just before we hit the quay. We were safe.

Dwindling attendance and income strain a congregation's capacity to raise or trim the sails or to fuel the motor. Without power to move forward, a church risks crashing on the leeward shore.[1] Although a pastor in prayer may perceive that God is calling a church to close, most pastors faithfully watch for the Holy Spirit's inclination within the sacred community. This watching and waiting is unique for each church. Like the seed that grows by itself, we know not how (Mark 4:26–27), the Holy Spirit may inspire congregational leaders to decide to close without their pastor's participation. On the other hand, when a treacherous end looms, God may call the pastor to seize the tiller and steer the church toward the sacred wind of transformation. This chapter describes pastoral leadership that brings a church safely home.

In truth, the Holy Spirit moves most congregations to closure without much pastoral initiative. In my study's written survey, more than 60 percent of lay leaders took a "great deal of" or "very much" initiative, compared with 46 percent for the pastor, 43 percent for members, and 36 percent for the judicatory. These statistics reflect congregations that made the decision on their own without pastoral leadership, as well as congregations in which responsibility for closure was shared with the pastor. In nearly a third of the churches in my study, the pastor indicated taking no or "very little" initiative; in these churches, only 10 to 20 percent of pastors experienced "the actual decision to close" as a "great challenge."

Laity who spearhead the closure process often take the lead by bravely facing what is actually taking place. For example, one pastor reported, "The final bump was in the fall before we closed, when the nominating committee started looking around the elderly congregation to say, 'Who will be an elder for next year?' Some of our younger, healthier ones were having health problems, or having to move. Or they just said, 'We don't think we have it in us.'" One congregation that had financial reserves but increasing maintenance expenses "had some people on council who were not afraid to say, 'We're running out of money. We need to close.'" One pastor said the church decided to "close instead of using the money that they had gotten from the sale of the parsonage."

Like a sailboat without wind or a motor to power it, an indecisive church community risks a precipitous and perilous closing. This and the following chapters describe some steps pastors may take to seek the wind of the Holy Spirit so that a congregation closes gracefully.[2]

This journey begins with seeking the Holy Spirit's creative, consoling wind in the congregation, then harnessing that power with transformational leadership skills that engage the entire congregation on a pilgrimage. Pastors' gifts include gathering the sacred community to listen for God's call, holding the congregation accountable for an inclusive process and ultimate decision, speaking the truth in love (with the assistance of the judicatory and neighboring churches as needed), and managing conflicts. When the sacred community completes all of these tasks well, pastor and congregation can gather at a final worship service to share authentic and loving good-byes, with sadness but also with peace and hope for a new future.[3]

In this survey, I found that when it is the pastor who initiates a process to gather the community to seek God's call, the most diffi-cult task becomes the actual decision to close, which was rated a "great challenge" by more than half of pastors in congregations where lead-ers and members took no initiative.[4] In response to the questionnaire, pastors also indicated that "dealing with members' difficult emotions," "initiating discernment," and "the process of discernment" were seri-ous challenges. Among the reasons was denial—that is, congregations fearing the loss of sustainability or vitality. One pastor described five churches close to each other: "My assessment was that they all had their own problems, but they avoided facing them by finding another church that had worse problems." Members also may have spiritual and emotional attachments to a church building, or a "theology of place," that may be hard to reconcile with a call to worship wherever God calls based on a "theology of journey."[5]

Deciding to close a church takes both faith and leadership. *When pastors gather their sacred communities to seek God's call, whether that is to revitalize, merge, close, or head for some other destination, they guide with their rudder—the gospel of resurrection faith—inviting their congre-gation to look to Jesus Christ and imagine for themselves a new future after death.* In one small church, the pastor noted, "It was a process—mostly through my preaching and going through Lent and Easter before, and tying that into the dying of a congregation and new life, but not point-edly. I still wanted them to come to that conclusion." The pastor led with faith as he held the congregation accountable for the decision.

Sometimes all it takes is listening for the movement of the Holy Spirit among church members. In a small rural church, the pastor lis-tened for some time to a founding family grappling with the church's future. "It was the matriarch's parents who started that church sixty-two years before, and this was painful—very, very," recalled the pastor. There they had married, raised their children, and now guided their grandchildren. "It was more helping them through that pain, trying to make it as easy as possible for them to come to that conclusion." Suddenly, "my gosh, they just said, 'OK, wrap it up. Close the door.'"

The church closed with a beautiful service one month after the family made the decision at home.

Pastors may publicly acknowledge a slight ripple on the water, a gentle puff on the sail's telltale, which may be all it takes for the congregation to embrace the actuality that will move the church to its calling. For example, in a small rural congregation when one lay leader told the pastor, "We don't know how long this is going to go on," the pastor acknowledged the individual's courageous remark with, "Let's look into that. Let's have a serious discussion about that." He gathered members in a meeting to review the purpose and mission of the church and the purpose of a pastor.

> They pretty much said, "Well, then I can go to a church closer to my house." I said, "Well, that's certainly an option." Then another lady said, "Well, if I don't come here, I can just watch preachers on TV." OK, that is an option. And we just talked about it. It turned out that two of the ladies, two widows, were pretty much taking care of 90 percent of the expenses of the church. And they were driving the furthest to get there just to sustain it, just for tradition's sake. Both of them told me in private that they would get involved in a same-denomination church in the bigger city because that's where they lived.

Perceiving hidden currents that were beating back a church's mission, this pastor called members onto the deck where they could see themselves clearly. Members had been hanging on because a monthly church supper was a reunion for people in the rural community and the many who had moved away. In order to continue the suppers, the judicatory agreed to donate the church to a local nonprofit; the decision to close followed easily. The church heeded the wind of the Holy Spirit in a journey that, to the pastor, felt like Easter.

In larger dwindling congregations, pastors may initiate a formal dialogue centered in Scripture to move toward a merger or dissolution. For example, when a neighboring church approached an aging congregation of about seventy people about purchasing their cathedral-sized building, the pastor wondered, "What is God calling them to do and to be?" They already leased space to several small congregations; although aging, they still had a large endowment. The pastor designed a "season of study and discernment, prayer and exploration of possibilities." The congregation formed task forces to explore possibilities, including merging with a neighboring church that already shared ministry with them. The pastor believed her respect for the congregation's agency was essential: "They trusted that I had no agenda. I was just with them and supporting this process and would support whatever they decided." The pilgrimage itself was healing: "They opened up to new possibilities. There was a growing trust. I think they learned to trust in a new way." Members visited other churches en masse without their pastor, eventually deciding to merge with a smaller congregation with young families, bringing nearly $2 million from the sale of the church building with them. "It was a miraculous process," said the pastor, "and I think it was partially because no one had an idea initially that we were going to close and sell the property. It wasn't even discussed in the beginning." It was "something that God led" in a pilgrimage the pastor likened to the season of Christmas.

Like many others, this pastor found that the Scripture readings appointed for each Sunday—with their sacred mysteries of God's presence with the Jewish people and of Jesus' birth, life, death, and resurrection—may blow a fresh, powerful, consoling wind into a congregation's sails.[6] During a church's decision process, one pastor urged others to "let the liturgical year help to create a theological frame, to develop one that's contextual and that's grounded in the wider traditions, beyond even your context." The pastor said that this helps "to bridge you beyond where you are to where you're going, wherever that may be. Be very open to mystery. Be real about what's difficult, to not try to pretend like that's not there."

For example, one minister in an indecisive, struggling congregation incorporated the story of the Annunciation in a "slow, methodical, intentional process over eighteen months of leadership team and congregation." He explained:

> The entirety of our faith lives are journeys with Christ from Annunciation to Pentecost. When a church closes, it prepares to hear anew the whole story of Jesus, the Christ, beginning with Annunciation and the anticipation of new life. The closing of a church is not a final event but a deepening in our shared life with Christ. It is striking that the words "Be not afraid" appear both in the Annunciation and in the resurrection narratives.

Watching and waiting for the Holy Spirit's guidance, members of his church participated in *lectio divina*, a reverential reading of Scripture that listens in silence for God's word, refraining from dialogue.[7] In the beginning, the minister recalled, members "sat in the church hall in a circle with everyone facing each other. We spent about six months praying in a *lectio divina* style and a full faith-sharing on the Annunciation text." Days or weeks after the leadership team prayed with the text, the congregation did too, using the World Café process as a setting for dialogue.[8] The prayer circle of sacred community became a place of healing: "There was an expressing of anger, but there was also expressing of peacefulness in that anger." The pastor felt that through this process, the closing of the church came to feel like Easter.

Pastors may root the spiritual journey of their congregation in diverse Scripture passages; for example, the parable of the Prodigal Son was used in one church where, reported the pastor, "they really didn't feel like a failure, but it's a sad thing, and so they sort of felt like God would greet them and be happy with them." They also recalled "where Moses didn't quite get over to the promised land. Every member could see that Moses knew God was with him." In their interviews with me, pastors affirmed that a pilgrimage of closure with scriptural study blesses the people with God's forgiveness, assurance of God's presence, and hope for a new future. Old Testament stories, psalms, and Gospel readings leverage the power of the Holy Spirit, strengthening the rudder and centerboard to stabilize the church as it moves through troubled waters.

Holding a congregation accountable for the ultimate decision means finding the right balance of agency between "I" the pastor, "you" the congregation, and "we" or "us" in collaboration. One risk is a pastor taking on too much responsibility. One pastor cautioned, "There's a balance between coming to a congregational meeting and saying, 'Look, this is what I think is best for you' and saying, 'Here are the options.' I'm not sure that I really did a good job at that."[9] One pastor serving two churches—one strong and one weak—found a healthy balance of "I" and "we": "The final blow: we had called a meeting for the weaker church—basically, it was just like a presentation. I showed them the revenues, I showed them what we had, and the inability to continue in this way: 'There's no other way to go.' There was no alternative for us." The pastor experienced their pilgrimage like the reflective season of Lent.

Just as going up on deck can relieve seasickness, an inclusive, transparent, aboveboard, faith-filled pilgrimage with one another and God may assuage angst. One pastor said, "I would say be patient. Nobody wants to be rushed into this sort of decision; that will make the process much worse, if you set a deadline like six months." It's about the sacred community—"it's not about the pastor." One pastor for whom the closing was like Easter took time in the process to make for "peace of mind and heart":

> It wasn't the moneyed people's idea; it wasn't the denomination's idea. What we strove for was consensus and sensing of what the Holy Spirit needed us to do. Well, we talked it to death. We beat the horse completely. If you go in there and kind of rush for a decision, that makes people anxious. When they're anxious, even if a decision is made, then there's probably not going to be consensus. They might go along to get along, but they don't have the sense of buy-in.

Another minister advised, "There's a whole lot more listening involved than there is talking. The listening is not only to each other, but it's listening to what the Spirit says. Every answer is tentative. It can change tomorrow." Listening shows respect and eventually reveals what has been hidden below water and the limited view from below deck. One pastor told me, "First of all, it's about the relationships. Second of all, it is about building bridges of understanding."[10] Listening to members of a congregation and building bridges of understanding among them are the fruits of faith that embody God's presence.

Gospel faith not only guides pastors to listen to and build bridges of understanding with members of their congregations; it also gives pastors courage to confront denial. One pastor urged others leading decision journeys in their congregations, "Don't stop trying. Don't stop fighting. Don't stop taking the risks. If you're not failing, you're not taking risks. If you're not taking risks, then you're not really sharing the gospel like I think we're called to do. Yeah, this is not a safe job that we have. It should not be a safe job that we have. It should be dangerous and risky, filled with a lot of mystery."

Although it may feel risky, a pastor's naming of a difficult truth may actually relieve a congregation's anxiety and release a clear decision. One congregation with forty members owed thousands of dollars for a new organ and was looking at well over $250,000 in deferred maintenance costs when a flood damaged the church. The pastor held back from naming the possibility of closure until the financial realities could sink in, then said, "Now it's time for me to say something and to be honest with you: what I hear and see is that you are too tired to continue on, and even though in your heart you want to, it's not going to go because you are just too overwhelmed now." Then, the pastor recalled, "one of them blurted out, 'Oh thank God, Pastor! I've been wanting to say that all the time!' and the rest of them agreed too." Over the next year and a half, they had several congregational meetings. "We gave them opportunities to talk and stand up when they spoke," said the pastor. They closed gracefully.

Similarly, power to spring forward was released when one pastor wrote a column in the church newsletter entitled "What Are We Doing Here?" He reported, "I was surprised at the result. I got feedback on that—like, positive feedback! People were wondering the same thing. What are we doing here?" The pastor learned there were "a number of people who were actually . . . thinking it's time to close the church and move on." He believes he "kind of gave them that voice to do it." Another pastor initiated a difficult conversation: "We had a little time in there, after I said, 'Good morning. We're going to worship God.' . . . [At the point of] sharing for the good of the family of faith, I said, 'Have you thought about this [possibility of closure]?'" The pastor commented, "I think they were relieved that I brought it up, and they were open—very open. Our treasurer was there, and he said, 'Yeah, we're having problems,' and we just [nodded] and everybody agreed." In this study, I saw that pastors would raise the question of closure when they sensed it might be a relief to talk about it.[11]

When faith-filled, transformational pastors still find their congregations apprehensive and indecisive, as a last measure some reach out for assistance from the coast guard—that is, the judicatory. For example, one pastor serving a stalled church invited the judicatory executive and the church's leaders to assemble a series of congregational meetings "for prayer and study and conversation." The judicatory executive led the first one, bringing in facilitators "who were outside of the congregation, community members from different walks of life," among them a UCC chaplain, an Episcopal priest from a neighboring congregation, and a social worker. About six or eight community leaders facilitated dialogue at tables where, the pastor explained, "we assigned people seats . . . like setting up the place cards for a wedding [so] that the conversations [could] happen in a way that would be healthy and helpful." In this intervention encouraging the congregation to take responsibility for the decision to revitalize or close, the judicatory executive used the story of the disciples crossing the sea in a storm as the Bible study text. "So where is this church on this journey? Are you ready to set out across the sea, or are you in the middle of the storm? Are you at a place where you recognize Jesus to be the one to worship and trust?" The judicatory leadership team asked the church, "What's your vision for the congregation five years down the line?" and "What is it that you're willing to do?" The judicatory team heard, "We just really want somebody to tell us what to do. We don't think this can survive. We're pretty confident [we're] done." The pastor observed "pessimism . . . but nobody wanted to say 'It's time to close.'" Bringing in consultants to facilitate what might be highly emotionally charged conversations enabled the pastor to be "the pastor" to everyone, rather than the messenger bearing bad news. The congregation eventually voted to close, having experienced the honest, healing, and consoling presence of Jesus on what the pastor described as their "Easter journey."

Because a judicatory is a fleet of churches, pastors may encourage hesitant congregations to explore mergers with or adoptions by nearby congregations; these choices preserve treasured relationships as they renew another congregation's mission.[12] For example, one pastor averred, "My job was . . . either to help turn [the congregation] around or help it to die with dignity." Noting that many members were "old-old" and disabled, he successfully proposed adoption by a flourishing congregation nearby,

> so for the members it wasn't a traumatic thing. It was just a natural procession. I wanted to make sure that the people in the church felt cared for . . . like life would continue on. I wanted to, as much as possible, kind of have them move en masse to another church rather than scatter to the wind, or end up, you know, a dozen different places in all, and we were able to accomplish that quite well.

As pastoral leaders, clergy in multichurch calls might more easily suggest merger or adoption because the pastor remains the same.[13] When an elder in one church died, a pastor appointed to two congregations sat down with leaders of the weaker church: "I've been thinking that one of the things we should pray about and think about doing is closing [this church]." She assured the congregation, "You can come over to the [other] church; it's only about five miles away. They come here to church to worship with you. They welcome you. It could be a really nice thing." They closed peaceably, and the receiving church grew.

Some congregations end with a merger—that is, two congregations "die" to become one congregation with a new name and identity. Merging is more difficult to negotiate than a process of adoption, but if successful, the process can feel like a festival season such as Easter. One such process was led by a pastor who had founded a rapidly growing congregation that was outgrowing its "small, nondescript brick ranch building." When their balloon payment on the mortgage was due, the pastor and lay leaders proposed to a nearby declining, older congregation in the same denomination that they would sell their building and unite with the older congregation, which had a more expansive building that was largely unused. Although the merger was challenging, their first shared worship service on Christmas Eve celebrated that "something new was being born." For the pastor, coming together was like Easter, with the new church adopting a new name selected by the united congregation. The pastor now sees God's hand at work: "We're two churches coming together, trying to be in harmony with each other, but we're also longing for that deeper harmony that comes from our experience of God and the faith we share."

Even with faith and the best leadership steps a pastor can provide, a pilgrimage to closure may not be a sunlit journey on calm seas. Everyone grieves differently, as one pastor noted:

> Some people feel, "OK, this makes the most sense, let's make it happen yesterday," and other people say, "I need to know everything." The many personalities: "But what about this?" "But what about that?"—like "Let's talk about it more." Keeping people on the same timing was really tough, the lag-behinds and the run-aheads. We're just going step by step. It feels fast to you. It feels slow to you. But we're just going step by step.

Pastors seeking to keep the community intact and healthy on a lengthy journey must manage conflict in a way that encompasses respect for everyone yet moves the vessel forward. To this end, pastors may extend the length of the discernment process by including in the leadership team opponents of closure to create more opportunities for discussion; they may even stimulate disagreements. For example, when community circumstances ended the possibility of renewal in one church, the pastor preached about what it means to be church; she also conveyed to the congregation that they would close, stirring up conflict. Despite their weariness, members found it difficult to imagine departure from a building "they loved with all their hearts." In this church's lengthy journey, the pastor invited a critic of closing to join the task force considering it. "Going to her and asking her to be on that seemed like it broke down some barriers and helped her to feel like she would have a say," said the pastor. This step affirmed that the body of Christ is inclusive. At one meeting, the leadership team addressed the congregation:

"This is where we are: the most faithful thing to do is to die and trust the Lord for resurrection and walk our different ways, not keep holding on to this thing that really is not church anymore." In their pilgrimage, which the pastor likened to Advent, Easter, and Pentecost, the congregation voted to close and celebrate its legacy.

Although a congregation's legacy might diminish, conflict can sometimes be averted by delay. For example, one pastor led a dying but stonewalled congregation through years of informal dialogue—potlucks, straw polls—pondering merging, federating, closing, and other options. The pastor recounted:

> You know, there were some people who just said, "Well, why can't we just all join another denomination, and we'll just join as a group?" Some people were in favor of that, and others didn't want to do that. So finally, after a couple of years of just not having official votes or formal meetings or anything—they decided, "No, we're just going to close it up entirely. People can go whichever way they want to go. Whatever assets we have after we've taken care of the building, we'll just divide that up as we choose."

Interviews with pastors revealed that when a congregation can bear loving and honest dialogue, faith and transformational leadership skills can come together to birth a decision everyone can live with, as one last story will show.

In this particular failing church, the interim pastor organized a "mission study" team that did research and "came up with 'either we rebirth and become a completely different church—or we close.'" The pastor preached how a church closing is like Jesus' death that "led to the resurrection" and found "they really gravitated towards that." In town hall–style meetings and one all-congregation Saturday gathering, "they were slowly moving towards closing, but there was a heaviness and they didn't want to move towards it." The pastor and the leadership team split the congregation into prayer groups "for a month or two, meeting and praying about these two pieces of discernment and rebirth." The church's mission study group "really saw and tried to impress on the rest of the congregation: 'This congregation will die, one way or the other. Something totally new needs to be born.' Most people didn't get that." Then halfway through, the death of a matriarch was followed by that of a forty-year-old man, also a key member. "And you could feel it sinking down," said the pastor.

A couple months went by, and I could sense they were moving towards closing, but it [was] too hard and scary. . . . I pulled out my last tool: I had the treasurer go and analyze the giving—who was giving what, by age. And I did some pie charts and bar graphs. And it pretty much showed what I knew, looking at them: 80 percent of giving was done by people seventy-five and over. One thirty-five-year-old single mother on food stamps isn't going to be giving much—but somehow it didn't seem to add up for people. I was surprised that the visioning team was so shocked by those numbers.

They continued the prayer groups and held another Saturday event. Finally, said the pastor, "one key member, who was the only living charter member, said she had had a dream. She said God spoke to her and told her they had to close; she said, 'I think we need to close.'" They voted then to close.

CHAPTER SUMMARY

Although many declining congregations make a clear decision to close on their own initiative, when the wind is dying, some need a nudge from the Holy Spirit. In churches in denial or that are uncertain of their future, my study showed that pastors often led a community's pilgrimage, designing interventions ranging in complexity from simply preaching resurrection hope and listening for the Holy Spirit's inclination among church members, to designing formal dialogues centered in Holy Scripture with a mix of leadership, small group, task force, and town hall meetings, some with judicatory assistance. No matter the congregation's size, pastors seeking an ending more like Easter than Good Friday held their church accountable for the decision to close by supporting their capacity to hear the call of God with resurrection hope. In some churches, the pastor's speaking a difficult truth in love became a turning point for the birth of a community decision. In a time of uncertainty, watching and waiting for the Holy Spirit's power can ensure order, protection, and guidance as a sacred community sails into the harbor of dissolution: a pilgrim people bearing God's powerful, healing presence into the world.

6

Stormy Weather

Conflict and Recourse

We were racing on San Francisco Bay in sustained winds of 30 knots (about 35 mph), gusting to the high 30s. The Golden Gate was to our right as we sailed upwind toward San Francisco. I was wrapped up like an Inupiat in the cold. About twenty minutes earlier, our skipper had handed the tiller to a new crew member who had joined us for the day. The sky was gray as winds tossed water in the air, drenching folks on the deck close to the bow. We were nearing a mark where we'd take a 180-degree turn. The wind that was before us would soon be behind us, with the 40-foot sail whipping overhead. The crew crawled over the deck to hang over the port rail for ballast on the new course. We got the warnings: "Prepare to jibe," then "Jibe ho!" The boat swirled and lurched to port. The rails went under, and water cascaded aboard. With all hell breaking loose, the boom cracked like a tree and the sail fluttered uselessly on the mast. Although the keel brought the boat upright, two crew members on the rail went under, their life vests automatically inflating to save them. They held on for their lives. Our skipper took over and yelled directions—I don't remember much of what he said, except to keep my head down and move back so those on the foredeck could move safely to the cockpit. "Is everyone safe?" the skipper shouted. With wind spilling off the sail, the boat slowed. After recovering our wet crew members, we abandoned the race, called the race committee, and motored to the marina. In the deafening silence, I said a prayer.

Sometimes leading a church feels like this. Church buildings can fail, but worse, the mutual trust of sacred community may suddenly be rent by gossip, rumor, secrecy, or inexplicable outrage. In my early tenure at the church that closed, a relative newcomer shared a secret with me: an elected church leader had told her I was "killing the church." My stomach went into knots. Newly ordained and naive, I didn't expect high drama in the church, but there it was.

At their best, pastors inquire, and judicatories inform them, about onerous contexts before their entry. But too often, challenging contexts are revealed only during the long journey of ministry; one pastor called these "kitchen conversations." In the church I served, for example, church members power washing the church building revealed a "secret" conflict that helped me understand their lack of trust in me. The power washing reminded me of baptismal water setting us free to speak the truth in love.

This chapter describes sources and signs of church conflict, the ways they affect pastoral leadership, and skills pastors bring to facilitate God's work of reconciling the differences. Church conflict can come from many directions—cultural differences within the congregation or with the wider church, relationship conflicts, conservative-progressive theological rifts, histories of pastoral or lay leadership addiction, sexual abuse or other boundary violations, financial mismanagement, and more. I was not alone in entering a conflicted congregation. In this study's written survey, about one-fifth of pastors had entered congregations with conflict they assessed as "more serious," "serious," or "greatest."

For example, cultural conflict prevailed when a majority Anglo congregation in this study had been poorly merged with an ethnic minority congregation: the two maintained separate services, finances, and cultural identities that the judicatory wanted to merge because neither congregation on its own was sustainable. The senior pastor explained:

> It got really harsh. We had meetings, especially between church leaders and others, that were really just yelling brawls. It was pretty bad. We ended up having co-chairs for the leadership team. We had tried to bring in as many co-chairs and tried to balance everything out as much as we possibly could balance out.

One person asked the senior pastor to force the majority immigrant church out; another "ordered" the pastor to sign a partisan letter. The judicatory got more involved as the pastor tried to restore sacred community. The pastor recounted:

> Initially, my striving was to try to bring the church together for what they were saying at times, like "Yes, we are working towards being a multicultural kind of a church," and I strove with them. I told them, "I don't know if it's going to work, but I'm going to give you everything I have to get you there." My striving in a sense really was to try to help them come together and see the gifts that each of them had and how they really could be a stronger congregation in a unified fashion.

Despite the best efforts of this faithful, well-differentiated pastor, the cultural conflict remained intractable, leading to the judicatory's assessment that they were not a viable congregation and should be closed, which is what eventually happened.

The signs of church conflict are many.[1] According to Speed Leas, a practical theologian, some indications include participation by only a few members; self-censorship and withdrawal from established relationships in the church; closed or deceitful expression of ideas and feelings; ignored contributions of many members who are devalued, disrespected, and treated lightly; ineffective sending and receiving communication skills; and ignored or suppressed differences in opinions and ideas.[2] These group dynamics indicate loss of mutually respectful relationships rather than conflicts over what tasks need to be accomplished or how to complete them—disagreements that actually might be constructive.[3]

In the grief and anxiety of a sacred community's impending dissolution, not only may church people contend with one another, but some factions also may draw the pastor into their unrest. This study encountered stories of how church people

— kept congregational secrets from the pastor;
— made physical threats against the pastor;
— invaded the pastor's personal space (person and office);
— spoke ill of the pastor in the church or the community;
— called the judicatory to complain about the pastor;
— refused to give the pastor access to church documents and other resources;
— sabotaged pastoral decisions (for example, location of altar candles or banners);

— scapegoated the pastor (for example, in replying to a pastor's complaint about not being paid, saying "That's not a very Christian attitude" or the pastor "was spending too much money [referring to salary, health insurance, and retirement contributions]" or "It's all her fault");

— shared uninhibited reactions in meetings (for example, storming out or yelling at the pastor);

— made authoritative decisions on behalf of the church without the pastor's knowledge or consent; and

— were rude to the pastor's family.

Halfway through my interviews I realized an unexpected sign of conflict—the pronouns clergy use to tell stories about their churches. Tumultuous journeys would sound like this: "They are more attached to their organist than they are to finding a better, more effective future style of worship for the church," or "They didn't want harmony; they wanted disharmony and confusion," or "They said I was only interested in bringing people in from outside." I call these "they (negative)" statements. "They (negative)" means that predicates associated with "they" are barriers to sacred community and mission.[4] In contrast, pastors whose sacred communities had integrity said things like "They envisioned their future," or "They knew who they were as disciples of Christ," or "They saw the handwriting on the wall"—what I call "they (positive)" narratives. "They (positive)" means that the predicates associated with "they" encourage sacred community and the church's mission. In describing these churches, pastors also used the collaborative "we" and "our" to describe acts of grace and blessings, whereas those in conflicted churches rarely did.

Relationship conflicts can impair a pastor's ability to exercise transformational leadership because they raise anxiety and resistance to change.[5] People dig in their heels as the challenge of fear deters the rational thought, commitment, and investment in shared tasks that a community needs in order to move toward its destination. Fear and accompanying anger may lead to such behaviors as avoidance, apathy, unfair fighting, and flight, all of which may contribute to erosion of respect for the pastor.

In this study, pastors who arrived in conflicted congregations experienced less respect from their congregations over the course of their ministry than did pastors serving in churches with less conflict. Nearly three-fourths of pastors in churches with little or no conflict experienced moderate to high respect, compared with only 17 percent of pastors in seriously conflicted congregations. Relatively newly ordained pastors (first or second call) were as likely to enter contentious congregations as those with more church leadership experience. Nevertheless, a few pastors entering at-odds churches were able to build trust and respectful relationships and sacred community, despite difficult beginnings.

Besides nurturing a congregation's faith and understanding of what it means to be the church, key tools for reconciliation include restoring respectful forms of communication and decision-making, clarifying the roles of the pastor and church leaders, and practicing empathy. Although some congregations, especially those in theological conflict, may collapse in irreconcilable chaos, pastoral leadership can provide order, protection, and guidance, enabling the congregation to arrive safely at closure and to move on with hope for a new future as the people of God.

A pastor's trust in God is essential in any situation, but especially in turbulent churches. One pastor admitted, "There's just no way I would have survived with sanity intact if God had not been with me the whole time. I don't believe the chaos was engendered by God or designed by God or anything else, but out of all the chaos that came, the God gifts that also came were so sustaining." There was not just "I" agency or "we" agency or "they" agency; there was God agency. Clergy trusted that in time, by grace, God would restore order, protection, and direction.

From my journal, six months before our church closed:

In Genesis's Tower of Babel, God "confused" humanity's speech. Even now in the church we misunderstand one another. A community that speaks and listens to one another with respect and dignity can do anything, and when they don't wish to speak and understand one another, they will not be able to accomplish anything. Jesus is the living water that quenches our thirst for power and control so we can respect and trust one another and work together for the common good.

In the face of division, pastors turned to God and struggled to restore the elements of sacred community, such as a lively faith and honest, mutually respectful relationships, to guide a conflicted church toward a "good enough" closure.[6] For example, in a church that had difficulty with a recent pastor, the pastor who followed realized that lively faith was missing: "It became very clear to me that the biggest problem was [that] they were nothing other than a Sunday social club. They did absolutely nothing during the week. It was clear to me that this was [not] about Jesus and the gospel." Describing his tenure, the pastor said, "I spent the first year trying to get them to be church. I spent the second year trying to get them to be church with someone else [in a merger]." When that failed, he continued, "I spent the third year convincing them that they needed to close." (Note the "they [negative]" statements.) Despite the congregation being disrespectful of the pastor at the end, he strove to maintain his dignity; with his leadership they closed charitably, giving away their endowment and leaving the building to the judicatory.

A lively faith that is shared is key to reconciliation and a "good enough" death; in this study, churches divided by a conservative-progressive theological rift among themselves or with the pastor often devolved into irreconcilable discord. For example, one pastor entered a church that "knew all the time what their aim was, and their aim was to close that church, kill it, then start their own church [in a different denomination]." The pastor didn't know their goal until the secret eventually slipped out. The pastor wanted to follow the church's finances, but, she said, "they wouldn't give me the books." At meetings "none of them really wanted to participate. They'd be passive-aggressive." (Note the "they [negative]" references in this narrative.) The pastor said, "I didn't know what the heck was going on." Without shared agreement on what faith in Jesus Christ means, pastors in churches like this were often unable to overcome destructive norms and either experienced the loss of large segments of the congregation before closure or were attacked as a symbol of the opposition, or both. In this instance, the judicatory extracted the faithful pastor from the harmful situation and assumed control of the closure and the building.

One of the tools pastors brought to the journey of a struggling, at-odds congregation was a variety of paths for spiritual growth, such as Bible study, book groups, and group spiritual direction. One pastor in a conflicted church was personally moved by the image of the transfiguration because of its mysterious sense of transformation, as well as by the paschal mystery of death and resurrection. He described how preaching on the mystery of God's power to transform Jesus in both of these stories "really served us and helped us open up . . . the conversation" about what it means for the church to die and be resurrected in new form. He concluded, "There was such an integrative element to it," bringing people together in their faith as it related to their own circumstance of closing. "It was theology on the ground, and it had a pastoral specificity, and it was much larger than that at the same time." The pastor's faith-filled leadership led this congregation to a harmonious Easter-like celebration of their ministry.

Leading with faith, some pastors also managed to repair conflicted relationships using various forms of spiritual direction. At the opening of leadership meetings, for example, one pastor encouraged listening for the Holy Spirit in prayer and in one another's speaking. She would "hand out a cross or a card or something that they could pass around" and keep for personal devotions. Then she said, "I would [read] some Scripture and then I would ask them to honestly say what they heard in the Scripture as it related to the church." She was intentionally teaching them to listen respectfully to one another. She continued: "As we got closer and closer to the time, like a year prior to the closing, I would ask them what was their joy about being here and what was their fear." By using Bible study that required listening to one another in silence, the pastor said, "they knew they had to listen to each other and take it in and make no response back to the other person. That was a great way of helping them start to process" the challenging dynamics of dissolution in a respectful way.

Another pastor who walked into a grieving quarrelsome congregation undertook "to have the members of the congregation, who would now be let loose to go to other congregations, [be] as spiritually healthy as they possibly could be." On arrival, she discovered a dearth of norms of sacred community, such as respect and forgiveness. As in many difficult church transitions, the congregation was conflicted as well as disappointed with the legacy of the previous minister. Even looking ahead, members were contentious about their hopes and expectations for the new pastor, with some not sure the church would remain open beyond a year. As the judicatory worked with the entire congregation, the pastor worked for about two and a half years with about twelve people who were really interested in their spiritual life, "practicing different ways of praying and, essentially, developing a mutual spiritual direction group among themselves." She also did some appreciative inquiry work "so that they knew who they were, and that each of them had a calling from God, a purpose of some sort so that, when they did make the vote, they knew who they were as disciples of Jesus."[7] Her pragmatic leadership clarified communication norms support-ing loving, honest relationships.[8] They closed peaceably in what, to the pastor, felt like the church season of Advent: "[In] Advent, you're always waiting for Jesus to show up. I was waiting for people to wake up to Jesus being present within themselves, Jesus being present in their lives. I was also waiting for Jesus in my own life through the whole thing."

This pastor recognized that respectful communication is key to respectful relationships. Family systems theorist Edwin Friedman identifies three ways you can identify "madness" in others or yourself: interfering in the relationships of others, unceasingly trying to con-vert others to one's own point of view, and being unable to relate to people with whom one does not agree.[9] Disrespectful communications such as gossip, rumor, and concealment are signs of inability to relate to others.

In responding to rumors about themselves, pastors may model non-reactivity so they will not hurt others, appear to take sides, or raise the anxiety of the system. As one pastor reported,

> I didn't lose my cool, I didn't respond in kind when people were really vicious. There was a rumor mill about me; I didn't respond. It's not that it wasn't painful, and it wasn't that I didn't want to respond [laughter]. I had a few choice things to say, but I knew it would not matter. It would just make it worse. I think that may be one of the first times in my life that I actually had been able to keep that commitment fully. I didn't react. So that was new. I think the gift of time has been that 80 percent of those people remain in our denomination.

The pastor's personal clarity helped the congregation grieve and move peacefully into resurrection life in other congregations of the denomination.[10]

Rumors about church members can be unveiled through honest, respectful communication. As one pastor remembered,

> I had to be honest with them. [I said in a meeting,] "It did not come to me directly, but I have heard the rumors that there is going to

be a movement to depose the current leadership chair and replace her with this person." Right about that time, the [church member] walked up and said, "Here are the ballots, and here's what we're going to do." The judicatory executive came in and said, "We can always have nominations from the floor. I am not going to use anyone's prepared ballots." By the time we were finished, I was on my third chairperson.

In another divided church, the pastor noticed "one group who, right before a service, met in the corner of the church," to plot the strategy they would take with the judicatory and the pastor—"pretty terrible things." The pastor met with folks privately to say, "The approach you're taking is not going to do you any good. It's going to actually hurt your process. The appearance you're giving to the judicatory executive or any committee from the outside is . . ." and she spoke the truth in love. The pastor took the tiller to steer clear of the shoals of contempt.

A minister who experienced moderate conflict at the beginning of his ministry shared that one of the transformational tools he brought to the church was "transparency . . . honest, open communications" within the boundaries of open meetings rather than privately:

> When I got there, they had an email system that some, but not all, of the members of the congregation were on. It was where they would air their disagreements initially. . . . Initially when I got there, we would have a church meeting, World Café style,[11] where we would just have a really great conversation. Then off to email most would go and there'd be a different agreement with a subset of the congregation and then they'd come back to the meeting and not share that, so communication was very dysfunctional, very fragmented. I basically shut down the email system and said we need to have conversations where we respect one another. Now the conversations are in the congregation as a whole. All are invited to all meetings. All members need to come to all meetings unless you're really sick or dying. But this is where our work is done, face to face.

One Ignatian tool that particularly facilitated this pastor's challenge with the congregation was detachment.[12] Being able himself to "let go" of attachment to a particular outcome such as closure, the pastor encouraged members of the congregation to let go of such things as having the last word, gossiping, or speaking over others—actions that distracted from the community's decision-making process.

The tool of another pastor who worked through conflict to a "good enough" death was to set clear boundaries for how disagreements should be aired. Although one church held open congregational meetings over a year and a half to dialogue about the church's future, one Sunday, a faithful and concerned member stood up at the prayers and said, "Pastor, I am seriously praying for you because I think you and the leadership team are moving in the wrong direction." After hearing this and other hard words, the pastor said, "OK, I hear your concerns, but this is not the place or the time. We will gather after worship, and anybody who is here who wants to stay and dialogue can do that." She noted, "That's where some of the anger started spilling out finally." With the pastor's exercise of empathy, transparency, and setting boundaries for appropriate communication, this church closed harmoniously, gladly selling its building to the majority immigrant congregation already worshiping in the space.

Sometimes trying to repair the sacred community's conflict does not work; for example, clarifying what healthy behavior looks like may not be sufficient for reconciliation. In one contentious congregation, a pastor tried restoring loving, honest relationships. Despite lack of agreement on matters of faith, the new pastor, hoping for reconciliation, worked with the leadership team to develop relationship norms to keep the church moving forward through dialogue. Only days after signing a document in a "beautiful ceremony" rededicating themselves to working together despite differences, one member of the congregation sabotaged the congregation's collaborative efforts. In the face of this challenge, the judicatory decided to close the church. Radical relationship transformation is difficult, and where a shared, lively faith and norms of respect don't exist, sometimes it is impossible.

But back to efforts to resolve conflict by clarifying norms for group process. *Differentiated pastors may need to clarify their own role and the role of church leaders.* One pastor said of her entry to a conflicted church, "Half of them expected to be able to get rid of me in a year so that they could just close the congregation and walk away from the whole thing. Even though the leadership had voted unanimously to call me, that was still their expectation. . . . The other half expected that I, not Jesus, would save them. I can't tell you how many times I said, 'I am not the Savior. You only have one Savior.'"

In another fragile congregation, where two women informally wielded control of most church activities, the pastor engaged the entire leadership team in a process to put in writing the roles and responsibilities associated with every aspect of church life; they soon realized that these two women had no accountability. At the same time, the pastor encouraged new leaders to take their place in reconstituted church committees. Clarifying church roles as well as norms restored the health of the sacred community before closure.

Another pastoral balm on a wounded church is practicing empathy. Although it cannot be the only response, listening to understand restores a sense of protection. One pastor who "walked into a lot of conflict" noted that leadership meetings went on for three hours and sometimes longer "because [the pastor] allowed them the time and space to rehearse over and over again all of the things that had gone wrong and all their feelings." As a result, the pastor recalled, "each meeting, there were fewer and fewer of them having to do that until we got to the point, about six months in, that there's only one person left who was still not willing to move on." Not being in sync with a spirit of reconciliation, this person left the church; later it closed with a spirit of goodwill.

Faithful clergy in my study made every effort to respect the dignity of even difficult people. One said, "I remained loving and caring toward them, I sat with them in their pain, I buried their dead, I went to the hospital when they were having surgery or whatever, I stood by them." He visited a woman and her troubled family in the hospital even when, he admitted, she "was about to drive me over the edge with all her antics." Another pastor called with condolences for the wife of a previous leadership team chair who had left the church in anger and later died. "At the very least, even beyond the closing of the church I let them know, 'I never stopped being there for you or walking with you,' even if it meant walking to the cross," said the pastor.

Despite a pastor's best efforts, some conflicts may remain unreconciled at closure. The written survey asked pastors, "If the process of closing your congregation was like a church season or holy day, it would be . . ." Not only were pastors serving in initially conflicted churches more likely to name the process of dissolution as "Good Friday" or "Holy Saturday" than were those in less conflicted churches

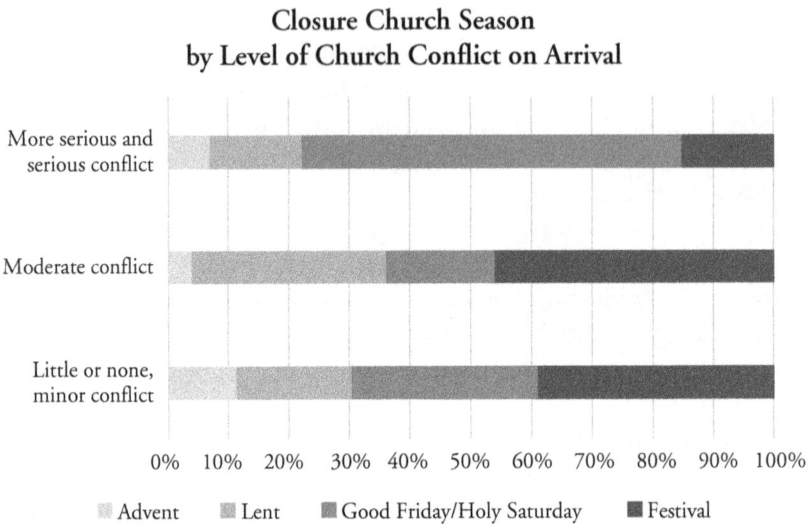

Closure Church Season
by Level of Church Conflict on Arrival

Figure 1. Pastors serving churches with more serious conflict on their arrival are more likely to describe their closure experience as the season of Good Friday or Holy Saturday rather than a festival season (such as Christmas, Epiphany, Easter, or Pentecost).

(figure 1); they also experienced less respect from their congregations.[13] This reflects not only conflict and a dearth of honest, mutually respectful relationships but also pastoral grief over the death, the pastor's loss of innocence, the pastor's loss of the few treasured friendships he or she had in the church, and in some cases, loss of vocational opportunities after serving a difficult parish.[14]

Said one pastor who called the closing of his conflicted church Good Friday, "It's something that I don't ever want to go through again. It's not easy on anybody, and nobody's happy about it, and it hurts everybody." He also opined, "It may be God's plan. How do you justify that a church closing could be God's plan? But it could. Rely on the faith that you had and realizing that, 'Hey, God, we're going to get through this together because it's definitely not what I wanted.'" Even in the midst of conflict, with faith in God and transformational leadership, this pastor was able to establish trust with many in the congregation before it closed.

CHAPTER SUMMARY

A conflicted church's journey to dissolution may see the hull breaking apart, people bruised and scarred, and hopes for the church as the hands and feet of Christ shattered. Sometimes even a pastor's best efforts to ensure a lively faith and restore respectful communication and decision-making fail, especially in the presence of theological divisions, and churches collapse in the midst of closing.

Given time and a pastor's faith and transformational leadership skills, it is possible for some conflicted churches to experience their pilgrimage like the festival season of Easter or Pentecost, or the reflective season of Lent or Advent. Other faith-filled remnants exit their beloved church with grief but gratitude for what has been, and with growing hope for what is to come. The next chapter explores the farewells that contribute to a "good enough" death for the body of Christ awaiting, if not experiencing, resurrection.

7

A "Good Enough" Death

Ceremonies, Preaching, and Legacy Giving

The afternoon our church closed, friends and strangers ambled slowly from the parking lot to the church under the wistful gaze of the worship leaders and children's choir, who waited in front of the parish house for the procession to begin. Tears of sorrow, anger, and confusion mingled with the joy that others had come to worship with us. Friends from the city and neighboring congregations with whom we had shared the founding and leadership of the food pantry, members and clergy of nearby churches, former members of the congregation who grieved with us, and even a newspaper reporter and photographer from the local paper joined the solemn assembly. At the back of the church, the retired bishop who had been our chaplain joined the procession, and his wife came over to give me a hug. The diocesan bishop didn't attend but delegated to the dean, a neighboring priest, the responsibility of reading an episcopal letter before the service. The organist began "Ye Holy Angels Bright." The acolyte led us down the aisle. It felt like Holy Saturday, this seventh Sunday of Easter.

Dissolving a church means the death of a sacred community.[1] The senior citizen who loves to welcome newcomers, the church member who bakes great cookies, the choir soloist called upon for every funeral, and countless others will lose the roles and identities they knew and counted on in their church.[2] This chapter explores the variety of church rites and rituals that can evoke God's consoling presence and compassion for those who mourn. Prayerful activities honor loss even as they promise the hope of new beginnings through grace. The distribution of legacy gifts to other churches and the community in honor and memory of their life together nurtures resurrection hope. Acts of remembrance may culminate in a final worship service with a sermon that speaks about the death with both a voice of vulnerability and a voice of consolation, and speaks about resurrection with conviction and hope. In addition, churches may assist parishioners in their time of loss by helping them find new spiritual communities.

Honoring a congregation's grief is like hospice ministry. One pastor observed, "You come to that point where you need to reassure people that . . . it's time. It's not going to be terrible, that there is life and life will continue. It will be different and it will be hard, but it's time." Understanding this dynamic, one judicatory asked a hospice chaplain to assume the role of closing pastor. *In recognition of death's theological significance, pastors draw on Scriptures and liturgies of the church to witness to God's presence and the hope of resurrection.*[3]

One pastor, who led with his rudder of faith, said, "The liturgical year is one of the best gifts to any church."[4] He elaborated:

We used the year with a sense that Pentecost is the sending forth. There clearly was going to be a closure. There was going to be a certain kind of death, and it was also going to be a certain kind of life for those who were going forth into new communities, knowing, too, that some might not go to new communities, depending on how they were feeling. Lent was a time of really fairly active grieving. That continued certainly beyond that, but then we took the fifty days of Easter to celebrate the community as well.

In assurance of God's presence, another pastor did a sermon series on Psalm 23 to close their time together as a church. Their next-to-the-last worship service was their big homecoming service, where everybody came back—including former pastors.

They still just wanted to come together and worship together one more time after the big blowout service. That Sunday was "Surely goodness and mercy will follow me the rest of my life." I don't know how that all came to me, but when I looked at how the verses broke down, it was clearly the Word of God to the people. Here's this great celebration and my cup overflows out into the community, to see where this church will lead, and will continue to overflow and overflow, then in the last moment just to know goodness and mercy are going to follow us wherever we go. It was definitely God's word.

Every season of the church year has its blessings for saying good-bye, even Christmas, as reported by another pastor:

People said they got totally into it, we were so lucky, full of grace. We hung greens. We knew it was the last Christmas, and the work party and the food everybody shared—it was really fun. I made a deliberate decision that it would be nothing but a celebration of our Lord's coming as a child. We all knew we were closing the church in five days [laughter]. We made a collective decision that we were going to celebrate Christmas. It really was—it was amazing.

Pastors and lay leaders honored grief with healing prayers in the weeks and months before dissolution. One pastor created a healing service that was used repeatedly in a new space the church used after leaving their former building but before deciding to close. They did "a lot of healing," said the pastor, "a lot of naming what had happened in the past. People were able to say, 'You know, that was 1970; are we really still mad?'" The pastor noted that "you could become less mad once you admitted that you were mad [at the church and the world]." The healing service always began with singing from a set of ten hymns, during which people came forward to a kneeler. "Two people put their hands on them and prayed for them. We would keep singing until the last person was up. Then we would always jump to the same victorious last hymn. We loved it." When the momentum for separate healing services waned, the pastor "moved components of the healing service to the Sunday worship, so then coming forward to get healing took place during Communion." The pastor recalled how "the flow of the service that we created ended on this victorious note."

Another congregation also incorporated healing as part of Sunday services before closure, a ritual that began with an ill member of the church requesting anointing and laying on of hands. The first time, the pastor anointed her. After that,

I also passed the oils to everyone to anoint her. Her children anointed her, her husband anointed her, the choir anointed. . . . In the background the choir was singing, "There was a healing balm in Gilead." From that day on, every Sunday for the next nine months until we closed, we had anointing and healing and laying on of hands. People were able to come forward in that healing process every Sunday to express what they were learning, feeling, and embodying through the discernment process. By the time we got to the last three months, every single member of the congregation was getting up for laying on of hands. Liturgy was really a powerful and important part of the whole process—healing, the liturgical aspect of healing and Eucharist and the turning about, looking to the resurrection.

In another congregation that began healing prayers, the pastor related how they "laid hands on my husband. It was a nice thing for that community to do to show their love since he also prayed for them." She concluded, "There were things like that that just kept the Spirit moving."

Storytelling is another way to honor the life of the sacred community that mourns. "Just about every time we came together, there were stories being told," said one pastor. She told church stories about hard times as well as happy ones, mentioning even bad decisions: "A certain family had control of the finances, and nobody else knew what was going on." Another pastor said, "I needed people to get up and say publicly—and this was not a group of people that were real comfortable doing public speaking, but they did it—what was most important to them about Cross and Crown [Church]. We did it on Sunday mornings." That was recorded, put on a CD with some choir hymns, and offered to all church members.

Another congregation "had an official book that was put together that had a lot of pictures and stories of the congregation and milestones along the way." They set up "a timeline in the sanctuary along one of the walls with different kinds of labels that people could fill out," noting baptisms and other events. "It just gave you a real sense of the changes and the challenges as a part of our life in close to forty-six years," said the pastor. For another, honoring parish members who died during the weeks and months before closure helped with grief. "I had several deaths to tend to of those wonderful people," recalled the pastor. "We shared those stories. As we bring closure to this, then it reminds us that we have wonderful memories, like we do with our friends that have passed away in the last two years, and our memories will never go away."

Photos of church history were gathered and shared. One pastor and her secretary went through every single photo the church kept and later distributed them, putting out "thousands of pictures in the hope that each person would remember something." She said, "People remembered their stories as they would choose pictures, and we copied them all for them, every single one that they wanted. It cost some hundreds of dollars, and we didn't care."

One pastor found a 150th-anniversary book celebrating how "several people in that area wanted a church that was close by because it was too hard to travel distances, how they came about purchasing that land, and what their focus and hope was at that time." The pastor was honest about aspects of church life described in the book that were not as inspiring: "There were some fights there too, even about what to name the church. And then the fights coming up as to closing it. It was a great, great spiritual and reflective resource." Throughout the two years before the church closed, the pastor "would pull that out and share that with them. Sometimes it would just fit in with the lectionary readings too." The pastor concludes: "That guided us from the beginning to the closure, in the struggle."

When it became clear that the judicatory was going to close our church, I knew I needed a chaplain, and the congregation would too. For the next six months, I met with our chaplain every few weeks. One evening he met with members of the congregation as they sat in a circle in the church, and he listened to their painful stories and feelings. He participated in the closing worship as well, sitting next to me in the front of the church. I couldn't have made it through the process or the service without him. I think it made a difference to our congregation too. God and the wider church were present in our grief.

Grief is often difficult to share, so one pastor shared her own grief first to encourage others to share theirs. At her congregation's last worship service in the church building, before moving to a storefront, she tried to get them to talk about what they would miss. "Oh no, it'll be fine, it'll be wonderful, it'll be perfect," they responded.

> I finally said, "Well, I'm going to miss having a piano." We had a grand piano. It wasn't going to fit in the new space. That got people starting to say things they would miss: having room to grow, having a separate office, having a piano—which then made people remember that they missed having a choir, having a baptismal well—giving that up was a loss. Then they started to talk about other stuff, about the building, about not having kids running around. The sacred stories were more remembering how to lament than learning how to celebrate.

Grief may evoke guilt or shame that pastors feel called to address. A pastor shared this:

> For a lot of people closure was a sign of defeat. I had to devote a lot

of energy helping people to understand that because a church closes doesn't mean that they have been unfaithful. A lot of people were feeling guilty, a lot of remorse . . . wishing they had done things differently. I just really tried to reinforce this notion that congregations are like people. Congregations die like people die.

It "doesn't mean that they have been unfaithful." The pastor worked to instill in the congregation "that we had been faithful—the ministry, the fact that we had been there—but it was time now for the congregation to move on and spread the seeds of our congregation into other churches and be like leaven in the bread of other congregations." A heartbroken pastor told members of his church, "If you know you've given everything you had, and I believe everybody in this room has, then there is no reason for regret." Another said, "It was really trying to find a way for them to accept that it wasn't their fault that it was closing, helping them to move on to another congregation."[5]

Grief was sometimes compounded by the loss of other community institutions, as has especially been seen in the rural Great Plains (Montana, North Dakota, South Dakota, Wyoming, Nebraska, Kansas, Colorado, Oklahoma, Texas, and New Mexico) and the Corn Belt (Iowa, Illinois, Indiana, and parts of Missouri, Ohio, Nebraska, Kansas, Minnesota, and Michigan).[6] One pastor in this area shared this:

> This has been a transition for ten years and more with the flooding. You're trying to help people cope with the fact that they're losing their farm, their house, their community. You're trying to help them deal with that and then finally help them through the inevitable decision that this place has to close. They have to come to that decision. Even though they all know it, they don't want to do it. But you know they know.

Sometimes, despite a pastor's best efforts, suffering moves people to leave the congregation before the last day. "Some actually did walk away early," said one pastor. "You know, they were just tired. I was straddling between people who just couldn't possibly think of closing and others who were out the door before we really were closed." The pastor did what he could to "keep the communication going and to care for people and do what we could—or," he added, "do what I could."

In the midst of grief, the disposition of church property in legacy gifts may nurture resurrection hope. One pastor remarked, "I think they felt that they at least were in charge of their destiny. I think their fear was that someone would come in and say, 'This just has to be, like it or lump it.'" Giving away something of value promises—and is a form of—resurrection after death. Gifting blesses the giver as much as or more than it blesses the receiver. Many congregations found deep consolation as they became "organ donors," and beloved buildings, altars, organs, and endowments nurtured new ministries.[7]

Depending on the denomination, church buildings and property can be gifted or sold at a low price to another congregation or a valued community organization. As one pastor reported, "The unexpected blessing is that there was an African American congregation who did not have a church, and this had been a historically white church. They needed a facility, and we were able to transition them into that facility. The mission of that church didn't cease; it just transitioned. It was a real blessing." Another congregation donated their building to a local youth services nonprofit with which the congregation had collaborated. As the pastor explained, "We all came together, and we talked about giving it to them. They had a big party and said, 'Thank you very much.'" Another gave their building to a community theatrical group whose director was able to procure funds from his employer to renovate the building. Some churches sold their buildings at below-market rates to struggling congregations that had been renting space. One majority white congregation wanted to gift their building to a renting majority immigrant congregation. Defying the judicatory, who wanted them to sell it at market price, they sold it at a low price to their brothers and sisters in Christ. Often a congregation will also gift church furniture, dishes, altar furnishings, and other assets with the building "so [the receiving church] would not have to buy new things for its ministry." Another majority Anglo church had an immigrant congregation as a tenant with whom they had developed a mutually respectful relationship and were united in mission, despite striking theological differences. "We still believe in the same God," the pastor said. When it came time to close, the immigrant congregation didn't have sufficient money to purchase the building, so the founding congregation accepted enough money to cover its debts and donated the interior furnishings. "We felt good about it because they were doing what we had hoped to do," said the pastor. "They had a connection with the food distributor out in the city, and they would distribute [food] to people who needed it in the area."

One "organ donor" church donated their Communion set to the

church where most of them would now be worshiping, and their organ, baptismal font, and pulpit to a church that was rebuilding after a fire. "Their philosophy was, this was intended for ministry; it needs to continue to be used in ministry," the pastor said. "I'm really reluctant to say the church died because it didn't. It just took on new life in different places." Another church gave away "the valuable things in the church to other churches in their city that were younger and struggling," and they gave away nonsacred things to a denominational home for children. One small, rural church had a parishioner who had founded a preschool in her town, but when that person moved away, it precipitated the church's closure; the congregation gave the preschool "boxes and boxes of things, crafts and things like that for the kids."

Legacy gifting to the community, wider church, and other nonprofits brought solace to many closing congregations. One church sold the property for $750,000 and sold the organ back to the manufacturer for $175,000, then gave away over $900,000 in legacy money. Another majority Anglo congregation gave a nest egg of $136,000 to the immigrant congregation following them. One gave to a small church that would continue their food ministry. One congregation that didn't want their money to go to the judicatory or denomination (there were a few like this) merged with or was "adopted" by a neighboring congregation, to which they donated their financial reserves. Another, with a commitment to food ministry, made a legacy gift of funds to churches with food grants.

One congregation chose to support a refugee house founded by a big, wealthy church that had tithed off of a capital campaign to pay for rent for three years. With the three years over, the house was about to close. As the pastor explained,

> The congregation took that as kind of a God thing; their legacy money would pick up. But then, they designated that they didn't want it to go to rent but to a down payment, and they asked the judicatory to raise the rest of the money to buy a house. It took about two and a half years to raise the rest of that money, but they bought a house, and it's called the Ruth House. So a lot of good came out of it.

The pastor said her congregation's decision still sends "chills down [my] spine."

There was also the congregation that brought $2 million to the church that "adopted" them, and another that brought $100,000 to the church with which they merged. In a denomination where congregations are required to give the bulk of their legacy to the judicatory, one church found hope in their freedom to tithe, or give 10 percent, to charities of the congregation's choosing, while another established an endowment fund with the judicatory. One endowed a judicatory's summer camp for children and youth.

Besides leaving a material legacy, churches can leave a ministry legacy. When one church closed and canon law required the church building, contents, and financial reserves to go to the judicatory, the congregation left a legacy in the form of ongoing, outwardly focused ministries. "All but one of their ministries—seven ministries—continued in [their community] after the close of the church," recalled the pastor. "They were able to recognize that joy and celebration that, yes, we did implement Total Ministry from a ministerial, baptismal way of being church, [even though] we didn't implement successfully the governance and the structure and the discernment process."

After the rituals of attending to grief and of legacy gifting are completed, *a closing service serves both as a funeral to mourn the death and as a proclamation of resurrection hope.* Although one pastor said pointedly, "It was not a funeral; 97 percent of those people are members of the local denominational church," most clergy did call it a funeral. "Colleagues and I talked about it as though we're giving them a funeral. I think that mentality helped," said one pastor. He went on to say their closing ceremony was "very funeral-like, and it was very moving. They loved the church, they loved the idea of what we were doing, and it was just time to move on." Another described

> [striving] to have a closing service in which, number one, we thanked God for the good blessings we had had, for the ministries we had had, for all of our past ministries and that God would guide us and teach us, as we would look for another church, each of us. If that didn't happen, and frankly, I didn't expect it to, then we would "be the church." That's what we tried to do. It was a thanksgiving, celebratory closing.

The closing service was significant for many "we" pastors, one of whom recounted it in two parts of the interview, through tears both times:

> The blessing of the closing service [was] just astonishing, and the blessing of the congregations that took care of us. Like the night of the closing service, we weren't even really sure, as we looked around

the room, we didn't see the people from the church up the road. We saw the pastor and a few other people. I was like, "Huh, that's interesting." Then I realized that that's because they were downstairs making the food.

At the last service, some churches displayed timelines that people had filled in, others displayed photos, and some took a walk through the sanctuary or grounds, like the stations of the cross, remembering and reenacting some of the ministries that had occurred there. One pastor put together a slideshow and DVDs of their history using all the scanned church photos that members had spent hours organizing. The pastor reported that the slideshow was "a big chunk of the last Sunday service . . . and it went through their history, with music, and all different songs. And that was really what made the last service, more than any sermon I did—that I put this together." After the service, everyone in the church got one of the DVDs. In another congregation, recalled the pastor, "somebody stood behind the altar and said, 'This is our altar, and this is what has happened here over the years, and this is what it means to me.' We said good-bye, and we walked around the church together, and the property together, and did that with everything and then walked out of the church together and locked the doors."

One pastor remembered how sacred objects were integrated into litanies of remembrance: "The person who was most involved in Christian education came up and talked—to tell a brief litany about education. The trustee person came out and held up the hammer and talked about that." Another walked with her congregation inside the church and through the cemetery outside and invited people to talk about what happened there and give thanks; they spoke easily because, as she explained, "we always met in a circle. . . . I would say like maybe a one- to three-minute kind of little homily, but then always end with a few questions, and then people just took off."

Acts of remembrance embraced historical church drama, photos, and music. One congregation "read a play that was written for an occasion back at the old building that rehearsed the history of how the congregation came [into being] . . . [back] to the end of the Civil War." The pastor recalled showing "pictures that we found from as far back as we could find pictures." It was multimedia: "We had never been able to get anybody that would write music or write songs, but we did find one that an early pastor had written. Terrible, terrible, but that's OK. We brought it out and we sang it."

The power of symbols was recognized in a Scandinavian congregation that closed, symbolically, on May 17, Norwegian Independence Day. They had been worshiping with an emerging Arabic church, to which they now gifted their building. After the Scandinavian congregation's closing service, the members went out to lunch, then returned "for the organization of the Arabic church," which the Scandinavian congregation's pastor described as "a wonderful, fabulous resurrection story." Although many people sought out different churches, some stayed. "Imagine the charter for this Arabic congregation," said the pastor. "You've got names like Jensen, Madsen, Holm. That was really, really special because it was their baby."

The transfer of sacred objects or the building itself is sometimes incorporated into the closing service. For example, one church in its closing service "recognized then the transfer of [the church building] ownership to the theatrical group that was going to own it." A congregation that merged with another one had also merged twenty-six years before, bringing with it a large painting that had hung in the sanctuary. "We had it removed and installed in the new merged congregation in their chapel," said the pastor. "It was very important to do that." The chief acolyte from the closing church symbolically "handed off a very nice processional cross to the acolyte of the church we were going to, and it was processed the ten blocks to the new church."

Sadly, in some congregations, conflict, financial circumstances, or a demoralizing downturn hastened closure and prevented a celebration of ministry. One congregation failed to have a closing service because suddenly the window for moving the church to another location was closing due to the weather, and they were unable to schedule a service.

While there are many guidelines for preaching at funerals, there seem to be none that address closing a church.[8] *In this study, I learned that in closing sermons, pastors speak in various voices—among them, a "voice of vulnerability" that shares painful events, losses, feelings of guilt and grief, fear or confusion, and a "voice of consolation" about God's presence in suffering, forgiveness, and compassion.*[9] Like biblical prophets, pastors may use a "voice of admonition," chiding, encouraging, and guiding the baptized. Finally, they often employ a "voice of promise and hope" that shares God's promise of new life in the church rising out of the ruins of broken dreams.

Speaking of grief is to use the voice of vulnerability, a courageous voice that dares to witness to experiences of "the cross." For example, one pastor shared this: "We've known this day is coming—wanted to push it away—to stop time if we could—but we can't. The reality is, this is the last time we will celebrate our faith in the risen Lord Jesus Christ in this place." Another asked, "How many of us woke up this morning with a feeling of dread? How many of us lay on our beds this morning and thought, 'Can I do this? Can I get up and face this day?' How many of us on our way to church this morning drove here with a pit in our stomach, a lump in our throat?"

Pastors related the grief of the congregation to Scripture passages about suffering and loss, such as the Exodus stories of the people wandering in the wilderness, the "valley of the shadow" in Psalm 23, the Babylonian exile, the destruction of Jerusalem, and the ascension of Elijah before Elisha's eyes. New Testament stories included the disciples after Jesus' death and St. Paul's being "blocked" by the Spirit from entering Asia. One pastor spoke of the chaos in the beginning of Genesis:

> The Hebrew words translated as "formless void" literally mean chaos or confusion: tohu wabbohu. Even the sound of it is scary. A forbidding darkness, distorted and muddled. That's all there was, says Genesis, until: "Then God said." It was written for people whose world had literally been torn apart. So when the priest sang, "Tohu wabbohu," they knew what he meant. It means those times in our lives that are very scary. You place the telephone back in its cradle and sit back down before you fall down. . . . What once seemed such a serene, ordered universe is sinking into the tohu wabbohu . . . sometimes only a phone call away. Those times when the earth beneath our feet begins to move quite literally or quite metaphorically. Whichever way, things are a mess and there appears to be no way out.

Biblical stories wove the congregation together with ancient peoples through the thread of a faith-based understanding that death happens, grief is real, and they are not alone; other good people of God have suffered.

Pastors also spoke with a voice of consolation as they tackled feelings of responsibility, guilt, or shame and affirmed their congregation's courage to die. One pastor recognized the cultural decline in religiosity and the fallibility of human nature: "New families moved in, but they didn't seem to be as interested in a neighborhood church. . . . The soil of this neighborhood no longer yields enough fruit to sustain the garden that once was." He added, "People didn't know what to do, so they did what they knew. Real outside-of-the-box change is hard for everyone, and even more difficult for groups and institutions."

Another pastor called the church to imitate Jesus:

> Risking death is . . . the very thing that frees Jesus to be all that God called him to be. Once Jesus is willing to risk death, all other risks seem minor. . . . As Christians, we are called to take risks. We are called to risk death on a cross. We are called to risk traveling to Jerusalem. We took a risk, and the result of that risk is different than we expected. We are a congregation that struggled and was renewed. We are a congregation that struggled and was healed. We are a congregation who has struggled, and will close. We took the risk.

Pastors told consoling stories of God's grace, such as the account of manna in the wilderness, the resurrection, the gift of the Holy Spirit at Pentecost, 1 Peter 2 on "living stones," and for one evangelical preacher, James 1:12: "Blessed is anyone who endures temptation. Such a one has stood the test and will receive the crown of life that the Lord has promised to those who love him." One pastor evoked the time when Captain Chesley "Sully" Sullenberger twice walked the center aisle of his plane that had been forced to land in the Hudson River to make sure all the passengers were safely out. The pastor then said, "Brothers and sisters in Christ, we too have a pilot like that. His name is Jesus. And he will not leave us. In fact, he is going with us—to wherever God calls us next." Walking slowly down and up the center aisle, he preached, "Please accept this prophetic action that I do now—so that you will always, always remember that the Word was made flesh, and dwelt among us, and that we have received the fullness of God's grace and truth." Returning to the pulpit, he ended, "Jesus says to each of us today, 'Lo, I am with you always, even to the end of the world.' God bless us, every one. Amen."

Closing sermons also included admonitions, a rhetorical form rooted in the Judaic tradition of prophecy as well in the Gospels, the letters of St. Paul, and the book of Revelation. Admonitions encourage action, embodying hope for the journey into a new creation that God has yet to reveal. In this study, nearly half of all sermons had inclusive "we" admonitions, such as "we are called" or "we must." One pastor preached,

> We're called, as Mary was, to be bearers of God's love to all creation, that Christ would be born in us today. Like Joseph, we're called to

act on the promises of God, focusing ourselves on Jesus' mission—God's determination—to save the world from sin and death: bringing good news to the poor, release to the captives, light to those who sit in deep darkness, freedom to the oppressed, establishing peace on earth, proclaiming the kingdom of God.

Related to call, another prominent theme of closing sermons is "What does it mean to be 'church' when our building is no longer there?" One Methodist preacher was quite clear: "You are the church, and regardless of what we do here next week, that will always be the case." The church is the sacred community called forth or sent out by God. Clergy would be "saddened to know that [their former parishioners] were not going to church somewhere." One pastor lamented that "the elderly folks that were left . . . didn't feel that they wanted to go to any other church. . . . That's sad that they don't have a connection with a church." Especially in conflicted churches or those closed by a judicatory's decision, people may leave organized religion because they have been hurt. On the other hand, pastors are comforted when the faithful join new church communities because "what is being closed is a building, not a relationship with God."[10]

Members' movement en masse to a new church after closure often offers pastors solace. A Christmas-like experience was reported by a pastor who saw two congregations move "independently—of their own volition—to this third congregation. So the third congregation . . . suddenly had the people power they needed, as well as the motivation. And that congregation continues to thrive." Another pastor witnessed two congregations in the city benefiting from an influx of people from his church "who actually knew who they were, knew who they are and what they're there for as baptized persons. One of them is now thriving, not just [in terms of] numbers, but because there are people who know what they're doing and care." Five other pastors reported that their congregations left en masse with their closing experiences expectant, reflective, even Easter-like.

Pastors sought pastoral care for their churches' frail seniors and people with disabilities. One was moved to tears as she said,

> One major thing that I was striving for was that each person would know where they could go, . . . and that there were communities out there [where] they could find a home, . . . and then to let people sit in their grief, and their anger, and their anxiety, and let everybody

tell every story that they wanted to tell, and to do a good hand-off to colleagues. I was able to say, "Here's my eight fragile elders; will you go see them?"

Another pastor said her congregation had aging and dying people in their seventies and eighties and "these younger fortyish—especially one particular member with disabilities" who found care in a "pretty vibrant theologically conservative church about two miles away, so the bulk of them went en masse there, which was good. [They've] got a congregation around him to support him."

Pastors saw resurrection when a singer went to a church with a strong music program, or an elder to a church where relatives worshiped, or a family to a church with a Sunday school. One pastor rejoiced when she saw that "some people who had been part of that parish their entire lives because their parents were . . . went on to other parishes, and their lives have grown and expanded in quite wonderful ways." She felt that "it may not have happened if they remained in that place" with its conflict. Another went to an annual church picnic held by former members and heard one of them say to others that they should have made the transition much earlier. The pastor explained, "She was talking about the church where she's worshiping now that has a youth group and it goes on mission trips—all of this life of the church that they missed out on for decades." The pastor noted, "She was completely consumed with trying to keep this little church going. [Now] she's able to sit on the back pew and decide which things she's involved in."

CHAPTER SUMMARY

Pastoral leadership in a dying church means walking a sort of pilgrimage to the cross. Pastors strive to provide a "good enough" death for the sacred community—one that celebrates the church's past and present ministries; thanks God and others; leaves a legacy; consoles people in a closing service honoring what they faithfully, courageously began and nurtured over the years; and encourages the people of God to be the church as they worship God in new spiritual communities.

It is not always possible to do *all* of these things. People grieve differently. Some church members will remain until the end, and some will leave as soon as the decision to close is made. Some will accept it, and some vow they never will. Even the most inclusive, respectful process may evoke inconsolable sadness or anger.

Pastors must navigate this process even as they navigate their own grief and loss. It is a taxing journey filled with unexpected challenges, especially for young pastors and those for whom it is their first call. Like me, they may wonder, "What is God calling me to be? To do?" On a dark night, even a seasoned minister may stumble or fall. Even if they have led a church through an Easter- or Christmas-like closing, the pastor's future in the church may be uncertain. It is to their vulnerability that the next chapter turns.

PART III

The Pastor's Transformation, Reflections, and Recommendations

8

Grief and Vulnerability

We raced around San Francisco Bay one spring day, with the waters calm, the warm wind strong enough to move us along, and the sun bright overhead. Sometimes serving a church feels like that.

I remember one Easter morning at our small church: children running around in their Sunday best, the scent of Easter lilies, a new family bringing their infant daughter for baptism, and youth singing a heartwarming anthem. These moments give resurrection hope to the body of Christ. Journeys in the closure of a church may be blessed with days like this. They may even end with an Easter "Alleluia!" as the congregation celebrates a merger with another congregation or the gifting of the building to an immigrant congregation.

In contrast, some days in a pastor's journey can feel like sailing in a wind-whipped storm, with waves flying over the deck; the crew cold, wet, and uncomfortable; and the skipper holding on to the tiller for dear life.

From my journal, three years before our church closed:

"I am the good shepherd. The good shepherd lays down his life for the sheep."

Dear Jesus, Shepherd, the sheep are restless and wandering away from you. I ask that you call them back into the fold to be at peace with one another. The angels are fighting and scaring the flock.

Help them to turn to you and know your grace and truth. I am at my wits' end. I can't do this by myself, but I will try to do your will with your help. What do I need to say? How do I say it? Help me to trust your presence in our community, the love that banishes fear. You have gotten me through hard times before. Help me to remember you are in the room with us. Help me to be an instrument of reconciliation. Love, Gail.

When asked to ascribe a church season to the closing of their churches, more than a third (36 percent) of pastors in the written survey for this book called this kind of journey Holy Week, Good Friday, or Holy Saturday. Even pastors who named reflective seasons such as Advent and Lent (30 percent) or festival seasons such as Christmas, Easter, or Pentecost (25 percent) experienced frightful days.

Both the surveys and the interviews with clergy who served churches through closure revealed unique pastoral challenges. This chapter shares how the pilgrim journey affected the well-being of clergy as they served their churches. It begins by identifying the challenges of closing a church, such as the demands of making the decision to dissolve, as well as encountering unexpected currents or storms that threaten a pastor's journey. It then examines how these may affect the pastor, focusing on various dimensions of stress, such as loneliness, feelings of failure, having doubts about oneself as a pastor, vocational questions, changes in physical and mental health, and grief after the church closes.

Closing a congregation is a daunting task, even for those prepared to do it. This study has previously shown that *the most challenging tasks for pastors closing their churches include initiating a discernment process, dealing with members' difficult feelings, and—the most challenging one—making the actual decision to close*, which was reported as a "great challenge" by 28 percent. "Adaptive challenges" such as these have no obvious solution, require everyone's participation or consent, threaten existing ways of being and doing, and represent cultural changes.[1] Closing tasks are added on top of other adaptive challenges a church may have already faced, such as deciding whether to add video screens in the sanctuary, use inclusive language for God, or let the administrative assistant go because church income has declined.

On the other hand, once the difficult decision to close is made, tasks such as the disposition of church property and facilitating transfer of members are less fraught; organizational theorists call these "technical" or "nonadaptive challenges" because they can be accomplished by staff or volunteers using their own expertise and church resources. Other technical challenges might be preparing a Sunday church bulletin, preparing the church for Sunday worship, and bookkeeping.

In addition to adaptive challenges such as managing dialogue about a church's future, when a pastor enters a congregation with hopes and expectations for its revitalization, the decision to close is like hitting a shoal and foundering. As they entered their congregation, more than half of pastors (56 percent) expected that they would revitalize it and help it grow, and another 30 percent expected to either plant a new church or serve a healthy congregation. Only one in ten pastors expected that they were there to dissolve the congregation with dignity. When I asked a pastor who said closure was like Good Friday, "What were your expectations and hopes for yourself as a pastor in that congregation?" he answered, "My expectations and hopes really were tied up in the idea that the church would become a vibrant, growing community, with some internal harmony, and an outreach into the community, and a vision for the world. It didn't happen the way that I expected or hoped."

Dashed hopes for renewal were common among pastors who said their closing journey was like Good Friday or Holy Saturday. "I would have loved to have stayed for long enough to turn both of those congregations from what I considered to be dying churches," said a young, enthusiastic church planter. Reflecting on being called to this new ministry, the pastor shared: "That was exciting, and I was glad to do it. I had a kind of enthusiasm. I'm a very creative person." When the church had to close, his hopes were dashed. When I asked another pastor, "How did you feel about yourself as a pastor after you left that area?" he replied, "Fragile. Fragile. I still felt and feel that call to ordained ministry. I could at the same time read through the ordination rite and say, yes, that is still what I am to be, but I was fragile."

In addition to navigating difficult conversations and broken dreams, *some pastors also encountered hidden congregational or judicatory currents that threatened a church's journey.* One pastor learned at his first leadership team meeting that before he arrived, "they even had to take out a big loan with the bank because they had like a ten- to eleven-thousand-dollar utility bill that they just hadn't managed to pay." Despite that, leaders wanted to "order that new sound system and the new mike system," saying, "we don't know how much longer [the judicatory is] going to support us." Further, the founding pastor had made no effort to make the property tax-exempt, and "the judicatory ended up footing the bill for thousands of dollars in taxes." The new pastor was uncovering a pattern: "What I kept finding was, 'Oh, we didn't know that.'"

A different kind of chaos results when the expectations congregations share with pastors in job interviews don't match up with reality. One pastor accepted a call with dreams of multicultural ministry "in a neighborhood that was trending up to three-quarters Latino in ethnicity." In interviews, the church said they hoped to minister to the neighborhood, but on arrival, the pastor was surprised that in his written job description, "none of the mutual expectations really had anything to do with multicultural ministry. Most of them had to do with caring for the people that were there." When he began outreach to the Latino community, conflicts began. However with leadership and grace, the church engaged with other congregations to have a legacy community ministry.

Difficult currents could also come when area congregations are not in position to merge with a pastor's church. One pastor's church explored merging with another congregation and was far down the road in that process when the other church pulled out. In disappointment, the other church offered an "adoption," not a merger, but the pastor's church decided to close.

Both the breadth of adaptive work required to close a church and the unexpected trials pastors may experience in fragile congregations make closing a church more stressful than other congregational ministries. In this study, I was able to compare stress among pastors who closed churches with another nationally representative sample of pastors serving all kinds of churches throughout the United States.[2] In that study, 39 percent of active pastors said they experienced stress "very often" or "fairly often" because of the challenges they faced in their congregations "over the past year." In contrast, nearly two-thirds (65 percent) of pastors in my study said they experienced these levels of stress when they "served the church that was closing." Further, only one in six active clergy (17 percent) in the other study felt "lonely and isolated" in their work fairly or very often over the previous year, whereas six in ten pastors (60 percent) who closed churches felt "lonely and isolated" in their work fairly or very often. One pastor who closed a church said, "It didn't come all at once, but I felt incredibly lonely. I experienced a lot of loss during that time."

Loneliness accompanies a pastor's self-isolation. "It wasn't the sort of thing that I could bring to a clergy colleague group or even to a support group and fully explain everything that was going on. It was just rampant all the time, constant dysfunction." This pastor didn't share his grief with others because he was "just overwhelmed at trying to communicate it." Loneliness may emerge from a sense of having failed to meet expectations—a pastor's own, the judicatory's, the congregation's, even God's. This study previously showed that judicatory expectations of growth significantly increased pastoral stress. That a clergyperson's role is referred to as a "call" also gives it weight not associated with other vocations. "Call" raises the stakes of failure to accomplish one's hopes and dreams.[3] Inasmuch as their work is sacred, pastors may risk overwork or exhaustion, which may isolate them from family, friends, and other supports.

From my journal, four years before our church closed:

> Precious Lord, I wonder if you want me to stay here. I don't know that I am the right person or that it is best for my family to stay here. I don't know what to do. I feel like a failure. I've not been smart enough, courageous enough, experienced enough to do what needed to be done when I first got here. I feel like I have let you down, that I haven't gotten the right medicine to the patient when it was needed, and the patient got sicker. I guess that someday I will understand. I weep for your people, and for your church, and for me. Why does it take so long? What am I missing? What don't I see? Help me to focus on you and to love your people. Amen.

Many pastors like me feel they failed. In interviews, more than two-thirds of pastors used the words "fail" (and related words, such as "failure"), "guilt," "shame," or "fault," although there were no interview questions using those words. They had experienced "fear of failure," felt others would view them as a failure, or said that "for a long time I felt like I was a failure." Closing a church, even under the best of circumstances, can feel like failure in the eyes of secular society, the eyes of the judicatory, and perhaps a pastor's own eyes.

A sense of failure disturbs a pastor's sense of identity and exacerbates isolation.[4] Said one pastor disappointed in judicatory support, "I felt abandoned. I felt betrayed. You know, I thought I was left to fend for myself. And I felt like I was a failure, that I should have been able to see the challenges, to have gathered the resources. I mean, I should've been able to do this." Even a pastor serving a closing church only at its final service can feel stigma. One pastor's two-point call included a small church that had decided to close before he even arrived; all he did was lead the closing worship and oversee the disposition of property. Despite that, at clergy meetings he felt obliged to tell his colleagues, "I really wasn't the pastor of Holy Cross when it closed." He reflected on the experience: "There's kind of a stigma about being a part of a church that then decided for whatever reason to not be a congregation anymore." He added, "There really is this affiliation with failure, that if you were a pastor of a church when it closed, that you failed. Others think I must not be a very good pastor. I might not be a very good preacher because this congregation didn't come back to life the way I expected it to."

Another pastor in a closing church compared his experience to the stigma of failure in the business world. "To be in a situation that looks like a failure, and a pretty spectacular one, was really hard," he said. Healing took a while as the pastor thought through questions: "How could I have done this differently? Did I do the right thing? Did I see the right thing here? Did I call on the right resource here?" He had to come to peace with all that was done and learn the lessons that were to be learned. "That was a little hard. My pride took a hit."

A sense of fault came up often in interviews. It is a more common issue than shame, although one-sixth of pastors said they had "very much" or "a great deal" of a "sense of shame" after the church closed. The level of shame was lower for pastors who served more than one church at a time, what may be referred to as a multipoint call. Although one church closed, the other or others survived, or even thrived as they accepted members from the closing congregation. Yet shaming and stigmatizing pastors in churches that eventually close may keep others from being fully present to them in their grief. "[People] don't recognize that you have grief going on too," one pastor voiced. "Even though I love them and felt called to listen and listen and listen, it was pretty exhausting to hear all of the stories, even though I wanted to, and treasure and honor them." Grieving with a congregation is hard work, especially for the pastor who has formed close "we," "us," and "our" bonds that will end with the closure.

Clergy may fear that being vulnerable among colleagues will mean the destruction of one's vocation or reputation. The stigma that fosters hidden grief increases loneliness.[5] One pastor stopped attending clergy meetings: "I felt myself emotionally spinning." For a pastor in a closing church who is experiencing other stresses simultaneously, such as divorce or being a parental caregiver or the parent of a child with a disability, the accumulation of grief and sense of shame can be overwhelming.

Many who witness the closing of a church fail to realize the *vocational questions* the closing raises for the pastor involved. Active clergy in this study (those who continued working) were half as likely as another national sample of active clergy to think of leaving for "another type of ministry" (22 percent, compared with 43 percent), but twice as likely to think of leaving "for a secular occupation" (11 percent, compared with 5 percent).[6] As with feelings of loneliness and doubt, those more likely to say they would think of leaving for a secular position were younger and more likely to be in their first or second call.

Experiencing loneliness and having doubts about oneself as a pastor afflicted younger and less experienced clergy more than those with years in the pulpit. Survey data (figure 2) show that more than half of pastors under forty-five years of age felt lonely and isolated "very often" in closing their churches, or almost four times as many as those sixty-five years old or older; nearly half of pastors in their first or second call were likely to feel lonely and isolated "very often" compared with

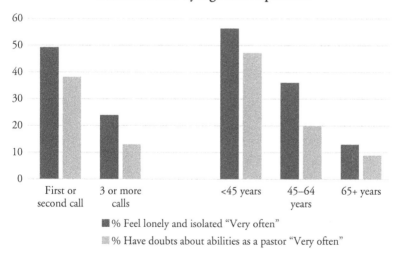

Pastoral Stress by Age and Experience

Figure 2. "When you served the church that was closing, how often did you 'feel lonely and isolated in your work' or 'have doubts about your abilities as a pastoral minister'?"

one-quarter of those with more experience. When you add the percent saying "fairly often" and "very often," eight in ten pastors under forty-five years of age had doubts about their abilities when serving a church that closed; nearly four times as many pastors under forty-five years of age as pastors sixty-five years or older had doubts about their abilities as a pastor "very often." In this study, younger and less experienced pastors are also more likely to leave congregational ministry for another form of ministry after their church closes.

Yet many pastors serving vulnerable churches (one-sixth of the study group) are young and inexperienced because economically fragile churches can compensate them more easily than they could a more experienced pastor. Bishops may respond to the desire of "dying" congregations to ask for younger clergy, especially those with children, hoping they will attract young families to join. However, placing younger, or even older but first- or second-call, pastors in these churches without judicatory support carries a risk of burning them out.[7]

People in all walks of life are affected by workplace stress—long work hours, high job demands, work-family conflict, low job control, low social support.[8] Many of these conditions characterize ministerial calls.[9] Recent research of UMC pastors shows that they have higher rates of depression than the U.S. population overall, and of obesity and related conditions than others in North Carolina, where the research was conducted.[10] Although clergy may have a support system that encourages a healthy balance of work, family, and recreation, *the challenges of dissolving a church or having conflicted relationships with a congregation or judicatory staff or colleagues can exacerbate preexisting medical conditions or cause new ones.* One pastor said, "It was a very traumatic thing. I wasn't at all well [when the church closed]."

Although one-half of pastors in the written survey said their health remained stable, three in ten pastors said their health worsened when they were serving the church that closed. After closure, one pastor recounted this: "I took time off to regroup. I can be a peaceful, spiritual presence to be present for others, but what I wasn't aware of until I was diagnosed [with an illness] is how the stress involved in closure was affecting my body. And I'm thinking I'm keeping cool, calm, and relaxed, but my body is absorbing it all. I wasn't handling it."

In interviews, clergy linked job stress to many medical conditions, including depression, anxiety, backaches, weight gain, lack of sleep, high blood pressure, exhaustion, chronic fatigue, acid reflux, eczema, type 2 diabetes, interstitial cystitis, migraines, heart attacks, fibromyalgia, kidney problems, addictions such as alcohol use or smok-ing, inexplicable limb pain, temporomandibular joint (TMJ) disorders, and cancer. Seventeen percent said they didn't know if serving a closing church affected their health, and a surprising 4 percent said their health improved over the time they served a closing church.

Pastors experiencing disrespectful relationships with either congre-gations or judicatories or both are more likely to report not only greater stress but also that their health worsened when serving the church that closed.[11] Worsening health was not related to a pastor's gender, call history, or presence in a solo or multichurch appointment. Difficult relationships were the primary correlate of health problems.[12]

Disrespect by church members can impair both mental and physical health. One pastor, subject to verbal abuse and shunning from church members and leaders, noted how hurtful actions affected her: "It's a sense of betrayal. I don't think anyone could have been prepared for that; it makes you not want to trust a whole lot of people. It affects your ability to trust." Another recalled phone calls from "strangers in town" saying things like "You need to get the heck out of here, because they're sitting in the local McDonald's and bad-mouthing [you] and planning how to connive so that you will fall flat on your face, or that you will get hurt. You need to watch your back." For a first-call pastor, these omens affected the pastor's sense of well-being: "I felt incredibly lonely. . . . I asked myself, Is it my fault? Could another pastor turn them around? Did I do this? Was I lazy? Could I have done something different? That plagues your mind."

A lack of judicatory respect increases stress as well as mental and physical health risks, especially among pastors working to facilitate a smooth transition for grieving congregations. One pastor with strong congregational bonds who experienced disrespectful actions by the wider church noted, "I have to say, for a long time I felt like I was a failure. I am a failure. I didn't keep a ministry going, I was pretty much a failure; I'm not really good at doing this and sort of felt that way." Another described the pain of hearing her judicatory executive tell her congregation, "I can close this congregation any time I want to. All I have to do is say I'm closing it," followed immediately by looking at the pastor and saying, "and I can remove your pastor at any time." Other clergy hear questioning of their competence: "Like somehow I didn't do enough or I didn't do the right thing."

One pastor said that neighboring clergy and judicatory leaders can "demonize the parishes when they go through grief and inadvertently stigmatize both the parishes and the priests who are leading them." In one judicatory, said another pastor, the executive "was at times almost making fun of me because I had been at a church that had closed. He brought it up in the judicatory meetings before all of my colleagues that he didn't close the church." Words like these matter, especially where there are undercurrents about improving "church vitality" or "getting rid of noneffective pastors."

The trials of dissolving a church may trigger even long-lasting mental and physical health effects.[13] In this study's written survey, clergy were asked about their current mental health and physical health (one to four years after their church closed) using questions similar to those in another clergy study.[14] Stress they reported while serving the church that closed was associated with worse mental health, regardless of how stress was measured. For example, twice as many pastors with "low" levels of spiritual challenges serving the church that closed scored "high" in mental health, compared with those experiencing "high" rates of spiritual challenges (39 percent, compared with 21 percent). Also, spiritually challenged pastors were less likely to report "good" or "excellent" physical health (42 percent) than pastors who reported less spiritual challenge (71 percent). Further, mental health scores and the percentage of pastors reporting "good" or "excellent" physical health decreased with stress on two other summary measures, although nearly all reported personal, spiritual, and vocational growth as well (see chapters 10 and 11).[15]

Additionally, difficult church dynamics may spill over and stress family members. One pastor said, "I put enormous, enormous stress on my marriage, and I feel that that was the worst thing that could have ever happened." Another pastor noted that both the congregation's and the judicatory's disrespect affected the spouse: "My family was devastated by the way I was treated and by my angst over 'Am I going to get ordained or am I not going to get ordained? All this is happening— what does it mean?'"

Even when a closing feels like Easter or Christmas, pastors may still grieve the loss of loving relationships, their congregation's unique gifts or character, or its mission and contribution to the community. One pastor said, "You have three churches. It's like having three kids; you love them all. But they're different, and they always treated me well, so I kind of miss them." One pastor was saddened by her husband's loss of "that core group of people. He would come and work alongside of them, and that was the closest, friendship-wise, that he ever experienced in a church. He felt like he belonged, so that [loss] was difficult for him."

One UMC minister explained why closing the first congregation he served, beginning in seminary, was so difficult: He built "deep and true relationships with those people." He said, "I went into the first one very open. 'This is who I am. I love you, you love me.' Going into the second one was 'You don't need to know everything about me. We don't need to be friends. I don't want to get to know you because it's just going to hurt when we have to leave.'" The pastor now sees that he can "open up and build those relationships a little bit better now, but also have some protection for me and my family."

Clergy may rue the loss of a congregation's special charisms. One pastor said, "When the Haiti earthquake took place, we just stopped everything and focused on lamenting with the people of Haiti. The congregation was able to open itself to do that, so I miss them." Another lamented the closure of "a teaching congregation that had a lot of people who were sponsored for ordination out of it"; yet another mentioned "a church that was looking out for the needy and trying to help everybody out." Food pantries, clothes closets, 12-step programs, ESL classes, and other ministries to a community's poor or homeless are "like a ripple in the water. It spreads out." As one pastor put it, "That church was, in its own way, a little light to the community around it, and that light got extinguished." One grieved that "that congregation was among a handful of congregations that were pioneering in their ministry with HIV/AIDS and with LGBT people at a time when that wasn't really happening. That's a loss of that history and a living link to it."

Grief extends to closure of congregations representing a denomination or tradition. In a predominantly evangelical community, one pastor ached for the loss of "an alternative way to worship and pray. That's sad." Another lamented that for "people who value the liturgy that the Episcopal Church has and value the dignity of the Eucharist, that's not there." Another said of a congregation that closed, "They were the only UCC church in town." One concluded, "I think it meant something to the God of the world. I think God was aware of that, and I think God was praising us and thanking us and being thankful with us." Another remarked, "If churches close all over the world, it would be a very sad day. For me, the church in serving the world is a moral conscience for the world. If we're not a good moral conscience for the world, there's nothing, nobody else, who's really trying to set a standard for the world to live up to."

Finally, pastors lament that when a church dies, especially without a reconciling process or worship service, church members may be stuck in unresolved grief, unable to move on to other churches. One pastor said, "There are only about a half a dozen or ten that are going to any church at all now. And that saddens me, that they've abandoned the faith over this." Another was sad that "the older members of the church don't have a connection." One church tried to worship in another congregation where they shortly felt unwelcome, and they just "dissipated." The pastor reported, "We were already grieving, and it just felt like it broke our hearts. I still grieve for that congregation. It's been difficult."

CHAPTER SUMMARY

We've seen in this chapter how serving a closing church can take an often-hidden toll. Caring for oneself was one of the greatest challenges for pastors. Because of self-isolation or stigmatization from colleagues, this study was the first time since their church doors closed that some pastors shared difficult thoughts and feelings. Adaptive tasks such as discerning whether to close or reconfigure ministry without the church building and coping with conflict or unexpected storms are particularly challenging. Some pastors were shaken by a lack of respect from their congregations, colleagues, or judicatory. Pastors associated workplace stress with worsening physical and mental health and less satisfaction with some aspects of their vocation, even one to three years after the church closed.

Serving a church that closed was more difficult for first-call and younger pastors than for others; they were more likely to feel lonely and isolated, to doubt their abilities as pastors, and to consider leaving the pastorate for a secular occupation. Besides being sad with and for their grieving congregations, many pastors, as other professionals might, feared what colleagues would think, that their story would overwhelm, or that there would be vocational repercussions for not being "over" their grief.[16] However, not all pastors grieve as deeply as some. Depending on their experience of God's presence and call, their pastoral or personal experience, their ability to differentiate from the congregation or the judicatory, and their social supports, clergy may have a healthy capacity to take verbal attacks, the closure of the church, or isolation from colleagues in stride.

This book supports the notion that suffering and grief over the closing church are not the end of the journey for these pastors. With the acceptance of death comes the beginning of new life in Christ.[17] A theology of the cross means that in despair we open our hearts to God and experience God's compassion.[18] In their desolation, many pastors I interviewed turned to God, sought out friends and family, immersed themselves in an avocation, or explored a new vocation. It is to consolations like these that the next chapter turns.

9

Consolation and Hope

I'm a fairly decent sailor, so I gladly signed up for our sailing club's cruise up San Rafael Creek. In the warm sun we enjoyed a gentle run up the creek and lunch together at a dockside restaurant before heading upwind back down the creek to San Pablo Bay, along with five other boats. Tack after endless tack, we struggled. Our friends pulled ahead of us, and suddenly I realized we were the last boat in the creek. I was at the tiller when I lost control and we headed into a pier and hit a tire. I shoved the boom and shouted to my husband, "Throw yourself to the other side!" With the weight shift, we managed to get back into the channel, only to find ourselves blown backward by the wind into rocks. I was afraid we'd never make it back to the boat ramp or, worse yet, would damage the hull. When we got back into the channel a second time, the boat listed to port and we did a 360. I handed the rudder to my husband, took out the oar, and began paddling. Looking out at the bay, I could see only open water. No sails in sight.

Then I heard an engine. Friends in a powerboat who had volunteered to accompany our club's cruise (a "crash boat") came around the corner. "Would you like a tow?" "Yes!" I shouted, along with epithets about the wind and the tide. As they tossed us a line, I looked to the rear of the boat and saw that the rudder had kicked up. It wasn't in the water. No wonder we had no control. Silently, I put the rudder down, hoping no one would notice. I let the crash boat tow us to our friends sailing in the bay.

Faith in God is a pastor's rudder—gifting stability, courage, and guidance when the winds are fierce or the waters riled. Faith is why and how we do ministry. Without it we struggle helplessly. The more frustrated and fearful I felt about the future of our church, the more it meant to me to pray the daily office or study for sermons. As I read in the morning about God's presence with God's people who felt abandoned, were exiled, or were fighting among themselves, I knew I could make it through the day. When our church-boat spun helplessly, work with others in our congregation strengthened me. God also was present through the "crash boat" of colleagues, family, friends, and others in the wider community who showed up to set us free. Even when the rudder kicks up, pastors do not journey alone. Jesus is near.

This chapter shares the many ways pastors find consolation and hope. *Clergy often find their faith nourished through spiritual disciplines.* Because Christianity is incarnational, *many clergy report finding consolation in work both alongside members of the sacred community and among the wider circle* of colleagues, family and friends, community leaders, spiritual directors, and therapists, who provide a rich network of relationships. This living human web leads stressed pastors to unexpected blessings, hope, and new life, even as they serve through difficult times in their churches.

God's consoling Spirit comes to pastors at all times, in unexpected places, and in unforeseen ways. "It's not in the past tense. I am continually in the process of learning. The Holy Spirit gives me what I need in the moment," said one pastor, whom God surprised with the gift of memorizing Scripture.

During that time, I got this craving to memorize Scripture. I memorized, oh my gosh, I bet I memorized about twenty chapters: Isaiah 53, and Psalms 1 and 90 and 3 and 100 and 150 and 21, Ephesians 6 and Romans 8. And the thing about memorizing Scripture is, you can't think of anything else. You can't. I tend to ruminate about things, and I also was at a point where I was driving long distances. That time alone in the car could have just been deadly for my spirit, just chewing all of this negativity. . . . One of my sisters in prayer said, "I think this is your life-saver. I think God has just thrown this out to you to keep your head above water." I really felt that Scripture taking up this much brain space as good food kept me from chewing on something that would have been deadly. I think the Spirit was looking out for me there.

For another pastor, God is present all day: "I'm not a prayer warrior type; it's more like Brother Lawrence practicing the presence of God.[1] In whatever I'm doing, I'm trying to do that in the midst of prayer, and God's beside me. We're working together."

One overwhelmed pastor in a conflicted church experienced God's faithfulness in a clergy continuing education event: "I resisted going, and then God showed up when I went." The pastor was placed in a small group with three other pastors, two of whom were on sabbatical. Through them, he was inspired to request a sabbatical, from which he ended up not returning. "Of the twenty-four people in the room, those two came together with me," he said. "I figured it was God's providence at that point."

One pastor was able, while praying, to "let go" of a failing church he had founded: "Honestly, it was one Sunday morning standing in worship, when I just really felt the presence of God, and God said, 'You're done.' I had closure that day." He was grateful for the blessings that had been realized through that church: "We saw lives change. We saw people come to Christ. We saw amazing things happen during our ministry. The decision to close was really mine, when it came down to it. It was my realization, and agreeing with God, and saying, 'OK, it's time to close the doors.'"

When grief over closure descended, another minister found a refuge: "Preparing sermons every week and doing Bible study kept me alive and helped me find the new gospel every week." Another, with a history of enduring verbal and mental abuse in a previous church, which had led to depression, offered, "I was afraid I was under such stress that it could happen again." She found that a gift for "recalling biblical stories" kept her healthy.

Besides prayer and Bible study, pastors during their difficult stretches also find God through nature, as one pastor reported:

During the time when the church was closing, and really at other times of hardship in life: "This is my Father's world. He speaks in all that's there. In the rustling grass, I can hear him pass. . . ." God speaks, has spoken to many vicissitudes of life. He did during my time of closing that church. We have a little state park here. And I walk in that state park every day and that's where I find God.

Because closing a church can seem like a failure to others, seeing God's presence in death and new life is consoling, as one pastor experienced: "Sometimes when I tell people I closed a church, they look at me as a failure. That's a struggle, but for me, really, that's not what it's about. It's about death and resurrection ministry and the fact that [the congregation] has to die for new things to be reborn." The pastor of one congregation had been "trying so hard to keep them alive and keep them viable," but, she recounted, "after a while, you can only push the rock up the hill so far. You have to get out of its way and let it go wherever it's going to go, and if it was going to go, it was because God wanted it to go. Sometimes God says to us, 'Things have to die in order for new life to come.' It's the Easter sermon all over again." Yet another pastor found consolation in the faith that God was fulfilling God's plan:

> God is doing this, and that's a beautiful thing. That gets the pressure off of me. Second of all, look at all the great things that are going on that couldn't have gone on if we stayed where we were. I feel like God saved my rear end there and redeemed the work. It wasn't work that just died. It was work that got transplanted and continued on and today continues to multiply, and so those are good. Those features were really redemptive . . . good grace.

Although a church may seem to fail in a human sense, death is the end of all living things. "Even in health care," said one interviewee, "we find that death is not the enemy, but it's the ultimate end of a course that has come to fruition." Another put it this way: "Why are there four Gospels? It's because they all contain Easter stories or the crucifixion. That's key to who we are as a people. Just because the church closed doesn't mean that church members failed." It also doesn't mean the pastor failed, as one learned: "I saw closure as something beyond myself, and that I was just part of the boat in the water. It wasn't my fault that it happened. It wasn't anybody's fault. It was just, you know, things come to an end in God's time, and I figured it was in God's time. It was not something I could beat myself up over."

One pastor, who had been called to grow a church that eventually dissolved, reaffirmed his commitment to follow God's call regardless of the risk: "Sometimes you fail. It doesn't mean you're a failure; it just means you failed. You can say that you have had situations in your life where you failed. You cannot be defined a failure, until your life is over."

Other pastors found consolation in a sense of faithfulness. As one commented, "I felt like I had done my best, that I was faithful. I didn't save us from closing. I felt we had a good plan. We gave a good fight; we put up a good fight." Another said this: "I never doubted my abilities as a pastor because I always figured that my abilities as a pastor came from the Holy Spirit. I never felt like I was neglectful in my ministry. I not only ran the church, but I ran a day school. I was headmaster. I generally worked sixty to eighty hours a week." Another reflected, "I had gotten past the failure deal and really was thinking I'd done some of the best ministry."

In the written survey, pastors were asked a series of questions about how they coped with challenges: "The following items deal with ways you coped when you were serving the church that closed. These items ask what you did to cope with this event. We want to know to what extent you did what the item says—*how much* or *how frequently.* Don't answer on the basis of what worked or not—just whether you did it."[2] Figure 3 shows the various ways in which pastors turned to God. Their intentions range from putting their plans into action with God to seeking help with anger.

Pastors' responses confirm that no matter how measured, the greater the stress, the more they turned to God for consolation. Figure 4 shows that when scores across all the "turning to God" items are added together to form a religious coping (RCOPE) scale, pastors turned more often to God (had higher RCOPE scores) when they served a church that was conflicted when they arrived, when they experienced moderate or

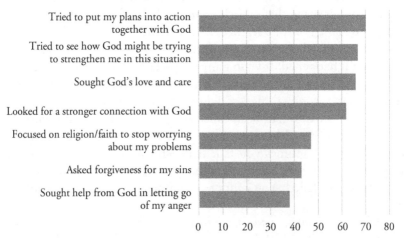

Figure 3. Ways in which pastors closing their churches turned to God (Components of Scale of Religious Coping, RCOPE)

high stress while serving, when their serving the church was a Good Friday–Holy Saturday experience, when they experienced worsened health, and when they experienced high stress after the church closed.[3] Other studies of clergy, as well as soldiers and people in other walks of life, show that reliance on prayer increases with fear or uncertainty, as reflected in the oft-quoted phrase "There are no atheists in foxholes."[4]

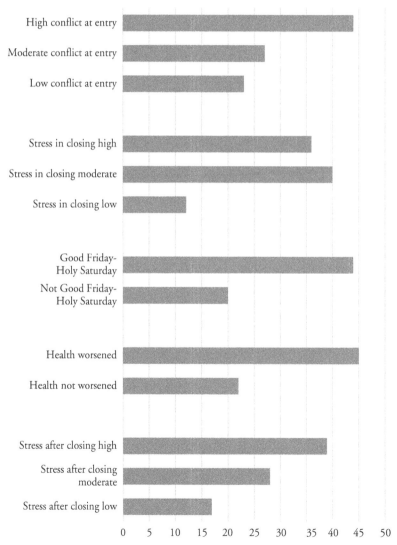

% High Religious Coping (RCOPE)

Figure 4. The greater the stress in closing a church, the more pastors turned to God

Besides knowing God's presence through prayer and worship, pastors in tough currents may be blessed in tangible ways such as through God's grace manifest among members of the church. Said one pastor of her time serving the church,

> There were times when [God] spoke to me very vividly and gave me guidance and would send people to me that would help me out. When we were trying to sell all the assets off, that would give us ideas, and it wasn't just me—it was other people, you know; it was like God was putting thoughts into people's heads and they were coming up with the ideas, so it wasn't just me leading. It was God leading. I think in the end, you know the very end, and looking back at it, I can see a lot of God's hand and the Holy Spirit moving in the group of seven.

In one of the most challenging burdens of pastoral leadership—discerning whether to close—pastors may experience grace in the willingness of their congregations to make the decision to dissolve themselves or, if they are not ready, to embark on a pilgrimage to hear God's call to new life and to make a bold decision.[5] One pastor was grateful that "it was not my decision; it was the congregation's." This pastor and others respected and were consoled by the autonomy and authority of the congregation to make their own decision to close.[6]

Many pastors found solace in what they were able to accomplish with the aid of their congregations. As one recalled, "When it came time to clean out the offices, there was suddenly this influx of bodies taking and pulling stuff apart and hauling stuff and trying to dispose of it. The money did not stop coming in. People didn't give it up." One pastor told of a helpful congregant who helped her create an office environment so the church could continue to function as a church. This parishioner's kindness helped the pastor function during the difficult time of closing the church. "God bless her soul. The goodness of her heart and her soul was just a great thing to have."

It is a blessing when a congregation affirms a pastor's call even when the church dissolves. One newly ordained pastor, who eventually closed all three churches in her first appointment after seminary, was grateful for their affirmation of her call: "From the beginning, they fairly quickly let me be their priest, which was affirming of who I am and of my call, even as we weren't sure what our future was together. And that continued until the end, and that was really wonderful."

Because pastors can become scapegoats for the decision to close, the *absence* of blame is a special comfort:

> Ten people made it clear all the time that this was not my fault, and ten others, that it was nothing but my fault. Everybody else was somewhere on the spectrum that didn't really blame me, but maybe I could have done something that would have helped. You know, it had to be somebody's fault. But those ten that were very affirming, many of them came with me. The churches were only about twelve miles apart. They said, "This is really not much to do with you at all. You need to keep that in mind. Whatever is said about you, just understand it's really not about you." I had some really good support.

Another pastor said, "They were who they were, and they are very good people. I didn't feel they blamed me at all. They just didn't make me feel bad. Some people would've, but it wasn't me that [caused the church to close]. It didn't spill over to me." Another said, "They didn't blame me or themselves, which is a huge way of supporting me." One pastor noted, "They had enough [shedding tears], not pride, but belief in themselves to not place blame. We didn't spend a lot of time finding fault with anyone or anything, other than the fiscal crisis of 2008." One congregation generously offered their pastor a year's salary as severance pay.

A congregation unable to afford severance may offer their minister compassion: "They were very loving and appreciative of my being there, my service. It was hard saying good-bye to the church and to the people, and I think everybody felt the same way." And another: "They loved me. They knew I was doing what had to be done, so they didn't blame me. I only felt love from all of them, so that was the blessing in it all." Another pastor reiterated:

> I think it was just the love, the intense love, of being with these people. I guess like a hospital chaplain must feel sometimes—the honor of being able to go through this with people, and the feeling that you have as a preacher at a funeral. To be the one bringing the good news in the midst of what looks like a completely closed grave.

When I asked about unexpected blessings, still another said, "Just the love." The pastor was concerned that the congregation would disappear after the decision to close was made, but reported,

We stuck together and we worshiped together and we loved each other. That Easter, it was an amazing Easter. They were looking at it like, "It's going to be our last Easter together," so they pulled together and they brought in a lot of family members. It was like four months of constant celebration. Those were wonderful, and it was a friends-for-life feeling, knowing that I was technically their last pastor. They teased me about that: "This will look good on your résumé; you closed a church," and things like that. But the love that we exchanged in that moment, it was well worth it.

From my journal, six months before our church closed:

God is surely with us. Sunday night Ben sent me his liturgy ideas, and today John [a neighboring priest] called. I called David [another colleague] and he called back. This morning as I went to pick up our recognition certificate from the Board of Supervisors for the food pantry, I went home saying, "Where do I turn with my fears and confusion about what to do? Who? Who do I turn to?" No clear answer came except to pray, and I did, and began to study the Scripture for Sunday because I am the spiritual leader and need to get fed. In the midst of that, John called—a prayer answered. I sobbed for the first time, really hard. I feel so inadequate, and John helped me feel respected and loved.

Just as Jesus journeyed with a small band of faithful followers whom he loved to the end, the Spirit, embodied in a rich network of relationships beyond the church, bears compassion, truth, and the promise of a new future. A congregation in denial, in conflict with the pastor, or overcome with grief may not support their pastor. However, when it feels like the rudder has kicked up, God may send a rescue vessel of clergy colleagues, family, friends, and others to bring comfort.[7]

In this study, *interviews revealed the diverse ways neighboring and other clergy supported pastors in their time of need.*[8] One pastor said, "I hadn't expected my peers would be as great as they were, and not just the last day. It was times leading up to the closing when I would attend a local clergy meeting. They were there. It was a lot like God being there, frankly." Another pastor said, "God was in the seminary colleague that moved near me. When I said, 'I can't do this anymore,' he said, 'So don't. You might have been called for this for a season, but . . .' He quoted back to me what I had said to him more than once: '*Christian* does not mean *doormat*.'"

Collegial support can bestow God's love. Moved to tears by a colleague's presence at closing worship, one pastor said after receiving the written survey, "I called my colleague and thanked her for being there because it triggered a lot of emotion." The pastor didn't usually associate with her, but "boy, did I value her presence. It just goes to show God works in mysterious ways." A pastor whose first church closed reported, "[I] was fortunate enough to have really good friends around me, who rallied around me and made sure I was OK, and they were checking on me on a regular basis. Without that, this would have been a totally different interview."

Clergy continuing education and support groups frequently offer empathetic listening and confidentiality. One pastor noted, "We would have conversations about how things were and weren't going. I was doing OK, but at the same time it's kind of a blow to your self-esteem. You come into the situation where you have a church that closes under your watch, and you've never done that before. It hurt." When being vulnerable with a bishop or colleague seems risky because it might jeopardize a future appointment, a shield of privacy is a blessing: "I was involved in a clergy covenant. I lived across the valley, technically in another jurisdiction, kind of freeing that I could talk about what was going on. You really did have that covenant of confidentiality."

In a storm of congregational conflict, caring colleagues are especially important. One pastor, whose members fought with each other and with her, valued "a close friend who was in seminary with me, right in this area." The pastor reported, "[She] would listen and support and encourage and take me out. I was really giving up. I was ready to give up. I was, 'I'm going to work in the container store. I'm giving up ministry and I'm going to work in the container store.' They supported me." "Container store" is an apt, and perhaps ironic, metaphor for refuge, especially when disrespectful actions among church members would not be contained.

Although a church dissolution can threaten one's vocation, one pastor found solace in his clergy prayer group: "Without them, if I had not had that solid group I was seeing every week, who would I have had to talk to? Just the judicatory folks. While, yes, they were taking my phone calls and, yes, they were totally supportive, without that peer support—ugh." Similarly, in the process of my church closing, my ecumenical women's clergy support group listened and laid hands on my head in prayer as I strained to find the wind for my sails.

Caring colleagues invited stressed pastors to lunch and affirmed their good pastoral work. One such pastor recalled, "A couple of really good clergy friends left me notes which were really nice, very help-ful—just coming in and finding a helpful little note." One overtaxed minister attended a judicatory workshop where a colleague he'd never met before spoke to him on the elevator: "'Hey, you're Bill, right?' I said, 'Yeah.' He said, 'I just want to thank you for how you handled the closing of your church. I've just heard stories about how well you've handled that, and I just really appreciate the fact that you're represent-ing young clergy the way you are.'" The pastor said, "I didn't realize I was handling it that well, I guess. You don't think about that."

One minister was grateful for a neighboring pastor who asked about how it felt to dissolve a church, and who then said,

> You know, I've noticed that the people from that congregation have really gone on to be part of a number of other congregations in our judicatory. The fact that they are in other congregations and are involved in other congregations and they haven't just gone off really says something about your pastoral care in that closure process because that doesn't always happen. I've seen it. There have been other closures and completely different outcomes.

The pastor added, "That meant a hell of a lot, because I worked very hard to help connect people to different congregations, but mostly to create a framework through which they could take the space to look through their own emotions."

The kinds of relationships that were most helpful to pastors were probed in the written survey with a question drawn from similar studies: "As you were serving the church, how important were the following [relationships] in your ministry?" Pastors could answer on a four-point scale from "of little importance" to "great importance." The most sustaining relationships for pastors were with family and friends; with spiritual disciplines such as Sabbath time, Scripture study, non-church-related hobbies, exercise, and contemplative prayer; with lay leaders in the congregation; and with colleagues in ministry. The interviews confirmed that intimate companions such as family, friends, spiritual directors, and therapists become more important with the emotional and spiritual tribulations of adaptive work. Their car-ing presence doesn't lessen stress, but it helps pastors bear it and work through it.[9]

Some marital relationships that could have been strained became a well of grace. One pastor noted that a caring spouse "knew who some of the difficult church members were," which became "a huge amount of support." A few families in the study were composed of married pastors. "We have a very deep spiritual relationship as a couple," one such pastor said. "It's the core of who we are. We're priests to each other as a part of our marriage." Another pastor spoke about how his wife "really did go through a mourning process, both for the churches and I sort of, you know, evolved into my own mess. There was certainly a point at which it was very painful for her, but she stuck by me."

Some pastors in troubled marriages went into counseling or recovery programs that helped them restore those relationships. One pastor learned much about his family system that later helped him with ministry: "My wife and I were in counseling. [The church closure] took a toll on the marriage, and I think that was really, really important to me—doing the family systems work. It led to devotional work. It allowed me to belch everything on the page."

Although not many pastors saw therapists or spiritual directors, the importance of therapists and spiritual directors in sustaining pastors in their ministry increased with the level of stress the pastor experienced.[10] Through the course of visiting a family systems therapist, one pastor said,

> I began realizing things about myself. It's basically the three voices that we all have: the scolding parent, the adult, and the child. I began to realize that the adult voice is the one I'm supposed to be listening to, but I've got to be the scolding parent or the spoiled child, and that was playing itself out in other aspects of my life. There was almost this fear of abandonment. Therapy pulled me through. I'm in a much different place today than I was when I was there.

When I asked her, "What unexpected blessings did you experience in that time?" she responded, "I didn't kill anyone!" and laughed. "That's a blessing. I think I developed a heightened sense of self-care. I knew what I needed to do to nurture me."[11]

The breadth of pastors' friendships blessed them with good listeners to help process the strains of ministry. One colleague empathized with a pastor who closed a church, lost a parent, and experienced multiple deaths in the first few months of her next church with, "I think you have death fatigue (compassion fatigue)." Another attested,

> In the middle of closing our church, God was with some really good friends who were there for me. Two of them are not even in the ministry, which is very helpful. I had dinner with one last night,

because she has a perspective that's outside the ministry. I think God was in them talking to me, listening to me, being there in the midst of that, comforting me, guiding me.

Besides relationships, even the geographic separation of church work and home can be a source of grace to burdened pastors. One shared this:

> I lived 150 miles away. I would drive over on a Saturday, and then I would drive to my home 150 miles away on Wednesday. Thursday and Friday were my weekends. Being 150 miles away, I had a buffer zone. My home became more of a sanctuary where I didn't have to deal with that other stuff. I think that was another factor that helped with my survival.

Another pastor said, "God was in the driving. Sometimes having the long distances to go meant I had time to decompress and I didn't dump so much on my husband." Even living in the next town was a buffer. "Fortunately, I didn't live in the town [where the church was]. I had my own home about fifteen, twenty minutes away." The pastor added, "That's where I have community and people that I like to be with and laugh with. It was and continues to be a great stress relief." Church interactions wouldn't break into private time. "I didn't encounter them except at church. That really does make a difference. It really was my job; it wasn't my whole life."

Relationships with the wider community also revealed God's loving-kindness. In the midst of their struggles, one congregation "adopted" a local junior high that had many needy children. When the church closed, the pastor was touched when a member "came over just in tears and said, 'I'm really going to miss what we got started as a connection between the school and the church.'" A church's legacy gifting to the community brings grace. One pastor, whose congregation's gift made possible the purchase of a home for refugees, said, "I feel like I've kind of done my one great thing, and maybe there'll be some other great things."

Our church's relationship with city neighbors was a wellspring of joy. In a last gasp for renewal, our congregation sought to prepare an acre of land beside the church for a community garden. In an act of goodwill, an agronomist from the local community college taught us the basics of organic gardening. The local tractor dealer identified a nearby farmer who drove his own machine through the suburban city to plow our acre-and-a-half field in the fall and the spring. Undergraduates in a university service club worked alongside members of the congregation to spread organic nutrients and seeds for the cover crop, then returned in the spring to dig ditches for water pipes, mark off beds, and cover pathways with mulch. Our small but eager congregation was overwhelmed with gratitude, as was I.

From my journal, three years before our church closed:

Reflection on "and with your blessing shall the house of your servant be blessed forever" (2 Sam. 7:29): God has revealed to David that he will bless his house forever, and David feels and expresses gratitude, and petitions for the fulfillment of the promise. God's blessings never seem enough! A river of generosity flows and I see the signs of it—winds for sailing, offers of help with our community garden's irrigation, farming, the parish house, water for tilling, how God is blessing our church with good things and good people—and still I feel the anxiety of whether there is enough. How like David I am, when there had been pain, the loss of Absalom, it is hard to trust. I understand that. I also see Paul's story in Acts: how the love of God in Jesus Christ reveals itself in amazing courage to keep on moving forward (Acts 18). With good news of God's love for all people, this is how I see the acts of Wendy, Mike, Frederique, Carl, Ron, and all others who have come forward to help this church. Amazing grace. Thank you, Jesus.

CHAPTER SUMMARY

Working in a church that closes can affirm God's presence in times of trial and soul wrenching. But in the midst of troubled waters, God embraces clergy with faith's gifts—spiritual disciplines such as prayer, sacraments, journal writing, walking in nature; an affirming claim on the authenticity and faithfulness of a pastor's call to ministry; the promise of resurrection after death for the congregation and the pastor. God's love may be revealed in the corporate actions of the church and incarnate in the pastor's relationships with colleagues, family, friends, spiritual companions such as spiritual directors or therapists, and the wider secular community.

These sources of grace cultivate clergypersons' hearts, minds, and bodies with the gifts from God that they need on the pilgrimage to closure. I remember the story of Joseph, torn by his brothers away from his family and sold into Egyptian service. He remained faithful to God, even in prison, and in God's time, the betrayal was redeemed by love that never ended. So it is with pastors tossed by wind and waves, yet faithful to the end by means of the compassion of God.

10

The Next Call

Vocational Transformations

From my journal, two months after our church closed:

Jesus is with the disciples. He tells them not to leave Jerusalem but to wait for the promise of the Father. And as they watch, he is lifted up, and a cloud takes him out of their sight. I imagine them standing there, wondering, "What do I do now? What will be my life now?" And I see myself in them—my life as a priest at Holy Family for nine years is over. The people and their ministry were honored [during our closing worship], and now what? It's funny, though. The mail brought hard news but also gave me hope—a friend cared enough to sit down and write pages of notes on my first attempt at an article for publication. Why did I think it would be easy? I can do this. I can take what [Jesus] said and do the work. God cares. Jesus is with me. This time is blessed. I consecrate it to God.

When church doors close, most pastors accept a new call or begin a congregational job search. Others, like me, retire or take a much-needed break to heal and decide whether to remain in local ministry. Although some choose new ministries, a few, even two or three years later, remain vocationally stuck. Closing a congregation, with its dashed hopes and expectations, interpersonal conflict, spiritual and emotional exhaustion, or stigma, can be what organizational psychologists call a "sense-breaking" event, or a "problematic disturbance" affecting personal and professional relationships, even a pastor's overall sense of call or vocation.[1] Clergy must make sense of what happened as they discern a new future by faith.

This chapter describes the vocational wake of a church's dissolution—*wake*, in the sense of the trace a boat or another moving object leaves behind. Interviews reveal that most pastors who have closed churches seek positions that will constitute a "good transition"—that is, a new call soon enough to minimize financial hardship, support their families, and contribute to healing and reconciliation. Accompanied by faith in their call to ministry, pastors may grow in their identity as a local congregational pastor; or they may transition into a "hybrid" pastoral identity, such as hospital or university chaplain, social worker, or nonprofit administrator; or they may discover a new identity outside the church. A few remain vocationally stuck on the sidelines.

In this study, among pastors who continued to work, about two-thirds served local congregations, most as solo pastors or intentional interims; about one-quarter retired; the rest took different paths. *Faith in their sense of call bears many clergy into new pastoral positions.* One pastor, though not a Methodist, cited the significance of the Wesley Covenant prayer: "If you'll use me, I'll go where you put me." He said, "That's really been my sense of call, and God's been good in the midst of that. I enjoy where I am and what I do." Good news from this written survey is that one to three years after their church closed, pastors in this study who were called to new parish positions are more satisfied with their personal and professional lives than an independent sample of pastors who left church ministry. On the other hand, there may be scars from their experience; their satisfaction was somewhat lower than that of another sample of pastors who likely didn't close a church.[2]

Finding their next position was easier in settings where bishops appoint clergy to churches (as in the UMC) than in a call system where clergy must participate in a judicatory or national search process (Episcopal, Lutheran, Presbyterian, and UCC). Compared with 12 percent of the pastors in an appointment system, nearly 40 percent of pastors in a call system experienced "very much" or "a great deal" of stress around the need to find another position. The survey showed that bivocational pastors or those in a multipoint call also found the transition easier. Said one, "Pastors in a failing church are isolated because everything they know is falling apart. I didn't experience that because I have another vital congregation."

Although an appointment system has its limitations, bishops and other judicatory leaders may aid in the transition of clergy with burnout or exhaustion. One pastor on disability after serving a conflicted congregation assisted a nonprofit board and networked; after that time, the judicatory gave him a "good assignment." Another also closing a church in discord admitted, "I was as burned out as I've ever been and emotionally drained. Spiritually, I was doing pretty good, but emotionally, physically—oh, my gosh—I was wiped out." Being confident in his family systems knowledge and pastoral skills, the minister explained to his bishop his hopes for a call with new opportunities for his family in "a town with a college or university or, preferably, multiple universities." He added, "It has to have McDonald's. It has to be a one-point charge in a place with a Walmart." The judicatory appointed him to a post like this, and he has grown.

About three-quarters of pastors in the four denominations with a call system actively searched for a congregational position. For many, the changeover was effortless. When one pastor's second church in a multichurch call closed, the pastor recalled, "I walked out the door, stepped into a moving van, and headed to my next call. And it is rare, but I also took it as God saying, 'I need you. I know that you have kids who need to eat. And bills that need to be paid.'" For another pastor, exercising initiative made for only a short gap:

> I actually took a road trip of ten days, traveled twelve hundred miles, and networked with seven different [judicatory] offices. A couple of months after, one of the [judicatories] called and said that they had a congregation that might be suitable. We did a Skype interview, then they flew [my family] out and we did another interview. The congregation had given me a three-month severance package. I had income through the end of March, and then I started the new call in May, so a little gap there in income, but for the most part, I was covered.

Like this pastor, those in "call" denominations with bishops (Episcopal and Lutheran) were helped more in a job search by the judicatory than by colleagues (who proved more useful than the judicatory to pastors in Presbyterian and UCC churches). The survey shows that 80 percent of pastors who were highly respected by their judicatory when serving the closing church found the judicatory "very useful" in their job search afterward. On the other hand, a complicated relationship with a bishop or judicatory staff hindered the vocational transition. A lack of respect was more commonly reported among women.

When a permanent charge wasn't open in the same area or wasn't feasible because the pastors were too emotionally burdened, many clergy accepted interim or supply positions. "I hadn't given up on ministry, and the fact that someone wanted me to supply preach kept my nose to the grindstone and my hand on the plow," one pastor recalled. Another said, "I did a couple of sabbatical and bridge pastorates that were short-term things, and I worked at [seminary] for a year. Then I got called to be the sabbatical interim pastor at [a church]." Several accepted interim or supply positions that turned out to be more or less permanent. One minister who faithfully closed a church quickly accepted a new call without consulting colleagues or doing research on the congregation beforehand. Family responsibilites were pressing, as the pastor recalled:

> There was nothing holy about this. I thanked Jesus but said, "I need this job. I need the money. I've got to pay the rent." Our savings were going down. I remember convincing myself, "You can do anything for a whole year. Give yourself a year. If you still hate it, you can handle it." Our judicatory has interim pastor meetings. I'd go there and listen to the verbatims [a shared written recollection of a pastoral encounter that encourages psychological, spiritual, and sociological reflection] and learn from that. I just did what I had to do. I loved it. I loved these people. I fell in love with everybody.

Retirement often proved a comfortable, alternative transition. Said one individual, "I'm sixty-three. I don't need to seek another parish. I took early retirement." For most, retirement was voluntary, although some felt their circumstances forced them to retire. "When the judicatory executive pulled the plug, he was going to carry my salary for six weeks and health care for three months, so I needed to do something," explained one former pastor. "I had to go on pension. I was eligible for that, so we did." Many planned well for retirement. One pastor and her husband bought a farm property to build a house with her adult children. "We closed the church on Easter Sunday, the moving van came on Thursday, and our stuff was delivered on Friday," she recalled. "On Saturday, we planted one hundred trees." Another retired pastor, who lives on a farm with a big garden, said, "Seven hours to mow the lawn . . . There are several hobbies I want to do, and it's nice to be unstructured."

For many, passage into a new church ministry goes well, but *for others, church closure means uncertainty, or even pain, that is sense-breaking and challenges a sense of God's call or presence.*[3] In my written survey, pastors were asked, "When the doors of the church closed, how much did you experience several sources of stress?" Among active (not retiring) pastors, the most prominent stresses after dissolution were feelings of loneliness and isolation (41 percent "very much" or "a great deal"). The need to find another job and financial strain came next (30 and 28 percent, respectively). Less common were a sense of shame (19 percent) and thinking or hearing that having closed a church would affect a job search (17 and 14 percent). First- and second-call clergy were subject to more spiritual stress (loneliness, shame) than were others. Many pastors with more challenging congregational experiences, with heavy stress while serving, or with experiences of disrespect from their judicatories continued to be anxious as they sought new positions. Men experienced significantly less vocational and financial hardship after the churches closed than did women.

Searching for explanations for the hardship of finding a position, one in five pastors thought that closing a church had hindered their job search. Colleagues and judicatory executives may attribute stigma. One pastor said, "I think one of the most helpful things is that people no longer remember that I closed that church. I said this before, but my colleagues were really creeped out: 'I don't want to be your friend because I might get tainted.'" Another pastor recalled a congregational job:

> I wrote to countless judicatory executives after I left my congregation and told them that I was deeply aware of this need to close churches. I offered my experience, my commitment, my spirituality. I have great empathy for judicatory leaders. It's a question they really don't want to deal with. I've heard so many say, "I will not close a church on my watch." That's a stupid comment. It has nothing to do with closing churches. How are you engaged with your congregations who are suffering? Your clergy who are suffering, who are out there on the front lines—how are you engaging that? But they're not engaging that.

Calls may be impaired not only by judicatory indifference but also by potential congregational employers who fear "the death of Christianity," as one pastor put it. One young female pastor said, "If I could have come to the end of that process so that I wasn't going to get branded this congregation-killer church closer . . . I've heard those

stories: 'They closed their last congregation. How good can they be?'"
Another reported:

> I went to one interview, and then I got an email from the chair
> saying I would not be continuing because the committee was afraid
> that I'd kill the church. And I sort of knew it at the time. People had
> warned me, "You close a church, and no one will want to hire you
> again." And then I got that email. Some people can't get past the
> fact that you "killed the church." They were in the same situation,
> very tiny.

Unwilling to leave the area where his spouse works, one pastor who had
difficulty finding a job now serves a vulnerable population in a secular
vocation. He said, "It's actually incredibly freeing to be making a living
outside of the church."

Financial stress often accompanied difficulty in finding a new position. Of those who stayed with a congregation until the end, 56 percent
received no severance pay. Some pastors worked without pay for a time
near the end of their service, and although some judicatories promised
back pay when the church building was sold, they did not always keep
their promise. The average search was five months, with 9 percent of
those pastors unable to find positions in a congregation. The gap was
only 1.3 months for UMC pastors, but 8.5 months for those in a call
system—a significant difference. Only 10 percent of retired pastors felt
financial strain "very much" or "a great deal," compared with nearly 30
percent of pastors who continued to be active. Nearly a third of clergy
in "call" denominations felt stress in searching due to financial strain.

A challenging job search with financial strain was more common
among women than men, not related to severance but to opportunities and demographics. Job-seeking took an average of 7.6 months for
women and 3.4 months for men, a significant difference. One-third of
female clergy experienced financial pressure "very much" or "a great
deal" after their church closed, compared with 18 percent of male
clergy. Although compensation inequality has been decreasing, there
remains a "glass ceiling" in the sense that large churches are less likely
to employ women, and in some denominations, women are paid less
for the same position.[4] Therefore, women have less opportunity to save
for a period of unemployment. In this study, women are also more
likely than men to be single or divorced (28 percent, compared with 8
percent of men) and unable to depend on a spouse's salary.

Women also reported less respect from their judicatories than did men, which created a sense-breaking experience. Said one:

> At a judicatory meeting, the executive announced that three pastors were coming into the judicatory for three churches looking for pastors. And I looked at one of the other females who was out of work, and she looked at me, and we talked afterward. Neither she nor I had even been allowed to see the information from those congregations. We may not have fit what they wanted; we may not have wanted the call. But we weren't even given the courtesy of them saying, "OK, we know you're seeking a call; we have three churches here that are looking for pastors. Would you be interested in any of them?" Totally ignored.

Regardless of gender, more than one pastor in a call system said, "Unfortunately, I used all my savings," or "It dealt a huge blow to my financial security. I'm just now pulling up out of it." Pastors may have to leave the manse the church provides: "My husband and I could not stay. We were allowed to stay at the parsonage for six months, but after that we had to move out. We got an apartment. Living in Chicago is very, very expensive. It was just very difficult for us." One pastor lost $30,000 on the sale of his house.

Only a few clergy received benefits such as accrued sabbatical leave, paid health insurance, or a love offering. Health insurance was a concern. "We no longer had insurance because my husband was insured through me; that was probably our biggest struggle," said one pastor. Searching for a new position in a call system, after leaving her beloved congregation, another pastor said, "I was told I had to pay my own insurance, so I've been taking money from my retirement fund." As she works part-time in a church, faith supports her:

> It was just one instance where it's a beautiful day and then all of a sudden, your boat is sinking. It was like that gospel story where in the midst of going under, Jesus is saying, "Keep faith." He turns around and calms the water. That's what happened to me in the midst of all that turmoil, physical sickness, and no real connection with people in power or with my colleagues. I was trying to stand for myself and for my congregation, and it was like that, like being in that boat, and then hearing that voice in the midst of things. I didn't give up, although there were many times I wanted to. But the voice and the presence were there. It was like being in the boat. I wasn't

the one who was screaming, "Help me, help me!" and "What's wrong with Jesus?" because I'm at a point in my life where I know Jesus is there. I know that God, the Holy One, is present in all of this stuff, and in the times that I faltered, I was able to return to that trust that even though this is crazy and I don't know what the heck's going on, I know that God is with me.

She values her call: "It's that call to be faithful and to recognize my call. We need to be in the process of identifying our call and helping each other find that call and then be about the process of going out in the world and acting out of that call."

After their churches closed, some pastors left ministry for a healing season. Like others serving contentious congregations with little outside support, one pastor served a closing church faithfully to the end but moved away for a healing season, far from the judicatory that ignored her plight as a first-call pastor:

> I was away from ministry for over two years. Then somebody I'd talked to [a couple years before] happened to remember my name and called from my new judicatory. "Are you still looking? I've got two congregations. I think you'd be good with them; I think they'd be good with you. Their pastor has just resigned. Are you willing to look at the information that they have?" And I said, "Sure." That was, again, God's work at that point. And they are totally the opposite of what I had in the first judicatory. And of course, I did say to the new judicatory office, "I'm not real trusting right now of my congregation, because they are so friendly, they are so loving." Now that I've had a chance to know them, yes, they really are that way. That was a growing edge for me; I had to learn to trust congregations all over again.

Although this pastor returned to congregational leadership, many others changed vocational direction, prompted by difficult relationships with the congregation they had closed or with the judicatory. Depending on the severity of the challenges and the adequacy of a pastor's faith and support system, identity threats may disrupt stability, continuity, and self-regard.[5]

The good news is that with faith, sense-breaking experiences may lead to "sense-making" experiences through what may be called the grace of resurrection transformation, the gift of consolation (in

Ignatian spirituality), or, in social psychological terms, "identity work."[6] Although pastors may protect their identity as pastors by blaming the congregation or judicatory, they may also emphasize the positive things they have accomplished or learned while serving their churches. What it means to them to be "called" may be transformed.

Following disappointment or trauma, a clergyperson may remain a local pastor and foster an identity as one who is "competent, resilient, transcendent, and holistically integrated" by emphasizing positive outcomes from the experience, or the clergyperson may gain a new identity.[7] Pastors' reflectivity on events and relationships is key to this adaptive work. These were challenges for the "I" aspect of differentiated pastors to navigate at the same time as they navigated closure with their congregations.

Most pastors who left congregational ministry embraced new "hybrid" identities as they moved into more specialized church or related ministries, such as "telling," "teaching," "tending," or others the Anglican Communion calls marks of a church: to proclaim the good news of the kingdom (tell); to teach, baptize, and nurture new believers (teach); to respond to human need by loving service (tend).[8] Only a few left ministry altogether for more secular work.

Changing ministries after stress is consistent with another national study of pastors who left congregational ministry.[9] To assume a new pastoral identity in whole or in part means letting go of old expectations and making vocational decisions by faith and with personal authenticity. After serving a conflicted church, one pastor applied for a judicatory grant to develop a special program for children with special needs, and received it. "It really has become an enormous call for me," she said. The pastor credits God as she put grant work together with interim jobs, eventually cofounding an ecumenical nonprofit to work with churches on adaptive curricula. "While doing interim work, I discovered that I have some gifts, understandably, for seeing potential sources of dysfunction and the potential ways in which a parish can fall apart." Through faith, she had the resilience to see the positive outcome from her difficult experience, what organizational theorist Jennifer Petriglieri would call "positive distinctness."[10]

> What do I most value about myself as a pastor? This may be an odd way to put it, but I think the thing I most find useful as a pastor now in myself is to be able to know that it's never the end of the world.

I see too many of my clergy friends who get really obsessed about a church member that doesn't like them or someone that doesn't agree with them or someone who's trying to block them in something or pull together some opposition. I look at that, and I think to myself, I have been through such an extreme example of this. I can tell you that at the end of this, the only thing you need to get through this is God. You can let go of worrying about these people. You have to be strategic. You have to look at the situation and do what you can. But in the end, if you are right with God, that's all you can do.

One pastor welcomed an invitation to lead a human service agency:

See, my thing is I don't see myself as a pastor. . . . I work as an executive for a nonprofit, and I don't see myself in the total frame of a pastor anymore. I see myself as a minister. This is a ministry, but I have the overlay of therapist and minister kind of wrapped together now. For me, this has been very good because it's a wrap. It's embellishing my whole being, so for me, the blend is back, where I'm both a minister and a therapist but I wrap it together. I don't call myself a pastor anymore. I call myself a health minister, and I see myself doing both. I see myself wrapped in both, so I have a totally different identity than I did when I was at the church. And for me, that's very helpful and healthy to see myself differently.

Faith has been essential to the pastor's transformation: "My favorite Scripture is 'I can do all things through Christ who strengthens me.' That has kind of always been my guiding piece—you know, I can do it, now I can do this. Christ will strengthen me, and I will make it through it, the whole thing."

One minister became a judicatory consultant, building on the painful experiences she had undergone and emphasizing the positives:

As it turns out, my experience of closing a church, I think, has caused me to be bolder and feel like nothing scares me. What's the worst that can happen? The church could close. Well, that's not that big a deal. . . . If we're going to keep holding on to these ancient structures with white knuckles, we're going to get buried with them. The Holy Spirit is going to steamroll right over that, one way or the other.

She went on:

I don't know which is harder, to die to yourself as a congregation and close a church or die to yourself as a congregation and stay open. I really don't. I really think it's actually much more difficult for a congregation to figure out how to do something different, how to let go of that, to be born in faith in a different way. That's really dying to yourself. That's what revitalization requires. It can't be, "Yeah, we're going to get lots of new people in here, but we're not going to change." That's not walking forward in faith. That's holding on to this idol of the past. You can't accept what the Lord has with closed hands. It really has prepared me uniquely for the job that I'm doing.

Other clergy stressed by their leadership experience chose "tending" positions apart from congregations, such as social work; counseling; hospice, nursing home, senior community, university, or hospital chaplaincy; or teaching in public or other schools.

Organizational studies show that job satisfaction among professionals, including clergy, is related to "meaning, recognition, autonomy, and remuneration."[11] After being isolated by his denomination as the church closed, one pastor remarked, "My sense of call at this time is, it's in the works. It's not as clear as I would like it to be at this point in time. I struggle with that." Pastors lacking mutually respectful relationships with the congregation and the wider church—what I call "double-jeopardy" pastors—lack these rewards. One double-jeopardy pastor turned to a secular "tending" vocation after a stressful closure. Faith has been the pastor's solace:

> God is still at work, in some way. There's always a bigger plan, and if we stay faithful, God reveals that in God's time. For me, it's about being faithful as God continues to work out this plan. I don't know what he's doing, but I don't need to know. I just need to know that he's doing something. That's what I live with. That works for me. That's good for me because I know God is faithful. He's provided blessings. There's always, I'm eating. I've got gas; I can drive my car. My house isn't going to be foreclosed on. God just continues to provide blessing after blessing after blessing, and I just keep trying to be faithful, faithful, faithful.

But even two to three years after closure, a few double-jeopardy pastors still felt vocationally stuck. One pastor, for example, felt his judicatory confined his search for a new call, and one still suffered financial strain: "Early on, it was very positive, but some financial struggles have hit. There's some bitterness. I'm more burned out, to be fully honest." Another said,

> I just kept looking and saying, "God is still there." I don't get it. It makes no sense. I don't like it. All of my dreams have been taken away. All of my hopes are gone. I don't know who I am anymore, or what I am, or how I am in the world. But something said, "Just keep walking," and that's what I've kept doing. I have not been to church since.

Consistent with other studies showing the importance of judicatory support, most every pastor in this study who felt vocationally stuck lacked mutually respectful relationships with denominational authorities and colleagues.[12] One said, "The only thing that struck me as odd was I never once talked to the big guy [the bishop]. If he could've just said, 'Samuel, I know you did a lot of work . . . I appreciate what you did'—that kind of thing—that would've meant a great deal to me." A few clergy had been removed from their posts for reasons such as church conflict or theological differences; some admitted they did not reach out to colleagues themselves, either because of geographic distance, personalities, thinking others might not understand, or some other reason.

Several stressed pastors turned to school or other training to hone skills, reflect on gifts and call, and explore a new vocation. Reflecting stigma sometimes associated with church closure, for example, one pastor from a severely conflicted church was challenged in finding the next call. Encouraged by the judicatory executive, the pastor enrolled in a continuing education program and now facilitates healthy church growth in a church without the "headaches of being the senior pastor who's having to make major decisions or play the politics":

> It took me a long time to get to where I am now, to say that I really feel healed about this. I know this is really human nature, probably nearly at its worst. It is not something that unusual that we should expect the church to be any different from any other institution. We would hope it would be, but we're all human, and we all sin and make mistakes and fall short. That's the kind of stuff at family systems training that you hear and you say, "OK, that's just the way it is. I happened to be stuck in the middle of a really bad situation for a while, that's all."

Another minister returned to school after dissolving a church. Before the pastor began serving the congregation, the judicatory executive hadn't shared intelligence about its collapsing finances and a former pastor's financial indiscretions. Feeling stonewalled by the executive, the pastor thought, "My God, you could at least have been my pastor for a bit." He returned to school to transition to a new hybrid identity as a ministry consultant for churches in a different denomination.

As of the time of our interviews, some pastors who sought a season of respite hoped to return to congregational ministry. One first-call pastor had arrived to find the congregation an "emotional mess." After a traumatic event caused the congregation's sudden death, the pastor turned to community service and a secular tending vocation. "Then after about six months, I started providing pulpit supply to a church about an hour away," the pastor said. "Then that ended. I have started dreaming again of being at the pulpit, so it's like, 'OK, God.'" As of that time, the pastor planned to start searching again more actively, strengthened by faith:

> All the miracles that Jesus performed, I really see as an expression of the person's faith. "Your faith has made you whole." That's kind of been a bit of a mantra for a while. In the parable of the wheat and the tares, the punch line there is "grow the wheat." We're not called to pull out the weeds. Focusing on the weeds is not what we're supposed to do. We need to be positive, look ahead, let God take care of the negativity.

CHAPTER SUMMARY

Most pastors who decided to remain with their congregation until the doors closed continued in local congregational ministry. The transition was shorter and less costly for those in the UMC appointment system than in a call system. Regardless of the denomination, dysfunctional relationships with judicatory executives, staff, and colleagues may impair searches. The most commonly chosen alternative for those who were eligible was retirement.

Interviews confirm that a smooth transition requires a call to another position soon enough to minimize financial hardship or, lacking that, a sustainable retirement plan. Pastors also seek a call that matches their gifts and hopes, and a good support system for themselves and their families. Finally, they long for a respectful relationship with the judicatory and colleagues, and opportunities for healing of grief and other wounds.

A minority of pastors, but especially women, suffer long searches and financial challenges after a church has closed. Most who had experienced conflicted situations needed and appreciated time for healing and reflection on their call to ministry. Returning to former occupations or interests or going back to school (whether secular or theological) with the grace of resurrection faith blesses pastors in difficult job searches and eases their journeys of vocational transformation after a sense-breaking experience.

The following chapter looks at variations in the spiritual and emotional consequences of closing a church, as well as the positive spiritual transformations pastors felt they experienced by taking this journey with their congregations.

11

Different on the Inside

Pastors' Spiritual and Personal Transformations

Advent

Outside the window
Seeds fly like snowflakes
On wings of unseen wind.
Layers of clouds march
Silently to the east,
Harbingers of healing rains.
The cat sits still, eyes
Falling closed,
Healing in her wounded body.
We await the coming of
The Lord—
We watch and witness
The gracious signs
Of impending birth
And breathe deep sighs
Of peace.

When I wrote this poem, I was deep in Advent preparations. I wasn't looking for Christmas decorations stored in the attic. Instead, I was clearing out closets and rooms and cleaning madly so our California daughter and her family could live in our home. The day after

Christmas, my husband and I would leave on a cross-country journey to live with our other daughter and her family in Boston, where I would spend a wintry semester going back to school to study practical theology. I wouldn't leave behind the grief of closing our church, which had taken place six months earlier. I would take it with me, tucked in a suitcase until I could unpack it safely on the other side of the country.

Although closing a church is a death, we've seen in this study that it is also a birth. It is God's call to leave the past and embrace a new future. Although the experience may leave some hurting even years later, for most, loss and grief lead to inner personal, spiritual, and professional growth that I tapped into in my interviews by asking, "How were you changed as a result of closing your church?"

Whereas the previous chapter described vocational changes, this chapter shares pastors' reports of inner transformation. When a church closes, a pastor may speak of a "dark night of the soul" or the hard work of healing, forgiveness, and discernment.[1] Clergy may also speak of hope fulfilled by resurrection and grace. Although difficult events may result in continuing distress, pastors told of healing through reflection and sharing in prayer with God and in safe spaces with others.

This chapter shows that the most prominent themes of inner change among the pastors I surveyed and interviewed are increasing trust in God, leading to greater confidence, courage, freedom, and humility than they had known before; greater self-differentiation, authenticity, and self-care in terms of pastoral identity; increased vocational skills, such as cultural sensitivity and the ability to respond more effectively to conflict; and, especially among those who experienced "double jeopardy" (lack of respect from both the congregation and the judicatory), decreased trust in judicatory and denominational leadership.

Many pastors noted greater trust in God, with its attendant gifts. One young pastor who felt like she had nobody to turn to in her judicatory sketched a picture of Jesus: "Around the perimeter I wrote, 'You're not alone. You are my beloved.'" Another pastor related, "My relationship with God . . . has become clearer. Things that I used to think I couldn't do, God has shown me that I can do them. I feel I have grown into the person he created me to be, and that's a very comfortable place to be." When I asked, "How have you changed as a result of your experience?" another said, "I think feeling more comfortable in God and God's ability to make good come out of everything. I'm more courageous now. I am more certain of who I am as a child of God, and that's valuable." Still another recounted, "If the Spirit says you need to say this in this sermon, for this congregation, that's OK. When you get to the next congregation, maybe you're going to say something different. I would never have been able to do that before."

When one first-call pastor was blindsided by her congregation's sudden decision to close, she turned to God:

> My father had painted—I think he was a young man, maybe an older boy or a young man—a painting of Jesus holding a sheep in his arms. That painting always hung over my grandmother's bed, and now it belongs to me. I think that image is what has helped me through all of my trials. I do believe I am being held in God's hands. I feel like I'm not as driven as I was, that I feel like I'm in a better place accepting the fact that God's in control, not me [laughter], and what will happen, will happen.

Another pastor, who struggled with her congregation, said in response to my question about change, "As strange as this may sound, I think feeling more comfortable in God and God's ability to make good come out of everything." A different pastor said, "For all that happened and for all the sadness and the lamentations, I believe deeply that God is at work at raising up new life for us. I believe that more than I did before." Another pastor saw God at work in her conflicted congregation: "I knew that God had us no matter what happened, and my faith is now even stronger in that direction."

Diminished anxiety, courage, and humility go together. "I think I'm more courageous than I was before," one pastor said. "I think I deal with anxiety a whole lot better. I still struggle from time to time, but actually, overall, I'm better at it. I think I handle conflict better than I did before." This pastor now realizes, "It's not all about me. The success or failure of the church doesn't really have as much to do with the success of the pastoral ministry, the office of the pastor, as I used to think it would." A more experienced pastor averred, "I have a lot more confidence in my priesthood and in my leadership. A lot more. I feel proud of what I did."

Another noted the gift of humility:

> Thomas Merton says you may not get any results, but you come to do the work more for the rightness, the value, and the truth of the work itself.[2] So more and more I feel like I've done a good thing, I've done the right thing, and I've done what I was supposed to do, and that it doesn't matter if anyone else notices it. That's kind of cool.

Another pastor put it this way: "It was a humbling experience. When I was going into it, I had much higher thoughts about who I was and what I could do. I think once I left, I realized I've got limitations and I don't think I recognized them all. I still don't." And another said this: "I certainly am more . . . just aware of my own weaknesses and awareness. That's OK because it's all I had. Sometimes it works well and sometimes it doesn't. There's a mystery beyond that."

Humility can look like this: "Once you've given your all in something, I'm not going to call it a failure, but once you've given your all and something has still ended, I think you just take yourself a lot less seriously." This pastor is no less serious about his call, but he admitted, "I don't consider myself a messiah in any way. You can have significant impact, but you don't have controlling impact, I guess is the best way to say it."

For one young, first-call pastor, the ability to deal with the stresses meant "the confidence, growing out of trust in God, that I can do the complicated, amorphous, very hard job of being a priest to a church. And that is a huge thing to walk out of your first position with." She said, "I closed three churches, ran a camp for the summer, and then moved to a foreign country where I'd never met anyone face to face. What can this do to me? If I can handle that stress, I can do this."

Besides spiritual growth, *clergy experienced their pastoral identity strengthened by greater self-differentiation and awareness of the need for self-care*, especially for those healing from conflict with both their congregation and the wider church. These gifts mattered especially to pastors who were emotionally attached to their congregations and narrated their stories primarily with "we" (the pastor and the congregation striving together), as in, "We gathered our history."

Increasingly aware of self-differentiation, several pastors realized they had assumed too much responsibility for their church. "I gave so much," one said. "Probably over-gave, you know? I loved this congregation and I really love them." Like me, this pastor found it difficult to close the church: "We didn't feel as if we were at the end of our ministry because we felt still that there was so much to be done." The stress of closing was so great that one pastor turned to a secular tending vocation: "I was such a cheerleader. I took on too much for myself, and part of that energy was not helpful." He would advise other pastors, "Try to stay cognizant of the difference between God's will and the power of your own will."

Another described increasing differentiation this way: "I'm much less sure I can save the world. And in many ways, that's a good, good, good change. That was the light turning on for me, that I was being the person who was doing everything." The pastor learned, "I can look back and say they actually were running their own meetings and I took over. I couldn't stand a bad meeting, and I took over. A bad meeting is better than a meeting in which the priest is in charge." Another noted, "I hope I'm more ready just to walk with people through whatever hardship they have, rather than feeling I need to solve it." One pastor put it this way: "I'm trying to be less responsible for a church's life, coming into a place that already has a history. It already has its own karma that I have to deal with but I didn't create. I'm a little less eager to take responsibility for someone else's stuff."

Part of increasing differentiation is recognizing the importance of self-care, as one pastor attested: "There's sort of a knack to figuring out how to balance what you have to do, what you want to do, and what you need to do, for your own health and sanity, against the expectations and hopes of your parish. I think I'm better at that than I used to be."

One pastor with a newfound faith grew in both self-differentiation and self-respect: "I am continually in the process of learning that the Holy Spirit gives me what I need in the moment. Maybe that's what people value. What people don't value is that I'm not running around trying to kill myself doing everything that needs to be done." Another admitted,

> Golly, I was just so naive, so naive. I really believed that things were going to work out for that congregation and that I could help them. . . . [Now I am] more true to myself and my relationship with God. I'm trying to get to know Jesus a little better, and the Holy Spirit, of course. I have to be true to who I am and not get subsumed in what it is that a congregation expects of a pastor. . . . That's another way that I've changed. I am glad for those boundaries.

As well as often leading to greater faith and self-differentiation, *closing a church can hone pastoral skills, awareness of church decline, and how to respond to church conflict.* "I think I've really grown a lot in my understanding and my acceptance of people," said one pastor. When asked how he had changed as a response to serving a church that closed, another noted increased awareness of cultural differences extended to economic reality: "Meeting working people in different economic strata and seeing the struggles of life in the area where the economy has collapsed and there are no jobs, and what it's like and just seeing that side of the reality of the church." These and other pastors valued the experience of serving in a small church. Another said, "It gave me experience in a small church, you know, just how things are done differently." One pastor, who was also a hospice chaplain, said, "When I come across elderly people who talk to me about how their church closed and they're very angry, I can let them spew that anger, saying, 'You know you'll miss it, yes, yes, you still were hurt and it's a grieving process, it's grief. And I'll walk with you.'"

Closing a church can enhance one's understanding of church decline, as this pastor discovered:

> I have changed in my understanding of the essentials of church groups, of not waiting too long to make a decision in a church that is either at its peak or in a decline. I think we wait too long. I think I did the same there. If we would have done something four or five years earlier, maybe it could have kept them going for four or five more years.

One pastor speaks openly now about signs of impending closure:

> People think of me as Typhoid Mary. But I did get to be where I am now. I think hearing those stories helped my new church hear where they were not, and that I would be able to tell when it was coming. And among the things I say to them now is, "You're OK now, but if we're not careful, we will not be OK." And we can't sit around and do nothing and just leave everything the way it is and hope that they see extra people—that they're going to walk through the doors on Sunday morning—and say, "Oh, yeah, they're going to come." I say, "No, they're not!"

Discerning and responding to conflict with more differentiation is a grace that, for some, redeems serving in such encounters. One avowed, "I have no patience for parking lot insurrection—none—the triangulation business of, if somebody doesn't like what I have to say, then they go out and complain to somebody else." In this pastor's new church,

> from the get-go I've said, "I don't work that way." Thanks be to God, I'm serving a congregation that doesn't work that way. If somebody has a problem with a sermon, they'll come and knock on my door. If they complain to somebody else around here, they're going to get told, "If you have a problem with Jane, you need to take

it up with Jane." The biggest marker I know of a healthy congregation is they fight fair.

Another pastor grew a "tougher skin" from her "wider experience with conflict and acting out" in her closing church. She values her hard-won transformational skill to describe and head off conflict by saying, for example, "This is the way something can go, so let's have a look at how we can make this healthy instead of getting to this point."

With the gifts of renewed faith and differentiation, some felt a renewed commitment to local church ministry. One pastor said, "I think it's just made me more faithful to being present and not throwing my [clerical] collar out. I just have such urgency to be part of this change while I'm still in ministry." After her church closed, a bivocational pastor felt ready to commit to full-time congregational ministry: "I was like, 'All right, you finally converted me. It's time for me to look for my own church.'" The pastor is now full-time and said this of her experience: "I did what oftentimes can be one of the most difficult things, which is to close a church. . . . I feel like together we did a good job of that. It helped me to experience myself as a pastor in a totally new and different way, so I think that was really good."

A prominent transformation theme among pastors who served in these stressful contexts is growing authenticity—"I think becoming even more myself" was the way one pastor put it.[3] Another remarked:

> There's not a lot of feel-good directly from that time. I think the blessings are longer-term: some exposure of my shortcomings and flaws, just sin and sin patterns, being driven deeper into the grace of God, and into dependency, and into, therefore, gratitude and joy and freedom. You know, that's a walk I still daily seek and struggle to live out, but it's more of an unmasking the false self and living into my true self in Christ. So that is a great blessing.

Still another said, "When people have been as vicious as some of that was at the end of that church closure, you develop a thicker skin." The pastor avowed, "I'm not as concerned if they like me or not. I don't want people to dislike me, but I can only be me, and if you can't like me as I am, I can't really do anything about that."

One pastor lamented "being too much of a lone ranger." He said,

> I had kind of this false sense of confidence. I mean, I had a confidence that I could do this, that I was going to make it happen. . . . I

had to prove something. I was newly ordained, and if this ministry failed, then I failed, and so I was not going to let that happen. . . . It's a weird phenomenon when you're not trying to prove yourself. That's when God takes over and God does the proving to you.

He moved into a new hybrid ministry: "[I had confidence] that God created me as a unique, creative child of God, that God's desire for me is to become fully human in that I'll not be the 'answer man,' the one who gets it all right. I want to be as authentic as I can be. It's a call to authenticity. It's a call to be fully human." He found spiritual strength in crisis.

Pastors who led closing churches also felt freer to be authentic outside of church settings. One pastor who now leads a congregation composed of many homeless people seeks to match inner authenticity with outward appearance: "I no longer wear robes or a collar. I don't do that; I can't. I'm a real person, and I think a pastor is only someone who is committed to the spiritual journey and continues to open to that." The pastor went on: "I don't like it when I hear other pastors become too rigid or too demanding, that it must be this way or that way. It's so important to be real and be with the people yourself and see what you can learn from them, not just what you can put onto them, so to speak." Another pastor was no longer afraid to order a beer with his pizza: "When I came here, the realization 'I've got to be me' has taken precedence over anything else, because if I can't offer me to others, then I'm not offering me to myself."

A lack of respect from the congregation or the judicatory or both can erode trust in the church. One first-call pastor who served a congregation that turned on her many times and a judicatory that left her on her own now separates "I" and "they" more easily:

I hate to say I'm not as trusting of people as I was, but I'm not as trusting in that I don't take what they say at face value anymore. I really look into what's really going on and see if they're just saying something because they think that's what I want to hear, or whether they're saying it because they mean it. . . . I try to let them control and review what's going on. I tell them it's our ministry, but if it's something they want to do, I'm there to support them and go along with it.

She values dialogue:

If I give them the time to marinate on what it is, then we may try it, or we may not try it. But they've had time to think it through, and then we can have a discussion on it. I've learned to be more intentional with them about talking about where do you see God in your life, where do I see God in my life, what is God doing with us here in this location?

For some pastors, the absence of a sense of sacred community in the wider church may leave a scar. "I trust the leadership of the judicatory far less," one admitted. "If I were really honest about it and if they wanted to hear from me, I would say, 'I trust you far less than I have in twenty-nine years.'" This pastor observed authorities suppressing discussion at an annual judicatory meeting and said, "Whether it's about another church closing and somebody raises a question and I hear, 'You are not going to question the committee which is recommending this,' I sit there saying, 'Then why are we here if we can't ask each other a question?'" The experience makes it difficult for the pastor to "just not sit there seething or say, 'You know what? I need to just walk out of here.' It's probably made me more angry. That's the largest piece I would say: I'm much less trusting of the judicatory leadership." Another reported, "I'm probably not as trusting of the judicatory, in that they really have my back. I struggle with believing anything they say, actually. Then I just want to be left alone."

Loss of trust in the judicatory extends to questions of ethical integrity. One minister said to the judicatory's budget committee, "You're having to cut money for ministries, but yet all the administrative staff is getting a cost-of-living increase. How many pastors regularly get a cost-of-living increase? But the administration and the hierarchy of the church get one. It doesn't make any sense." Other ministers see an "either/or" or an "us and them" mentality in a judicatory funding preference for urban over rural ministries. One pastor whose church was closed abruptly by the judicatory without consultation with the pastor or the congregation said, "I have been respectful to my judicatory executive over time, but I just felt torn apart by the church, frankly." Another confessed, "I think I got a little more cynical, and at this point I'm really hard-pressed to get up on a Sunday morning and go to church because it just doesn't work for me. I'm just very, very discouraged about the state of the church."

One pastor's challenging experience with closing led to closer scrutiny not only of his judiciary but also of his denomination. He left "a church that, if, you know, you don't buy into their philosophies, theologies, you're nothing." He "felt very betrayed" also by the judicatory executive who silenced "traditional theological pastors" like him.

When a church fails amid conflict, particularly with a judicatory, pastors may not share their sadness or anger with colleagues or executives out of fear that they will be judged: they should be "over" their grief, they should be more dispassionate, they should have a stronger resurrection faith, they should have left sooner, they should not have gotten enmeshed—the list goes on. Shame may cause pastors in relational conflict to hide their grief in such a way that it becomes "disenfranchised grief" or hidden sorrow.[4] When grief remains unresolved, pastors may be led by God and confidence in their call to explore other ministries, sacred and secular, besides congregational leadership. Sadly, a few leave the church without vocational clarity.[5]

By the grace of God, however, many pastors serving in conflicted situations do heal. Said one double-jeopardy pastor who began a new church ministry, "I'm grounded in prayer, and God will take care of me. What I need is to be able to express this call, you know, to be out there doing, talking about it, and expressing what I believe God is doing in the world." One pastor still exploring what to do said, "I think for right now, I'm tending to go more to use my gifts where God puts me. I'm just following God's lead at this point."

Now working in a church-related nonprofit, another double-jeopardy pastor shared this:

> I am free to be less agenda-driven and more led. . . . As I listen, it's like the Holy Spirit does the work. I'm not claiming any special anything, but I'm just more able to say, "OK, Lord, this is your game and your thing, and you've got this," and just kind of sit back and relax and listen—listen to what the person is saying and listen for what I believe the Holy Spirit might be saying, and then just ask questions or offer prayer, or whatever seems to be the thing at the moment.

One pastor has valued the grace of God after successive, challenging closures: "This experience has clarified for me that, yes, God is who Christ said he was and who I have said that he was, that I really was called to this. Now that my woundedness has healed, my passion for this has not subsided." This pastor's faith has supported him in a new form of pastoral ministry that he likens to being the point of the spear, not the shaft:

> I had prayed, "Lord, put me on the point of the spear. I want to be where the point cuts flesh. I want to experience conversions. I want to experience life change. I want to see your Spirit change people's lives." I've gotten a front-row seat for what God is doing, and I speak a language outside the walls that my compatriots don't. I walk through the grocery store and have a conversation with the checker. I feel more at ministry there than I do leading Bible study.

Feeling marginalized by the church, a few clergy sought secular work. When one congregation suggested a pastor seeking a new call might "kill" their church, the pastor journeyed through the emptiness of Holy Saturday, or what has been called a "vacuum" in role transitions to a new identity apart from the church:[6]

> I really don't feel like I'm part of the church anymore. I'm still slightly in, but on the very, very fringe. I don't walk into a church service and feel like this is for me, that I'm a part of this. [Ever since] I made a decision to launch a secular business, I don't really see myself working any amount of time in a congregational setting again.

Another pastor now serves in a secular "tending" organization serving marginalized populations threatened by social inequality. She adds, "I'm not quite sure yet about 'in the church' because the church as it is today is not meeting the needs that are out there. If there's a possibility of being a part of or creating something that is very different, that would be great." Claiming the gift of resiliency, this pastor entrusts God with her future:

> I don't have an official status as pastor. I continue to serve in a pastoring role to people. As the outreach ministry strengthens, my desire would be to find a way to connect it to the judicatory and put it under that banner. Yeah, resiliency and faith, or faith and resiliency. They both go. . . . The source of the resiliency is just faith. I could have just curled up and packed my bags and said, "I give up. I'm out of here, done with it all."

After a healing season, I wrote this poem one year after our church closed:

The Fountain

A trio of ibises by pond's edge
flies over the fountain,
one by one,
with one left by the side
of water poured out
to heal a broken heart,
bearing ashes
on its back,
heavy with itself,
not knowing
what to do
but hold them,
till splashing
its wings in
comedic dance
to clean itself
not once
or twice
but over and over,
at last it takes wing
and leaves behind
the grief it bore.

CHAPTER SUMMARY

Closing a church can be a threat to a pastor's sense of identity. Like professionals who worked at Enron, Arthur Andersen, or any other company that imploded, pastors whose congregations close must discern a way to reconcile their experience with their own expectations and hopes for the future. Pastors in my study discovered greater trust in God by embracing God's mercy, grace, and the seemingly elusive mystery of redemption. Many have been strengthened by the experience for a new vocational journey, growing in faith and skills. A few, however, remain stranded on the shore.

In this study, many clergy who dissolved their congregations turned to God to ask where God was calling them. Reporting strengthened trust in God, they grew in confidence, courage, and freedom, as well as in humility, they became more differentiated from their congregations and judicatories, and they acquired new vocational skills and a stronger sense of who they are, or what many called their "authenticity."

Pastoral differentiation contributes to resilience and hope. If "we" (the congregation and pastor acting together) and "I" (the pastor as separate from "them," the congregation) are separate, then "I" can move on with my own grief without "we," but with "my" own issues and supports. Moreover, differentiation creates the space for the congregation to own their own responsibility and for the pastor to own his or hers. It encourages pastors to realize their individual contributions and gifts apart from those of their congregations.

Still, colleagues and judicatory staff and executives may complicate a closing pastor's celebration of a good ministry, a "good enough" death, openness to call, and embrace of new life. The stigmatizing and isolating of clergy who had taken risks to serve a vulnerable congregation were more common in my study than one would hope. Clergy who experienced hurtful actions and comments at the hands of the judicatory became more cynical about the institutional church's integrity. A few felt pushed out of ministry altogether.

What I found is that secular models of coping with identity threats misjudge the power of faith to interpret a church closure. It is not failure; it is a life-changing event on a spiritual journey with God and the sacred communities we inhabit. Faith-filled pastors may end their ministries worn out, tired, even sick from stresses they experienced. But by the grace of God, they may also retain their passion for ministry, be reinvigorated and strengthened, and feel bolder and more courageous because of the storms they endured and outlasted. For them, death is not the victor. The journey goes on.

12

The Ship's Log

Hard-Won Lessons

From my journal, two months after our church closed:

> Acts 23:11. The Imprisonment of Paul. "That night the Lord stood near him and said, 'Keep up your courage! For just as you have testified to me in Jerusalem, so you must bear witness also in Rome.'" To me, this is what writing a book will be—a testimony to Jesus in another country.

Like me, many pastors keep a journal as a spiritual discipline to reflect on whether our rudder is sound and in the water. I have found my interviews with pastors to be also like journal entries, bearing witness to their experience of Jesus in another country. They have advice for other pastors serving struggling churches, for judicatories, and for seminaries. Thus, this chapter is like a ship's log documenting pastors' hard-won lessons, in the hope of easing the final journey that other churches and pastors will make.

For clergy, prominent recommendations of those who have closed a church center around caring for oneself. "Talk to God a lot; listen to God," and "Find time alone with God, whether it be walking or in a sanctuary somewhere." Another is to have a supportive network of colleagues, family, and friends and to participate in continuing education. Begin with faith, recommends one pastor: "It's always helpful to know where the hope is—in your own life and in the life of the people and in the life of what's going to happen. Hold on to that." Another pastor counseled, "Maintain your self-differentiation. Make sure that you have a strong devotional life and that you have a regular exercise regimen and some method of self-care, because if you don't have those things in serving a church like that, there's no way you can survive it." This also means: "Keep your spiritual center strong. What you can do is exist as an island of peace and an island of God-centeredness in the midst of this chaos."

Serenity comes also with an awareness of systemic challenges. One pastor counseled, "It's not your fault. This is all part of what the Holy Spirit is doing in reshaping the church in the United States. They're part of something much bigger than what they see. The church is going to go on and on." Another reminded us that we are called to be "faithful, not successful." And one said this: "It's not something to be ashamed of."

Blaming others can be toxic. One pastor whose congregation was closed by the judicatory without participation of the laity or the clergy got angry but shared this wisdom:

> Let's not give in to anger. . . . It can take over you. That's where you can actually open the door to some evil coming in. Even when you've been wronged and you're righteously angry, you have to be real about that but not taken over. Find a way to take care of that. It's very easy in these situations to sort of join with angry persons and feel dissed and cast aside, and don't do that. Do not do that.

For pastors, discernment of personal motives, interests, and gifts is key. One said, "Make sure that you're turning over to God your expectations for the church, and try to stay cognizant of the difference between God's will and the power of your own will. Our emotions can be so powerful that we think, 'Surely it's God speaking to me.'" Another added, "Ask yourself some hard questions of whether you are naive or unrealistic, to what degree do you see yourself accurately, what's the best thing, and what truly is God's will for this church and for you?" Humility means sharing agency with the congregation. One pastor suggested, "Do it in tandem with an administrative commission or a group of people so that it's not all on you."

Pastors need to build networks of spiritual support. "Do not isolate yourself!" warned one. They need to find mentors, spiritual directors, coaches, and consultants. As one pastor said, "Seek out all the help that you can get—for example, my meeting with the hospice chaplain." Another pastor summarized this theme: "Theologically, spiritually, and pastorally, I would tell them they need to locate a spiritual director or a mentor that they can really trust and use as a sounding board, and discuss all the little things that come up. And a prayer partner to help them, to pray for them for guidance." Colleagues may help pastors realize it is not their fault, as one pastor noted:

> Find some colleagues that have been down the path. There were at least three that were within this judicatory that I was in who had been involved in church closings. And all three of them, it was also their first call. And so they were very, very helpful. They kept reiterating to me that it's not me; it's them. And I think that's really important because it's very easy to fall into that "It's my fault" if this congregation closed.

Many noted the assistance of training and coaching in family systems theory. "I would definitely recommend they go to a family systems workshop and take interim training, but to be sure and take the second section, which is on genealogical makeup." Another pastor recommended that a neighboring young pastor "read books on church systems," which the older pastor described as "kind of my Bible." This pastor then continued with more advice: "Either go somewhere for coaching, or figure out how do you lead a process, because it's about leading a process as a non-anxious leader; it's not about making something happen; it's having the people do the work."

One pastor said of an eighteen-month continuing education course on pastoral effectiveness and family systems, "That, in my opinion, is what prepared me to deal with some of the stresses that came from that church. I think having that understanding of family systems and practicing self-differentiation and what-have-you is probably what saved my ministry, saved me."

Pastors unable to participate in formal training may consider hiring a coach. According to one pastor,

> The coach was a safe person outside of the denomination that I could talk to. [She] would guide me in how to be politically savvy [laughter] in the judicatory and in the midst of other people. She knew I did not like to play those games, but she said at some point I needed to do it that way, and she was right. She would also guide me, coach me, with the problems I was facing in the congregation

and how to go back and address these issues, or how to look down the road and start getting ready.

Clergy offered advice about entering and leaving a fragile church. Before entering, one pastor counseled, learn the church's context from denominational authorities and others: "Know the written history, as well as the unwritten history, and don't allow yourself to be consumed by the triangulations." And another said, "You need to speak to other pastors in the area and find out what's been happening there, and truly why did the last pastor leave, and if somehow that information could be available." About leaving, one pastor offered this: "You'd better prepare your résumé so that there is life beyond that church." Another added, "From the minute the first red flag goes up, they should open themselves up to possibly moving and looking. It's not going to get any better once you start to see the red flags."

Clergy offered even more recommendations for judicatories, beginning with confronting religious realities. For example, in one judicatory meeting a map of churches was displayed, prompting this comment: "You can see the cluster of churches around us, three miles between churches here, four miles there, three miles there, and that doesn't make any sense these days." Recognizing denial of religious realities, one pastor voiced:

> There hasn't been a lot of truth telling in the church. It's been too nice . . . , but Jesus wasn't nice. He told people the truth. "Man, go over there and wash in Siloam, then come back." I think more truth needs to be told in the churches and in the judicatory. It's very hard to get that. The bishop's very skittish about that.

Another pastor said, "It's not much different than having a conversation about 'How do we keep our beloved relative alive, and at what cost do we do that?'" She stressed that judicatories need to think about hospice with its "care and comforts and all the spiritual implications," adding, "If more judicatories would think like that and get away from the bottom line and the fear that the ground is disappearing under their feet, I think that it would guide everyone to a better place." Another pastor said, "There's a sense that if we close a church, it's a failure—that it looks like we're dying and so there's a fight that we're going to close the church as the absolute last resort rather than saying, 'It's OK, you know, it served its life.'"

Mainline denominations need to accept that churches will continue to close for decades to come. One pastor remarked, "I see that especially from bishops: 'If I close a church, it looks bad.' Bishops don't want to have to report to other bishops, 'We closed five churches this year.' They want to fight that tooth and nail, and that's just craziness to me." Thus, some denominations and their judicatories are failing to have inclusive, transparent dialogue about what God is calling the church to be and become. For example, one pastor asked, "How proactive do we be in helping a church to define what is church? At what point are we no longer a church?" One pastor laments denial: "One of the churches that I'm closing right now, there's the pastor, his wife is the organist, his daughter is the congregation's lay leader, and there were two other people. Should somebody have helped them at some earlier point to discern, 'Are we a church? Are there better ways for these resources to be used?'"

Although some denominations—for example, the UMC and the ELCA—offer nationally normed measures of vitality and sustainability to assess churches, some question their value. "Using benchmarks like church attendance, whether they pay their apportionment on time, and whatever debt they've incurred over the years—those things should not be the benchmarks used to determine whether a church should remain open or be closed," one pastor stated. Another said, "Vitality isn't only about numbers. It's about serving and loving and reaching people. We all have gifts to give." One pastor expressed: "They need to stop worrying about how many people are in the pews. That's the wrong thing to worry about." Yet another pastor said, "They need to better assess which churches are at that point, if they're still healthy, and find out how to help them stay healthy. I think what happens is that we wait—as a denomination, we wait too long."

Judicatories must recognize that what it means to be church is changing. As one pastor put it, "We need to look at how to be the church in a different way, nontraditionally. I think we need to help the people see that being the church isn't just that one hour on Sunday morning, and I think we need to help them name that." For this pastor, "handing out food or whatever you're doing, that's the church. Just because you're not in the sanctuary for an hour on Sunday morning doesn't mean you're not the church." Another pastor noted that years ago "you had a little church in every little community because there wasn't transportation." Now we need to "keep looking for possibilities instead of looking backwards."

Further, although judicatories are diverse, many clergy describe a systemic culture of suppressing difficult conversations concerning distributive justice when resources are diminishing. Several noted, for example, that judicatories financially favor urban churches. "I think it's sinful," one said. "It just sets up this dichotomy that churches in the rural areas, who are basically the staple of America, are less than folks in urban America. Why can't churches in urban areas live within their means, pool their resources so that rural areas can be serviced better?" Echoing a call for clarity of financial support, one pastor noted, "It's mostly little rural churches that are biting the bullet and going under. I think the judiciary needs to be sensitive." One pastor who noted greater financial support for immigrant churches than majority Anglo ones in his judicatory recommended this: "You should have the same formula for every church." On the other hand, one lamented, "We probably need to do a better job addressing the needs of a Native American church."

Other divisions remain undiscussed, as noted by this pastor: "When I go to denominational meetings, judicatory meetings, it's all about new church start, new church start, new church start. It raises my anxiety about new church start because I'm not in a new church start. I'm sitting around with a bunch of old people." Although a new church start in an urban setting will provide new ways of worship to new communities, the pastor continued, "there's a whole army of retired people that feel a little bit left behind. They don't know what to do because they're not young, because all the emphasis in the leadership of the church seems to be what we can do to motivate the young adults." Judicatory cleavages like these need to be aired.

In the absence of consensus about what it means to be a church, one pastor said, "What I'm hearing people say is, 'The reason you're closing all these churches is so they can just get all the money and support the judicatory.' Whether that's accurate or not, that's the impression people are beginning to live by." Another noted to me,

They may be trying to do some good things, but the impression is "They just want to steal our money. They want to take our property." There was never a real sense that they were a strong part of the judicatory or what that means. The judicatory really needs to figure out a way of, "What does it mean for us to be a judicatory?" Honestly, I've talked to you more about it than I have anybody within this judicatory.

With suppression of dialogue, one pastor blamed "cronyism" for decisions: "There wasn't enough objective individual conversation before decisions were made that really seriously affected people who were working hard out there in the trenches."

In other words, God calls judicatories to remember they are sacred communities called to a lively faith and loving, honest relationships as well as modern bureaucracies with budgets to balance and canonical authority to act. For example, judicatories closed some churches without including their people or pastor in the decision-making. In this context, the people of God may hear, "I have no need of you," and struggle with a sense of betrayal of trust. Some will never join another church. In this study, many pastors whose churches were closed without the congregation's advice and consent left congregational ministry. Yet pastors have acquired wisdom in their service that can be used elsewhere, and the baptized have faith and gifts that God needs in the world. Pastors call on the "admiralty" of their denominations and judicatories to be differentiated, transformational leaders with resurrection hope, willing to engage the people of God in dialogue, to risk conflict, and to nurture the faith and lives of all affected by closures, both pastors and laypeople.

When judicatories fail to engage in difficult conversations, fragile churches may close on a stormy sea without the "coast guard's" guidance and protection. As one pastor reflected, "I think sometimes the hierarchy wants the pastor to do it alone because the hierarchy often doesn't want any more lip from anybody about anything, because they get plenty about everything. But it's their job." Another affirmed how a judicatory official could instead take a more transparent approach and "explain to a pastor, 'You're going to be going to this situation, and you might very well be closing a church. And we're going to support you in that.'" This is a matter of ethics, as the pastor offered a potential response: "If you are sending me to close these churches up, that's fine, but I want to know going into it because there's a difference in how I minister to that church. You don't give false hope to a terminally ill patient. You need to be honest about where they are." The pastor continued:

> When I went into that church, I was full of hope for them. I said, "Hey, we're going to do big things here. We're going to grow this church." You've got a nice new young pastor here. We're going to revitalize this church. We're going to get stuff going here. To all of

a sudden, "Hey, we got to have a talk here. We're going to have to close the doors." There's no preparation. There's no ahead-of-time to be talking about it or even leading in sermons or looking for discernment, looking for understanding of what's going to happen.

When pastoral work gets tough, one pastor noted how "judicatory leaders need to be connecting and saying 'How are you doing? What can I do? Is there any way we can help you?' and truly mean it." This pastor went on:

> I can see a lot of people coming out of seminary and then being thrown into the small, part-time church and not being fully aware of what they're getting into, and the judicatory knowing it but not warning people, or saying, "I will be support for you and this is who you can talk to, or this is where you can find information on what you need."

Empathetic listening and assistance take many forms. One pastor suggested that judicatories provide

> someone specific . . . to be the contact person in the synodical office or the diocese or the presbytery or whatever, someone for you to go to who would be your shoulder to cry on, and the one to give you advice. They could at least say, "Let me get back to you" rather than saying, "We don't know; you'll have to do this by yourself." I did not realize that my judicatory executive even heard what I was saying, that anyone heard, so when your letter [about the research on which this book is based] arrived and my name was given to you, it was out of the blue. They never acknowledged what I had done. It's not like you close a church every day.

Another pastor lamented the lack of gratitude: "I'm just appalled by the judicatory, for the judicatory executive's office to not communicate anything: 'Job well done. I know it was hard.' Anything. Anything. I am just so appalled by that, and if that's what our church had come to . . ."

Some judicatory leaders themselves lack needed expertise. One pastor observed, "They're not properly dealing with church conflict. They're trying to, [they] think they are, but they aren't." The pastor lamented that the judicatory is "not willing to pay out the money to have the proper training for a mediation team." Another noted that in his judicatory, "there are people who needed stronger managerial skills, who needed stronger skills in terms of how to get the best from people when you've asked them to go into situations. . . . [I] got a lot of 'I don't know, I don't know, I don't know' as I asked questions." Technical issues remain unaddressed. "I didn't need guidance on how to be a compassionate presence," said one pastor, "but I needed other pastors to be a support for me, and the judicatory I looked to for the logistical stuff"—such as legal advice on dissolution of endowments, property deeds, church employees, and other issues.

Judicatories must aid pastors after churches close—for example, providing job search assistance as "some way of supporting pastors who are willing to stay to the bitter end." Another pastor remarked:

> The judicatory is doing very little about extremely low morale. They're not helping, in any positive sense, helping pastors, whether they maybe say, "We're going to give you a sabbatical," "We're going to give you this," helping them in the sense of, "This process can be more devastating than you might realize or we've given credit for, and we're here for you."

In the absence of judicatory affirmation of pastoral calls and debriefing of closing pastors, both notably rare among pastors in this study, one minister suggested setting up a sustainable model of support groups for grieving clergy in different locations around the country so that pastors wouldn't have to travel, that would be some sort of grief counseling for the pastors who have just closed a church: "Because it is a death, of a sort; it's not the same as a death of a member of the congregation. It's not the same as any other kind of death. It takes on a whole larger meaning." The model could become self-sustaining by paying it forward so that every pastor had a chance to talk without, as one pastor put it, "feeling like somebody that's never been through it is looking at you like you've got horns on, and be able to say, 'I've been through it; this is what happened to me and this is how I got over it.'" It's not just the pastor who needs care; it's the next congregation she serves, so that, as this pastor continued, "when we do get into a healthy congregation, we're not necessarily looking for those underlying things that happened at the last church that had to close. I don't think the pastors get the chance to realize that it's OK for us to mourn. We don't have anybody to talk to that's been through it."

The cost of not closing well means the risk of a turbulent, painful journey for church members as well as clergy. One pastor reported, "I ran into a family at soccer the other day. 'Where are you all going to church now?' And they said, 'We haven't been anywhere. It's just too painful.' They're still, for years, not churched." One pastor reminds us to "count the cost" of closing churches:

> It would not surprise me if in fact what we are doing is erasing the blackboard. We need to acknowledge that when we close a church, we are going to lose everybody. We may have a very small percentage of the supercommitted people who will hang around. It wouldn't surprise me in the least if we lost 90 percent of the people who were in congregations that closed, certainly to our denomination, if not to organized Christianity.

Clergy who have closed churches also hope to strengthen seminaries, noting holes in curricula for church growth, administration, and spiritual formation. For example, seminaries often lack twenty-first-century church models, as noted by one pastor:

> The "attractional model" is that you just do the programming, build the buildings, they will come. The "missional model" is that you go out and look for the people that need church and you bring them in. I mean it's a different—it's a little different bent. Our denominations are not helping us make these moves, and part of it is because the denomination is built on the attractional model and the structures are not easily shifted.

As one pastor said, seminaries need to help new pastors understand that "closure is not necessarily your failure. It may not be your personality, it may not be your doing, it may have nothing to do with your gifts. You may be called there for this time or season to help them get through it." This relates to the absence of "management training, in terms of what to expect as a manager and how to approach that in terms of the information you need: What are the goals here? What are the objectives? What are you asking me to do?"

Pastors need ways to understand the hidden and frustrating dynamics of congregations. What does it mean, for example, to be "a healthy congregation"? Family systems and related theories need to be taught. "So many of our congregations are in very dysfunctional relationships, and they mirror sometimes the dysfunction of their clergy," lamented one pastor. "We need to deal with those, with the systems stuff, and we need to have positive parameters for how to be healers." One pastor noted the weakness of a seminary class he had on church conflict: "I don't know that the professor had ever served any extended length of time in a local congregation, and he did not have any clue or knowledge of family systems. Family systems stuff was so prevalent in the church I closed that it was just scary."

Although as one pastor noted, "It's really spiritual resources, trust in God that gets you through the ministry," some pastors found seminary to be largely an academic experience. One recalled, "They didn't feel really any obligation to really help teach a person to 'be'—their spiritual life. It was really more of how much history, how many ideas, can we put into your mind?" One pastor noted that when one of his classmates with experience in meditation offered to teach a class on it, the dean refused: "You know what the students did? We went there anyway. Took our own time. We never got points for that. We benefited by that, but the dean's not recognizing the value of that was a shame."

Besides introducing new clergy to the possibilities of being church, seminaries can offer opportunities for active or retired pastors to debrief their experiences closing churches. One pastor recommended that seminaries provide opportunities for pastors to "just spill out their reminiscence of ministry for the last ten years. Don't let it ferment. Articulate it. When we retire, have somebody call up and say, 'Tell me about your last forty years.' Seminaries could do that."

CHAPTER SUMMARY

The log of pastors' recommendations for clergy, denominations, judicatories, and seminaries is lengthy but timely. Clergy can learn from the mistakes and successes of pastors who have sailed on a most challenging sea. It takes a lively faith and loving companions, as well as transformational leadership skills. At the same time, wider church bodies such as denominations, judicatories, and seminaries have been caught up in powerful riptides of cultural and religious change. It is human to deny impending church deaths, but congregations and their pastors need colleagues, as well as admirals and other leaders of the fleet, to be honest, courageous, and compassionate transformational leaders nonetheless.

Judicatories need to strengthen relationships of trust, especially in the face of cultural diversity and bureaucratic imperatives such as balanced budgets. Open dialogue about competing values such as compassion on the one hand and commitments to equality, mission, or stewardship on the other will strengthen the body of Christ. In truth, judicatories are sacred communities that, like congregations, must strive for a lively, vital faith; loving, honest relationships; curiosity and the capacity to try something new, as well as values and ways of being on which there is consensus. Seminaries must strengthen curriculum, particularly around family systems theory and management of healthy congregations, missional focus, formation of new churches and how to manage church closure, and clergy spiritual formation.

These hard-won lessons are prophetic wisdom for the wider church in the face of its numerical decline.[1] Many denominations, judicatories, and seminaries already address these issues, while others lag behind, with fear being one of the greatest obstacles. With God's help, transformational leadership is possible at all levels of the church and in all parts of the country.

13

Closing Thoughts

And So We Sail On

A call to ministry is a call to proclaim a gospel of resurrection hope in the midst of death. Yet closing a church is a daunting task, even for those with this faith—for experienced sailors, as it were. Lines, booms, and GPS may break; unexpected currents will threaten the course; passengers will become anxious about the approaching storm. The overarching finding of this study is that when we open our hearts in prayer and to others in our time of need, we discover that we are not condemned to sail in circles or crash on the rocks but are drawn by God's wind and led by the Spirit into new life. Pastors who have led their churches to the destination of death by the grace of order, protection, and the wisdom of God know this. Their reflections teach us about the unique pastoral leadership of this context, with its diverse challenges such as conflict, grief, and loss.

The purpose of this research was to understand the experience of pastors leading their congregations to closure. The study explored their call to serve a fragile congregation, how their transformational leadership brought their congregation to its final destination whether that was a "good enough death" or not, and how the journey's challenges and triumphs affected their lives. This research has identified the unique ways in which this call to serve the gospel stretches a pastor's spirit, mind, and body; the costs of this ministry; its rewards; and recommendations for the future.

Closing a church can become a more perilous journey than many others. A church losing vitality and sustainability is often caught in rough waters, vulnerable to a precipitous and painful shipwreck. An aging congregation, a failing building, and decreasing energy to serve a church's neighbors present broad and deep questions without easy answers. My church faced questions such as these: "When we can afford to pay our pastor for only one-quarter time, can we still expect her to lead worship both Saturday afternoon and Sunday morning?" "How can we clean the church when we can't afford a sexton?" And the one question that resulted in the diocesan decision to sell the building: "How can we repair the leaking roof when we have no savings?"

Questions like these are adaptive challenges that one person's skill or authority cannot decide; they require the sacred community to come together to understand the facts and ask, "What is God calling us to do and to be?" The sacred journey of inquiry itself, and any of its decisions, will provoke change. Familiar ways of being and doing will be altered, often leading to disappointment, sadness, anxiety, and anger for everyone in the church. Transformational change requires gospel faith in resurrection following the "little deaths," like ending a cherished second worship service, as well as the "big one"—the decision to dissolve a congregation.

Change means loss, and with loss comes grief, especially among church members. Although pastors realize that their call to ordained ministry transcends a particular community, people in a congregation develop a deep attachment to their church building; their identity is often not that of a pilgrim on a spiritual journey but of a settler with a home in a sacred space and intimate attachments to others who have shared their joys and sorrows, often for a lifetime. Calling this the difference between a "theology of journey" and a "theology of place" recognizes what has been found in secular work contexts—that people who identify more with their place of work (for example, Enron) than with their occupational identity (for example, engineer) will suffer greater loss and grief when leaving a position.[1] It helps explain why moving en masse to another congregation consoles both the people of God and the pastor—the sacred community is preserved.

Several pastors in this study reported the pain of the slow, slow decline of their congregations. The absence of visible signs of new life such as children running around, a new couple or family, or someone with a passion for an exciting new ministry is wearing on the soul. Also, living with awareness of loss for a long period of time makes the ministry of closing a church like hospice ministry, yet it's more challenging because it involves a community. People grieve differently—some keep their tears to themselves, some rant, and others manage to give voice to sadness with respectful maturity.

And on top of all that, pastors have their own grief.[2] Closing a church, especially one crashing against an unexpected shore, can trigger feelings of failure, fault, or guilt; loss of a sense of vocational safety because of stigma; or sadness for the loss of a church's beloved people or ministries. Clergy families may grieve over disrespect they or the pastor have experienced, the loss of stability for children and others in having to move, or sorrow at losing friends. Pastors often hide this grief from their congregations but seek help from family, friends, spiritual directors, therapists, and trusted colleagues. On the other hand, some pastors share signs of grief over the church's closure publicly in order to normalize the grieving process and facilitate transparency. These are among the costs of pastoral leadership at the tiller of a closing church.

Yet one more stressor for pastors serving closing congregations is conflict, when some in the church are unwilling to love others and/ or the pastor as themselves. Differences not handled with respect can shred the web of sacred community, leading to a loss of understanding, of willingness to give others a second chance, of compassion, and of trust.[3] When church members fight, as they are likely to do in times of adaptive change or grief, they can "fight fair" with emotional maturity, or they can resort to less respectful behaviors such as gossiping, rumor-mongering, and scapegoating.[4] This research has shown that congregations with greater emotional maturity are more peaceable and less stressful for pastors to serve, as well as more likely to have a festival ending that feels like Christmas, Easter, or Pentecost rather than one like Good Friday or Holy Week.

Pastors in the throes of congregational conflict as well as the stress of managing transformational change and grief need the spiritual, emotional, and material support of others, especially colleagues and denominational superiors. Yet this research has shown that judicatory respect is often lacking, with one-quarter to one-third of pastors less than satisfied with the degree to which or manner in which the judicatory acknowledged their concerns, was accountable, spoke honestly, showed them understanding, had compassion, expressed gratitude for their ministry, or provided "safety in speaking [their] truth"—all of which led them to feel isolated, or even stigmatized and ostracized. Stress related to a judicatory's lack of respect is greater among younger and first- or second-call pastors, as well as among female clergy.

From the perspective of clergy who feel let down, judicatories need to face the reality of their dual structures. As an expression of the wider church, they promise to be sacred communities with a lively faith; loving, honest relationships regardless of theological or cultural differences; curiosity about God's will; and a willingness to take risks for the sake of the gospel. However, these larger geographic bodies are likely to be culturally and theologically diverse. Many are also bureaucracies, like the coast guard, with committees, commissions, departments, and staff. Depending on the denomination, bishops or executive committees may function like admirals with ultimate authority over clergy qualifications, deployment, support, and discipline. Just as trees and hills create "wind shadows" blocking or slowing the wind sailors need, so these complicated aspects of judicatories may block or slow the healing, reconciling movement of the Holy Spirit over closing churches. It's no wonder that clergy and churches alike may be reluctant to invite members of their judicatory to participate in difficult decisions such as closing, or that some have disappointing experiences.

The principal aim of this book is to describe what it is like when the Holy Spirit is present with closing churches and their pastors, as well as when hope is dim and the way forward unclear. Whenever we experience challenging currents or unexpected gales, by God's grace we pray and work for God's compassionate wind because it is always there— wind that gifts the church and the judicatory to which it belongs with a lively faith; loving, honest relationships; and transformational leadership skills equipping pastors to console, heal, guide, and sustain fragile congregations.

The good news is that despite profound grief, decisions to close are more often made by faith-filled, courageous congregations and lay leaders than initiated by clergy or the judicatory. Most congregations have both resurrection faith and emotional maturity to participate respectfully in the difficult conversations needed in order to hear and respond to God's call to dissolve.[5] This book shares not only the challenges but also the grace-filled journeys of these and other congregations.

This book has only hinted at answers to the important question of how closing a church affects the congregation and its community. Not only is there profound loss—pastors lamented the loss of community ministries, members' grief that remains unresolved years later, and decisions to leave the institutional church altogether—but clergy also occasionally shared the blessings of closing for members of their churches: for example, being able to sit in a pew without worrying about the leaking roof, having an opportunity to fulfill one's call to be a children's Sunday school teacher, or blossoming in faith by leaving the church in which one was born and raised and joining a new worshiping community. Asking church communities and their neighborhoods about their experiences in closing a church is an essential task for others to assume.

Finally, although the book names the complexity and strain of judicatory issues from the point of view of the pastor, it does not systematically explore the hopes, expectations, and challenges of judicatory officers and their staff, as well as clergy colleagues—that is, the coast guard of the wider church. My perspective is limited by this omission, and those equipped to pursue this research are needed.

When I was serving Holy Family Episcopal Church, the emotional work was rewarding but often overwhelming. I found myself not only living in the present but reliving traumas and graces I had experienced earlier in life and in the church. My memory of God's love for me in the midst of earlier church traumas bore me through many a storm. I recalled that when I was discerning whether God was calling me to become a priest, a compassionate bishop told me, "Not yet," and invited me to take care of the grief over my father's death (which occurred when I was six) and then return because, as the bishop put it, "you have gifts the church needs." When a conflicted church that hired me fresh out of seminary decided they no longer had need of me and a bishop told me he would never ordain me a priest, grace upon grace followed. God called my husband and me to California, where I was ordained a priest before being called to Holy Family, which I served with joy (and holy angst) for nine mostly good years.

The process of research and of writing this book has blown additional blessings of the Holy Spirit's renewing wind over the "little deaths" of my life. The greatest has been witnessing the pilgrim journeys of other pastors called to the ministry of minding the tiller of a church that closes. Our vows as pastors ordained to love God and our neighbors as ourselves as we lead a congregation on its pilgrimage to death proved, for most clergy, to be indelible despite the tears of grief and tumultuous seas. In anxiety and pain, in satisfaction and joy, we abided in Christ through Word and sacrament and leadership of sacred communities, at various times resented, feared, and beloved. We came to see God's hand as we discerned the route and experienced God's redemption. The wider church may sometimes disappoint our congregations and us in our plights, but we grow in faith and in our vocation through the experience.

The twenty-first-century church will sail many uncharted seas. Navigating our rapidly shifting religious and cultural waters will feel at times like rounding Cape Horn in treacherous hurricane-force winds, sitting stuck in the equator's doldrums, or sailing "in the groove" on San Francisco Bay. Wherever they sail, the church as the people of God and pastors at the tiller seek and welcome the gracious, empowering wind of the Holy Spirit to lift their boat safely to its destination. My prayer is that the log of these pastors' journeys will inform and strengthen congregations and pastors who follow us into new life in Christ.

Acknowledgments

For nearly six years, I have been blessed by the encouragement and wisdom of Dean Mary Elizabeth Moore, Bryan Stone, and Claire Wolfteich of the Center for Practical Theology; Nancy Ammerman and Renee Spencer in sociology and social work at Boston University School of Theology; Bishop Susan Hassinger; and seminarians, graduate students, and staff. My appointment as a visiting researcher offered me friendship, the opportunity to sit in on classes, and the use of a valuable theology library for four snowy winters and beyond. I am also eternally grateful to Jack Chan, Amod Lele, Robert Putnam, and Emily Lawrence in BU's IT department, who kept my computer working and patiently answered software questions. Eager theology students stuffed over 250 written surveys into envelopes for me. Thanks especially to research assistants Kaitlyn Martin-Fox, Colin Cushman, Greylyn Hydinger, and Kristen Hydinger, all of whom assisted with word processing, data entry, and programming.

I am grateful to denominational researchers in the Lutheran (ELCA), Episcopal (TEC), Presbyterian (PC(USA)), United Church of Christ (UCC), and United Methodist (UMC) denominations for their cooperation and assistance in sharing data as well as offering valuable insight, especially Adam DeHoek and Marty Smith of the ELCA; Kirk Hadaway and Matthew Price of TEC; Deborah Coe, Ida Smith, and Cynthia Woolever of the PC(USA); Kristina Lizardi-Hajbi of the UCC; and Lauren Arieux, Laura Chambers, and Whitney Washington of the UMC. Ellie Smerlas at DataStar Inc., in Waltham, Massachusetts, provided outstanding data entry of written surveys. I'm deeply grateful to anonymous transcribers of all interviews at Rev.com.

A faithful writing group, including Sarah Lee and Bill Fritz, contributed invaluable honest feedback, as did clergy readers Linda Bobbitt, Sarah Conner, Joseph Duggan, David Eagle, Cliff Haggenjos, Susan Hassinger, George Hunt, Gail Irwin, Margaret Payne, Richard Pitt, Don Richter, David Schoen, David Schlafer, Peter Stebinger, and others I may have omitted.

I thank my wise and patient Westminster John Knox Press editor, David Maxwell, as well as Barbara Gage Coogan, whose developmental editing taught me how to become a better writer; and Catherine Priestley, Robbi Sommers Bryant, and Heidi Mann, whose editing expertise put the manuscript in final form.

The Church of the Roses Presbyterian Church in Santa Rosa, California, and Pastor Cindy Alloway, as well as the Church of the Incarnation in Santa Rosa and St. Nicholas Episcopal Church in Tahoe City, California, and their gracious staff and volunteers, shared quiet space in which to write this book. I thank Starbucks #3470, Acre Coffee, Peet's Coffee in Copperfield's Books in Santa Rosa, and Tahoe House, Tahoe City, for welcoming baristas and writing sanctuaries.

This research was financially supported in part by 2013 and 2014 continuing education grants from the Episcopal Diocese of Northern California, and also by a 2015 Louisville Institute Project Grant for Researchers: "The Last Pastor: Adaptive Challenges and Well-Being among Protestant Clergy Closing Their Churches."

This study would not have been undertaken without my journey with the people of Holy Family Episcopal Church in Rohnert Park, California. They faithfully served God and the world for more than twenty-five years in that place; said good-bye on May 20, 2012; and continue to bring me joy whenever I remember or witness their love of God and neighbor.

Throughout my ministry at Holy Family and my research for this book, these ecumenical women clergy friends encouraged and prayed for me: Cindy Alloway, Kate Clayton, Sue Fleenor, Amy Seymour Haney, Sally Hubbell, Laurie McHugh, and Pat Moore. Bless you!

Through celebrations of victories, capsizes, and rescues, members of the Santa Rosa Sailing Club and *Nancy*'s skipper taught me, and still teach me, how to capture the wind.

When I began this study, my husband was close to retirement. I upended his trajectory by asking him to leave our home in Northern California to spend four winters in Boston. Without hesitation, he agreed. We set off in an overloaded car for Boston in January 2013, encountering whiteout conditions in a snowstorm outside Flagstaff, Arizona. We made it through safely, and he has been faithfully by my side, back and forth to Boston four times, and home in California. I could not have completed this book without him. I am also grateful to our Boston daughter, Lisa, and her family for graciously hosting us in their home the first winter, and to our Santa Rosa daughter, Heather, and her family for living in or watching over our home when we were away. I thank them both for love in the hard times, and for cheers at each milestone on our journey. The journey really is "ours." These past years, my husband has written a book as well, albeit on a different subject.

Most of all, I would like to thank the pastors in this study who courageously offered to share their journeys. I bear witness that they served God and God's people faithfully through the death of their churches and beyond into new life. This book is dedicated to them.

Appendix A
Questionnaire

First, some questions about the church that closed:

1. Average Sunday attendance:

    just before it closed: _____

    2 years before: _____

    5 years before: _____

    10 years before: _____

2. In the year that it closed,

    What percent of the regular adult Sunday attendees in your congregation were white and non-Hispanic? _____

    What percent were Black or African American? _____

    What percent were Hispanic or Latino? _____

    What percent were Asian or Pacific Islander? _____

    What percent were American Indian? _____

    Any other ethnic groups? (specify) _____

3. The church was located in:

    ☐ urbanized area (50,000 or more)

    ☐ small town or city (2,500 to 50,000)

    ☐ rural area (SOURCE: 2010 U.S. Census categories)

4. About how many miles away was the closest church of your denomination?

    _____

5. U.S. State where the church was located: _____

6. Age of the congregation: _____ years

7. When you entered this congregation, what were the expectations? (check all that apply)

	Judicatory's	Congregation's	Mine, as pastor
Plant a new congregation	☐	☐	☐
Serve a healthy congregation	☐	☐	☐

	Judicatory's	Congregation's	Mine, as pastor
Revitalize a congregation and help it grow	☐	☐	☐
Discern whether the congregation could be revitalized and if not, close it with dignity	☐	☐	☐
Close the church by merging with another congregation	☐	☐	☐
Dissolve the congregation with dignity	☐	☐	☐
Other (*specify*): _____	☐	☐	☐

8. When you arrived, how would you describe the congregation?

	Strongly agree	Agree	Neutral	Disagree	Strongly disagree
Having a clear mission and purpose	☐	☐	☐	☐	☐
Ready to try something new	☐	☐	☐	☐	☐
Spiritually vital and alive	☐	☐	☐	☐	☐
Having a sense of excitement about the church's future	☐	☐	☐	☐	☐
Leaders willing to change programs and structures	☐	☐	☐	☐	☐
Viable and sustainable	☐	☐	☐	☐	☐

9. When you arrived, what level was the congregation's vitality in the following areas?

	Excellent	Very good	Good	Fair	Poor
Administrative practices	☐	☐	☐	☐	☐
Finances	☐	☐	☐	☐	☐
Buildings and grounds	☐	☐	☐	☐	☐
Relationships with the judicatory	☐	☐	☐	☐	☐
Ministries in the community	☐	☐	☐	☐	☐
Pastoral care programs	☐	☐	☐	☐	☐
Worship services	☐	☐	☐	☐	☐
Christian education programs	☐	☐	☐	☐	☐

10. Was there conflict in the congregation when you arrived?

Little or none	Minor	Moderate	More serious	Serious	Greatest
☐	☐	☐	☐	☐	☐

11. When you arrived, was the congregation receiving financial support from the judicatory (grants, loans)?

☐ No   ☐ Yes Estimated total outstanding? $_____

12. In discerning the decision to close the church, how much initiative came from the following?

	Great deal	Very much	Somewhat	Very little	Not at all
The congregation's leaders	☐	☐	☐	☐	☐
The congregation's members	☐	☐	☐	☐	☐
The judicatory	☐	☐	☐	☐	☐
The previous pastorate	☐	☐	☐	☐	☐
Your pastoral leadership	☐	☐	☐	☐	☐

13. Thinking about your role in closing the church, how challenging were the following?

	Great challenge	Somewhat of a challenge	Very little challenge	No challenge
Initiating discernment	☐	☐	☐	☐
The process of discernment	☐	☐	☐	☐
The actual decision to close	☐	☐	☐	☐
Disposition of church property	☐	☐	☐	☐
Facilitating transfer of members to another congregation	☐	☐	☐	☐
Dealing with member conflict	☐	☐	☐	☐
Dealing with members' difficult emotions	☐	☐	☐	☐
Spiritual care of the congregation	☐	☐	☐	☐
Your relationship with the judicatory	☐	☐	☐	☐
Caring for yourself	☐	☐	☐	☐

14. Before the church closed, how satisfied were you with the judicatory in the following areas?

	Very satisfied	Somewhat satisfied	Somewhat dissatisfied	Very dissatisfied
Acceptance of the congregation's identity	☐	☐	☐	☐
Inclusion of the church in decision-making	☐	☐	☐	☐
Safety in speaking their truth	☐	☐	☐	☐
Acknowledging the congregation's concerns	☐	☐	☐	☐
Gratitude for the congregation's ministry	☐	☐	☐	☐
Fairness with the congregation	☐	☐	☐	☐
Considering the congregation to be trustworthy	☐	☐	☐	☐
Understanding the congregation	☐	☐	☐	☐
Encouraging the congregation's independence	☐	☐	☐	☐
Accountability to the congregation	☐	☐	☐	☐
Keeping promises to the congregation	☐	☐	☐	☐
Speaking honestly with the congregation	☐	☐	☐	☐
Compassion for the congregation	☐	☐	☐	☐

15. As a pastor, how satisfied were you with the judicatory in the following areas?

	Very satisfied	Somewhat satisfied	Somewhat dissatisfied	Very dissatisfied
Acceptance of your pastoral identity	☐	☐	☐	☐
Inclusion of you in decision-making	☐	☐	☐	☐
Safety in speaking your truth	☐	☐	☐	☐

	Very satisfied	Somewhat satisfied	Somewhat dissatisfied	Very dissatisfied
Acknowledging your concerns	☐	☐	☐	☐
Gratitude for your ministry	☐	☐	☐	☐
Fairness with you	☐	☐	☐	☐
Considering you to be trustworthy	☐	☐	☐	☐
Understanding you	☐	☐	☐	☐
Encouraging your independence	☐	☐	☐	☐
Accountability to you	☐	☐	☐	☐
Keeping promises to you	☐	☐	☐	☐
Speaking honestly with you	☐	☐	☐	☐
Compassion for you	☐	☐	☐	☐

16. Overall as a pastor, how satisfied were you with the congregation's:

	Very satisfied	Somewhat satisfied	Somewhat dissatisfied	Very dissatisfied
Acceptance of your pastoral identity	☐	☐	☐	☐
Inclusion of you in decision-making	☐	☐	☐	☐
Safety in speaking your truth	☐	☐	☐	☐
Acknowledging your concerns	☐	☐	☐	☐
Gratitude for your ministry	☐	☐	☐	☐
Fairness with you	☐	☐	☐	☐
Considering you to be trustworthy	☐	☐	☐	☐
Understanding you	☐	☐	☐	☐
Encouraging your independence	☐	☐	☐	☐
Accountability to you	☐	☐	☐	☐
Keeping promises to you	☐	☐	☐	☐
Speaking honestly with you	☐	☐	☐	☐
Compassion for you	☐	☐	☐	☐

17. Members of congregations may express a range of emotions in the process of closing. How skillful were members in communicating:

	Excellent	Good	Adequate	Fair	Inadequate
Fear	☐	☐	☐	☐	☐
Anger	☐	☐	☐	☐	☐
Sadness	☐	☐	☐	☐	☐
Tenderness	☐	☐	☐	☐	☐
Acceptance	☐	☐	☐	☐	☐
Gladness	☐	☐	☐	☐	☐

18. When you served the church that was closing, how often did you:

	Very often	Fairly often	Once in a while	Never	N/A
Experience stress because of the challenges in that congregation?	☐	☐	☐	☐	
Feel lonely and isolated in your work?	☐	☐	☐	☐	
Have doubts about your abilities as a pastoral minister?	☐	☐	☐	☐	
Seriously think of leaving for a secular occupation?	☐	☐	☐	☐	
Seriously think of leaving for another type of ministry?	☐	☐	☐	☐	
Seriously think of retiring?	☐	☐	☐	☐	☐

19. In your opinion, how did serving in this church affect your health?

☐ My health improved

☐ My health remained stable

☐ My health worsened

☐ I don't know if it affected my health

20. As you were serving the church, how important were the following in sustaining you in your ministry?

	Great importance	Somewhat important	Somewhat unimportant	Of little importance	N/A
Intentional family/ couple time, if applicable	☐	☐	☐	☐	☐
Exercise	☐	☐	☐	☐	
Scripture study/ daily office	☐	☐	☐	☐	
Journaling	☐	☐	☐	☐	
Contemplative prayer	☐	☐	☐	☐	
Sabbath time	☐	☐	☐	☐	
Non-church-related hobbies	☐	☐	☐	☐	
Personal friendships	☐	☐	☐	☐	
Clergy study/ support group	☐	☐	☐	☐	
Relationships with lay leaders in your congregation	☐	☐	☐	☐	
Relationships with local clergy	☐	☐	☐	☐	
Therapist	☐	☐	☐	☐	
Spiritual director	☐	☐	☐	☐	
Mentor	☐	☐	☐	☐	
Judicatory executive	☐	☐	☐	☐	
Other judicatory support	☐	☐	☐	☐	
Other (*specify*): _____	☐	☐	☐	☐	

21. The following items deal with ways you coped when you were serving the church that closed. These items ask what you did to cope with this event. We want to know to what extent you did what the item says—*how much* or *how frequently*. Don't answer on the basis of what worked or not—just whether you did it.

	Not at all	Somewhat	Quite a bit	A great deal
Looked for a stronger connection with God	☐	☐	☐	☐
Sought God's love and care	☐	☐	☐	☐
Sought help from God in letting go of my anger	☐	☐	☐	☐
Tried to put my plans into action together with God	☐	☐	☐	☐
Tried to see how God might be trying to strengthen me in this situation	☐	☐	☐	☐
Asked forgiveness for my sins	☐	☐	☐	☐
Focused on religion/faith to stop worrying about my problems	☐	☐	☐	☐

22. If the process of closing your congregation was like a church season or holy day, it would be:

	For the congregation	For me, as pastor
Advent	☐	☐
Christmas	☐	☐
Epiphany	☐	☐
Lent	☐	☐
Good Friday	☐	☐
Holy Saturday	☐	☐
Easter	☐	☐
Pentecost	☐	☐
Other (*specify*): _____	☐	☐

23. When this church closed, did you receive any severance pay or other financial support?

☐ Severance (*specify*): _____months

☐ Other financial support (*specify*):_____

☐ No financial support

24. When the doors of church closed, how much did you:

	Not at all	Very little	Somewhat	Very much	A great deal
Experience stress because of the need to find another position?	☐	☐	☐	☐	☐
Hear that closing a church would hinder your search for another pastoral position?	☐	☐	☐	☐	☐
Think the experience of closing a church hindered your job search?	☐	☐	☐	☐	☐
Have a sense of shame?	☐	☐	☐	☐	☐
Experience financial strain?	☐	☐	☐	☐	☐
Feel lonely and isolated?	☐	☐	☐	☐	☐

25. Did you seek another pastoral position?

☐ No, I didn't seek other pastoral positions
   (*Please go to Question #28*)

☐ Yes

26. How useful were the following in your discernment process or helping you find a pastoral position?

When you were called to serve this congregation that closed:	Very useful	Somewhat useful	Not useful
The judicatory (synod, presbytery, diocese)	☐	☐	☐
The denomination's search process	☐	☐	☐
Seminary deans, faculty and staff	☐	☐	☐
Colleagues and personal networking	☐	☐	☐
After you left this church:			
The judicatory (synod, presbytery, diocese)	☐	☐	☐
The denomination's search process	☐	☐	☐
Seminary deans, faculty and staff	☐	☐	☐
Colleagues and personal networking	☐	☐	☐

27. How long was the interval between the time you left the church and obtained a new pastoral position?

_____ months   _____ I have not found another pastoral position

28. At present, what is your level of satisfaction with:

	Very satisfied	Somewhat satisfied	Somewhat dissatisfied	Very dissatisfied	N/A
Housing or living arrangements	☐	☐	☐	☐	
Your spiritual life	☐	☐	☐	☐	
Opportunities for continuing theological education	☐	☐	☐	☐	
Support from your denominational officials, if applicable	☐	☐	☐	☐	☐
Relationships with other clergy	☐	☐	☐	☐	☐
Relationships with members and leaders of your current church, if applicable	☐	☐	☐	☐	☐
Your salary and benefits	☐	☐	☐	☐	☐
Your family life, if applicable	☐	☐	☐	☐	☐
Your personal life	☐	☐	☐	☐	
Your current ministry	☐	☐	☐	☐	☐
Your overall effectiveness as a pastor in your current congregation, if applicable	☐	☐	☐	☐	☐

29. In general, would you say your health now is:

☐ Excellent ☐ Very Good ☐ Good ☐ Fair ☐ Poor

30. The following questions are about how you feel and how things have been with you *during the past four weeks.* For each question, please give the one answer that comes closest to the way you have been feeling. How much of the time *during the past four weeks*:

	All of the time	Most of the time	Some of the time	A little of the time	None of the time
Have you felt calm and peaceful?	☐	☐	☐	☐	☐
Did you have a lot of energy?	☐	☐	☐	☐	☐
Have you felt downhearted and depressed?	☐	☐	☐	☐	☐
Did you feel worn out?	☐	☐	☐	☐	☐
Have you been happy?	☐	☐	☐	☐	☐

31. What was your greatest satisfaction in serving the church that closed?

_____

_____

_____

32. Overall, what are the 3 most important issues judicatories and denominations need to address in the next 10 years? Try to be as specific as possible.

1._____

2._____

3._____

33. Remembering the challenges you faced, what do seminaries, clergy conferences and continuing education need to address so that pastors are prepared for ministry in a vulnerable congregation?

_____

_____

_____

Finally, I would like to ask a few brief background questions.

34. Your gender is: ☐ Female   ☐ Male

35. Your age is: _____

36. What race or ethnicity are you?

☐ White   ☐ Asian or Pacific Islander

☐ Black or African American   ☐ Other

☐ Hispanic

37. If ordained, the # of years since your ordination: _____
    ☐ Not applicable (*Please go to Question #41*)

38. Your highest degree in theological education:
    ☐ Bachelor Div.   ☐ M. Div.   ☐ D. Min
    Other (*specify*):_____

39. Your # years in paid ordained ministry (today): _____

40. The number of salaried calls you had before the church that closed:

    _____

41. Your employment in the church when it closed:
    ☐ Full-time   ☐ Part-time

42. Your number of years working in this church:_____

43. Were you a bi-vocational pastor when you served in this church?
    ☐ Yes   ☐ No

44. Did you have a multi-point appointment (serve another church at the same time you served the church that closed)?
    ☐ Yes   ☐ No

45. Did you serve this church through its last worship service ?
    ☐ Yes   ☐ No (*see below*)

    If no, how long before its closure did you leave?

    _____

46. Your present position (*check all that apply*):
    ☐ Retired (*Please go to Question #49*)
    ☐ Solo pastor
    ☐ Senior pastor
    ☐ Co-pastor
    ☐ Intentional interim minister or pastor
    ☐ Interim minister or pastor seeking a permanent position
    ☐ Associate or assistant minister or pastor
    ☐ Other kind of work (*please specify*):_____
    ☐ Not employed at this time (*Please go to Question #49*)

47. You are presently working:
    ☐ Full-time   ☐ Part-time

48. You work _____ hours per week in work related to your congregation or other current employment.

49. Your marital status:

    ☐ Single   ☐ Married or in a committed relationship   ☐ Divorced

50. Your denomination: _____

51. Would you be willing to participate in a confidential follow-up interview about your experience?

    ☐ Yes ☐ No

If yes, this is how best to contact me:

Email:_____ Phone:_____

Church name/diocese:_____

THANK YOU VERY MUCH FOR YOUR PARTICIPATION IN THIS SURVEY!

Please feel free to add any additional comments and suggestions here *or on the following page*:

_____

_____

_____

_____

_____

_____

Appendix B
Interview Guide

With few exceptions, the author conducted all interviews by telephone. The interview format is intentionally flexible to allow the pastor to engage the topics in whatever order they wished (they did not know the order listed here, which is only a suggestion). For example, a pastor might answer a question about how the church closed, then skip to the topic about their relationship with the judicatory, and I followed them, then backtracked to cover missing topics. Interviews were taped with permission, transcribed by a firm assuring HIPPA-level confidentiality, and uploaded into NVivo software. Thematic analysis and successive readings of each interview were integrated with survey data from the same pastor. Statistical findings informed the thematic analysis, and vice versa.

Church entry
— Overall, how many years have you been in the ordained ministry for which you were paid a salary?
— In how many different positions, including your current one, have you served as a paid ordained pastor?
— Did you work full-time at one or more other occupations before entering the ministry? If yes, for how long?
— What was your last occupation before becoming a priest/pastor/minister?
— What is the highest level of theological training you have obtained?
— When did you receive your first theological degree?

Pastor's sense of agency
— How did you come to this church?
— How long did you expect to stay?
— What were your expectations and hopes for yourself as a pastor in this church? for your relationships with the judicatory/denominational executives? for the congregation?
— What did the congregation expect from you? What did the judicatory/denomination expect?
— What did it mean to be a pastor/priest/minister entering this congregation? What was your role here?
— [If minority*] What does it mean to be a pastor in your culture? What images of the pastor resonate with your culture?

Can you tell me how your church came to close?
— The closing of a church often means making difficult decisions. How did the church make the final decision to close? What was your role? What did you strive for? What did you hope for?
— Can you tell me about your relationship with (a) judicatory/executives in the closing of your church? (b) colleagues? (c) members of your congregation? What did you expect? How did you experience support from them? Were there things you wished were different? Did these relationships change in the closing process? How?
— Moral sense: What do you lament?
— Did you or your congregation experience any dignity violations in the process of closing your church?
— What does it mean for the world that this church closed? (If minority*) What does it mean for your culture that this church closed?
— Can you share with me any significant sacred stories and images that touched your congregation in closing? that touched you as a pastor?
— You said in your survey that closing your church was like [church season]. Can you please tell me something about that?

Pastor's sense of agency
— What did it mean for you as their priest/pastor/minister to be a "responsible person" in the process of closing your church? Can you tell me how you navigated a particular challenge? (*explore how you thought and felt when . . .*)
— Probe for "Identity Work" (thoughts/feelings about challenges to pastoral identity: e.g., stigma, isolation and any actions taken in response): how the pastor makes sense of challenges.
— What was trying, hard, or wearing for you? Why or how was it hard?
— How did you care for yourself? Did you seek out any new supports? Where was God for you?
— What unexpected blessings did you experience, and how did they affect you?
— How did you live the Gospel?
— How did you talk about God in your church? Ask for closing sermon.

Reconstructing pastoral identity
— How did closing your church affect your family? Did it affect your health? Did you receive severance pay or another kind of compensation after your church closed? Did being a pastor who closed a church affect your financial security?
— What did you do when the doors closed?
— How did you feel about yourself as a pastor/minister/priest and your abilities after the church closed?
— How did you reach a decision about what to do afterward?
— How did you come to your current position (probe for supports of new identity)?

— What sacred stories and symbols have supported your identity as a pastor since the closing?

— Who or what has been most helpful to your healing or wholeness in the time since you closed your church?

— Commitment to pastoral identity: Have you ever thought of leaving pastoral ministry in the past five years?

— What does it mean to be a pastor of a church that closed?

Reflections

— How have you changed?

— How would you describe yourself as a pastor now?

— Would you ever do this again, and if so, what would you bring with you from this experience?

— What do you most value about yourself now?

— What do others most value in you (as a pastor)?

— What advice would you give a pastor like yourself facing a similar church closing?

— What issues do denominations and judicatories need to address?

— Where do you expect to be in five years?

— What are your hopes for the future?

Personal context

— Age, marital status, children

Closing questions

— How was this interview for you?

— Is there anything else you think I should know to understand how closing a church affects a pastor?

— Is there anything you would like to ask me?

Thank you very much for all you have shared.

Notes

Introduction

1. Books that describe church closing from a case study, pastoral care, or journalistic perspective include Gaede, *Ending with Hope*; Irwin, *Toward the Better Country*; Hilliard and Switzer, *Finishing with Grace*; Seitz, *No Closure*; Guthrie, *Grace of Everyday Saints*.

2. I sought to learn from as many pastors as I could gather from those five denominations—Episcopal (TEC), Lutheran (ELCA), Methodist (UMC), Presbyterian (PC(USA)) and United Church of Christ (UCC)—whose denominational leaders supported my research by providing contact information for clergy who had closed churches over a two- to four-year period. Not surprisingly, the churches served by these pastors had been in decline for a number of years. The year they closed, the average Sunday attendance was twenty-five. Two years before, the average was thirty-four; five years before, worship attendance was forty-five; and ten years before, it was fifty-eight. (See appendix A for the questionnaire and appendix B for the interview schedule. Questionnaires were analyzed with SPSS software, and thematic analysis of interviews was done with NVivo software.)

3. As a social scientist, I would typically indicate elisions in quoted interviews with ". . ." and insertions of connectors and articles like "and" or "the" with brackets (e.g., [and]), but these marks distracted early readers; I omitted them except when needed to clarify meaning.

4. Pilgrimage and journey are powerful metaphors for the process of closing a church. For contemporary literature on pilgrimage, see Webb-Mitchell, *Practicing Pilgrimage*; Olson, *Claiming Resurrection in the Dying Church*; Rendle, *Leading Change in the Congregation*.

5. On practical theology, see Miller-McLemore, *Wiley-Blackwell Companion to Practical Theology*; Moore, "Purposes of Practical Theology"; and Poling, *Rethinking Faith*. Pastoral leadership studies that inform this book include Friedman, *Generation to Generation*; Friedman, *Failure of Nerve*; Heifetz, *Leadership without Easy Answers*; Heifetz and Linsky, "Leadership on the Line"; Frank, "Leadership and Administration"; Gooty et al., "Leadership, Affect, and Emotions"; and Steinke, *Congregational Leadership in Anxious Times*. Studies of clergy wellness that relate to this topic include Carroll, *God's Potters*; Warren, *Cracked Pot*; and Proeschold-Bell and Byassee, *Faithful and Fractured*.

6. Frank, "Leadership and Administration."

7. The term *judicatory* refers to the middle administrative layer of a denomination, called a "diocese" in the Episcopal Church, a "synod" in the Evangelical Lutheran Church in America, a "presbytery" in the Presbyterian Church (U.S.A.), and a "conference" in the United Methodist Church and the United Church of Christ. To preserve confidentiality, in the book these specific terms are replaced by the generic word *judicatory*.

Chapter 1. The Pastor: Minding the Tiller

1. Peyton and Gatrell, "Sacrificial Embrace."

2. Rumsey, *Parish*.

Chapter 2. The Sacred Community: Sailing in the Groove

1. Heifetz and Linsky, "Leadership on the Line"; Heifetz, *Leadership without Easy Answers*.

2. Practical theologians offer tools to measure congregations' quality of relationships, worship and prayer life, Christian formation, and other dimensions of ministry that represent sailing in the groove. See Bobbitt, "Congregational Vitality in the ELCA"; Bobbitt, "Competing Frameworks"; Gifford, *Turnaround Church*; Hadaway, "Facts on Growth: 2010"; R. Bass, *www.CongregationalResources.org*. See also Schwartz and Schalk, *Natural Church Development*.

3. Heifetz, *Leadership without Easy Answers*; Heifetz and Linsky, "Leadership on the Line"; Steinke, *How Your Church Family Works*; Steinke, *Healthy Congregations*; Friedman, *Generation to Generation*.

4. Kondrath, *Facing Feelings in Faith Communities*.

5. Cafferata, "Respect, Challenges, and Stress." See chapter 6 for stories of leadership in churches with lesser respect for their pastor, and chapter 8 for some consequences of low respect.

Chapter 3. The Judicatory: The "Coast Guard"

1. See chapter 9 for greater detail on judicatory support.

2. Cafferata, "Respect, Challenges, and Stress."

3. Ibid.

4. Becker, *Denial of Death*.

5. The excised paragraph read, "A harsh reality is confronting congregations today as they struggle to stay afloat on the rocky seas of the current economy and seek ways to minister to the ever-secularizing population. This reality has never been as apparent to many of us as it has been recently made at Faith Church, due to discontinue its ministry at its current location. Extensive damage to the sanctuary's roof prompted the difficult decision that the judicatory and the church

are no longer able to maintain the property, which is now on the market." The newsletter said simply, "In the face of adversity, the people of Faith Church are strengthened by and celebrate their faith."

6. Cafferata, "Respect, Challenges, and Stress."

7. Ibid.

8. Episcopal Church, *Book of Common Prayer*, 305.

9. Koopman, "Towards an Ecumenicity of Inclusivity"; Armentrout, "Chronology and Bibliography of Lutheran-Episcopal Dialogues"; World Council of Churches, Commission on Faith and Order, *Baptism, Eucharist, and Ministry*. For further discussion of this topic, see chapter 12.

Chapter 4. Leadership Gifts of a Transformational Pastor

1. Friedman, *Failure of Nerve*, 183.

2. See Weber, *Economy and Society*, 212–15.

3. On a church's DNA, see Bobbitt, "Competing Frameworks"; Reformed Church in America, "Determining a Church's DNA."

4. On respect, see Lawrence-Lightfoot, *Respect*; Dyck, *On Human Care*; and Hicks, *Dignity*.

5. Donne, "Now This Bell Tolling Softly for Another, Says to Me: Thou Must Die."

6. Friedman, *Generation to Generation*.

7. Fleming, *What Is Ignatian Spirituality?*.

8. Steinke, *How Your Church Family Works*; M. Smith, *Transitional Ministry*.

9. Cafferata, "Respect, Challenges, and Stress."

10. Friedman, *Generation to Generation*.

11. Ury, *Getting Past No*.

12. See Van Quaquebeke and Eckloff, "Defining Respectful Leadership"; Kant, *Metaphysics of Morals*; and Buber, *Writings of Martin Buber*.

13. Peterson, *Under the Unpredictable Plant*.

Chapter 5. The Pilgrimage to a Grace-Filled Closure

1. Vitality and sustainability are essential topics of denominational study and research across traditions. See especially Bobbitt, "Creating Shorter Scales to Measure Congregational Vitality"; D. Bass, *Christianity for the Rest of Us*; Mann, *Can Our Church Live?*; Gifford, *Turnaround Church*; Schwartz and Schalk, *Natural Church Development*; and Zscheile, *Agile Church*.

2. Chapter 6 describes decision-making among congregations in conflict with one another or the pastor, or with the judicatory, while chapter 7 describes the tasks that ensue when a church has decided to close, such as assisting members with grief and transitions to other churches, honoring the church's ministry and journey, and creating a legacy.

3. This chapter is from the point of view of the pastor, not the congregation. Other books have shared case studies of congregational experiences. See, for example, Gaede, *Ending with Hope*; and Irwin, *Toward the Better Country*.

4. For readers for whom this matters, statistical probability is significant at p<.01.

5. See also chapter 1.

6. See also Merton, *Seasons of Celebration*; Olsen, *Wisdom of the Seasons*; Vogel, *Syncopated Grace*.

7. Pennington, *Lectio Divina*. See also https://www.ignatianspirituality.com /ignatian-prayer/the-what-how-why-of-prayer/praying-with-scripture.

8. See http://www.theworldcafe.com.

9. Church planters may exercise more "I" initiative or agency than other pastors. As his new church was failing, one pastor said that he "just got to a place where I just felt like I'm running out of gas here, I don't feel like this is going anywhere." When a judicatory representative came, "all of us . . . we cared and kind of had [an] . . . 'air our grievances' kind of a meeting. I think that was [a] pretty healthy process just to let people do that." The church closed gracefully.

10. See Blount and Carroll, "Overcome Resistance to Change with Two Conversations."

11. Just as there is "art" in sharing bad news in medicine, so there is "art" in sharing difficult truths in a congregation. One isolated poverty-stricken rural congregation resisted closing until the minister said, "We're not going to pay the bills, we're not going to have electricity, we're not going to have water. . . ." The pastor hadn't been receiving a salary from this church for about six months, but kept serving, thinking, "Oh, I love those old folks." She finally said, "'Listen, we have to face the truth that this is the end of the road.'" They voted to close in what the pastor experienced as the season of Epiphany: "They knew I was doing what had to be done, so they didn't blame me. I only felt love from all of them."

12. Bandy and Brooks, *Church Mergers*; Tomberlin and Bird, *Better Together*.

13. Pastors in multichurch appointments experienced significantly less stress when serving churches that close than pastors in single-church appointments. Cafferata, "Respect, Challenges, and Stress."

Chapter 6. Stormy Weather: Conflict and Recourse

1. See, for example, Edgell, *Congregations in Conflict*; Ellison et al., "Size, Conflict, and Opportunities for Interaction"; Ellison et al., "Does Negative Interaction in the Church Increase Psychological Distress?"; Cosgrove and Hatfield, *Church Conflict*; Hoge and Wenger, *Pastors in Transition*.

2. Leas, *Moving Your Church through Conflict*.

3. De Wit, Greer, and Jehn, "Paradox of Intragroup Conflict: A Meta-Analysis."

4. One other sign of distress in interviews was the pastor's use of the pronoun

"me" as the object of a disrespectful action by someone in the congregation, as in, "There was a rumor mill about me."

5. Parsons, *Understanding Your Congregation as a System*; Heifetz, *Leadership without Easy Answers*; Heifetz and Linsky, "Leadership on the Line"; Steinke, *Healthy Congregations*; Steinke, *Congregational Leadership in Anxious Times*.

6. A broken sacred community takes time to heal, perhaps more time than some churches have. One management consultant, Heifetz, writes, "The deeper the change and the greater the amount of new learning required, the more resistance there will be and, thus, the greater the danger to those who lead" (Heifetz and Linsky, "Leadership on the Line," 14). Healing a sacred community with broken relationships requires the hard work of eliminating destructive conflict as a norm by upholding values of sacred community such as inclusion, making clear decisions, accountability, respect, and transparency. Shortcuts such as blaming (the pastor who abandoned them, those who disagree with "us"), herding ("we have to stay together as the opposition"), or reactivity (avoiding people with whom you disagree, simply empathizing) simply relieve anxiety in the short run (Friedman, *Failure of Nerve*, 54).

7. See Bendroth, *Interim Ministry in Action* for a description of the appreciative inquiry process.

8. See Kotlyar, Karakowsky, and Ng, "Leader Behaviors, Conflict, and Member Commitment" for further elaboration of pragmatic leadership.

9. Friedman, *Failure of Nerve*, 121.

10. Pastoral differentiation means not only having the capacity to see the other as different ("they") but also the capacity not to be emotionally or spiritually dependent on the action of the other—that is, to let go of the congregation as a source of affection and affirmation. Challenged clergy are vulnerable to being emotionally manipulated and swept into an emotionally dependent, undifferentiated "we." One experienced pastor was called to an urban congregation in a new judicatory, not anticipating the full extent of the congregation's dysfunction. The pastor was soon in the middle of a tug of war with one lay leader when another said, "I'm going to help you, because you don't have a friend on that [leadership team]. You don't have anyone to give you any support, to help this church be vital." He was sucked quickly into the riptide of church dysfunction, trying to please them ("I worked my tail off"), but soon realized it was foolish to try. Needless to say, this pastor felt low respect from the congregation but was supported by the judicatory in the ensuing chaos.

11. World Café Community Foundation, "The World Cafe," http://www.theworldcafe.com/.

12. Some call this "active passivity," a "spirituality of attentiveness, of watching and waiting, or noticing the ebb and flow of our feeling and inner dispositions," not necessarily acting immediately on them (Fleming, *What Is Ignatian Spirituality?*, 40). See also Vinita Hampton Wright, "The Inner Process of Letting Go," http://www.ignatianspirituality.com/24471/inner-process-of-letting-go.

13. For readers for whom this matters, this is statistically significant at p<.05.

14. See chapter 10 for vocational difficulties experienced after a closing.

Chapter 7. A "Good Enough" Death: Ceremonies, Preaching, and Legacy Giving

1. Denominational resources for congregations and pastors ending a congregation are scarce but growing. See, for example, Schoen, *Facing Your Church's Uncertain Future*.

2. Mitchell, *All Our Losses, All Our Griefs*.

3. Joyce, "Final Gifts"; (UCC), "Living Legacy"; Gaede, *Ending with Hope*; Irwin, *Toward the Better Country*.

4. See also Olsen, *Wisdom of the Seasons*.

5. Pastors addressed their congregations' sense of failure informally as well as in the closing sermon, even as they may have needed to deal with their own sense of failure (see chapters 8–9).

6. Jones, Kandel, and Parker, "Population Dynamics Are Changing the Profile of Rural Areas."

7. See Yonat Shimron, "Legacy Ministries to Dying Churches Give Congregations a Way to End Well," *Faith and Leadership*, September 5, 2017, https://www.faithandleadership.com/legacy-ministries-dying-churches-give-congregations-way-end-well.

8. Hoffacker, *Matter of Life and Death*; Schlafer, *What Makes This Day Different?*; Long, *Accompany Them with Singing*.

9. For the concept of "voice" see Gilligan et al., "On the Listening Guide."

10. For a Roman Catholic example of this transition, see Chimelis, "After Decision to Close Our Lady of the Rosary Church."

Chapter 8. Grief and Vulnerability

1. See Cafferata, "Respect, Challenges, and Stress" for details on the challenges faced by clergy in this study. For the concept of "adaptive challenges," see Friedman, *A Failure of Nerve*; Heifetz, *Leadership without Easy Answers*; Steinke, *How Your Church Family Works*.

2. Carroll, *God's Potters*.

3. See Proeschold-Bell and Byassee, *Faithful and Fractured*, chapter 2; and Warren, *Cracked Pot*, chapter 7.

4. Petriglieri. "Under Threat."

5. Doka, *Disenfranchised Grief*.

6. Carroll, *God's Potters*. His sample was asked, "In the past five years, how often have you thought of leaving pastoral ministry to enter a secular occupation?" and "In the past five years, how often have you thought of leaving pastoral ministry in a congregation for another type of ministry position?" Our survey

changed the context: "When you served the church that was closing, how often did you seriously think of leaving for a secular occupation?" and "seriously think of leaving for another type of ministry?"

7. Younger pastors who closed churches actually did leave local church ministry more often than older ones.

8. Pfeffer, *Dying for a Paycheck*.

9. Ellison et al., "Religious Resources, Spiritual Struggles, and Mental Health"; "Called to Serve"; General Board of Pension and Health Benefits of The United Methodist Church, "Annual Clergy Health Survey"; Carroll, *God's Potters*.

10. Proeschold-Bell and Byassee, *Faithful and Fractured*.

11. Source is survey data in this study. Clergy may not feel safe in sharing congregational challenges with colleagues or giving difficult feedback to a bishop or other executive who has authority over future placement.

12. Ibid. These relationships persist with statistical controls.

13. See Stets, "Identity Theory."

14. Mental health was measured with a summary scale used in another study (Carroll, *God's Potters*): "The following questions are about how you feel and how things have been with you *during the past four weeks*. For each question, please give the one answer that comes closest to the way you have been feeling. How much of the time *during the past four weeks*: Have you felt calm and peaceful? Did you have a lot of energy? Have you felt downhearted and depressed? Did you feel worn out? Have you been happy?"

15. The statistical significance of the correlations: spiritual challenges and mental health ($p<.05$), spiritual challenges and physical health ($p<.01$), stress "serving the church that closed" and mental health ($p<.001$), stress "after closing" and mental health ($p<.001$), stress "after closing" and physical health ($p<.05$).

16. See James, *With Joyful Acceptance, Maybe*; Kelley, *Grief*; Ellison et al., "Religious Resources, Spiritual Struggles, and Mental Health in a Nationwide Sample of PCUSA Clergy"; McCarroll, *End of Hope—the Beginning*.

17. Moltmann, *In the End—the Beginning*; Rambo, *Resurrecting Wounds*; W. Farley, *Wounding and Healing of Desire*.

18. Hoffacker, *Matter of Life and Death*; Owens and Robinson, "Dark Night of the Church."

Chapter 9. Consolation and Hope

1. Lawrence, *Practice of the Presence of God*.

2. This question replicates items from the positive RCOPE scale created by Pargament, Koenig, and Perez, "Many Methods of Religious Coping."

3. "Was there conflict in the congregation when you arrived?" The choices were "little or none," "minor," "moderate," "more serious," "serious," and "greatest." "Stress closing" was a summary scale asking how often did the pastor: Experience stress because of the challenges in that congregation? Feel lonely and

isolated in your work? Have doubts about your abilities as a pastoral minister? Seriously think of leaving for a secular occupation? Seriously think of leaving for another type of ministry? "Stress after" was a summary scale asking how much did the pastor: Experience stress because of the need to find another position? Hear that closing a church would hinder your search for another pastoral position? Think the experience of closing a church hindered your job search? Have a sense of shame? Experience financial strain? Feel lonely and isolated? All correlations were significant at p<.05 or less.

4. See research on faith and stress such as Ellison et al., "Religious Resources, Spiritual Struggles, and Mental Health."

5. For the concept of a "bold decision," see *Living Legacy* (UCC).

6. Cafferata, "Respect, Challenges, and Stress."

7. Proeschold-Bell and Byassee, *Faithful and Fractured*; Peyton and Gatrell, "Sacrificial Embrace"; Peyton and Gatrell, *Managing Clergy Lives.*

8. For other studies of clergy supports, see Proeschold-Bell and Byassee, *Faithful and Fractured*; Warren, *The Cracked Pot*; Doolittle, "The Impact of Behaviors upon Burnout among Parish-Based Clergy"; "Called to Serve."

9. Besides the above, see Cafferata, "Respect, Challenges, and Stress."

10. All relationships are significant at p<.05 or less.

11. See also Greene-McCreight, *Darkness Is My Only Companion.*

Chapter 10. The Next Call: Vocational Transformations

1. See Van Quaquebeke and Eckloff, "Defining Respectful Leadership."

2. For those who left church see Hoge and Wenger, *Pastors in Transition*; for those in active pastoral ministry see Carroll, *God's Potters.*

3. For a broader perspective on challenges in securing another position see Ashforth, Harrison, and Corley, "Identification in Organizations."

4. "Called to Serve"; Price and Hurst, "2014 Church Compensation Report"; Lizardi-Hajbi, "Gender Pay Gaps for UCC Clergy."

5. Petriglieri, "Under Threat."

6. Kreiner, Hollensbe, and Sheep, "Where Is the 'Me' among the 'We'?"

7. Petriglieri, "Under Threat." See also Calhoun and Tedeschi, *Handbook of Posttraumatic Growth.*

8. Episcopal News Service, "The Five Marks of Mission: A Checklist for Mission," https://www.episcopalchurch.org/library/article/five-marks-mission-checklist-mission; Society of St. John the Evangelist, "5 Marks of Love," http://www.5marksoflove.org.

9. Hoge and Wenger, *Pastors in Transition.*

10. Petriglieri, "Under Threat."

11. Hoge and Wenger, *Pastors in Transition*, 13. See also Van Quaquebeke and Eckloff, "Defining Respectful Leadership."

12. Cafferata, "Respect, Challenges, and Stress;"; Peyton and Gatrell, "The Sacrifical Embrace"; Warren, *Cracked Pot*; Hoge and Wenger, *Pastors in Transition*.

Chapter 11. Different on the Inside: Pastors' Spiritual and Personal Transformations

1. Owens and Robinson, "Dark Night of the Church."
2. Merton, *New Seeds of Contemplation*, 19.
3. See Peyton and Gatrell, *Managing Clergy Lives* for an expanded discussion of authenticity in ministry.
4. Doka, *Disenfranchised Grief*; Helsel, "Liminality in Death Care."
5. See chapter 10 for examples.
6. Rambo, *Spirit and Trauma*; Ebaugh, *Becoming an Ex*.

Chapter 12. The Ship's Log: Hard-Won Lessons

1. The United States is facing a tsunami of church closings. The number of Protestant adherents has decreased steadily since reaching peaks in the 1950s and 1960s, and precipitously since the 1980s. Church membership is in decline not only in the United States but also in our northern neighbor, so much so that one scholar says, "Christendom in Canada is no longer a reality" (Clarke and Macdonald, "How Are Canada's Five Largest Denominations Faring?," 530). In 2014 one-quarter of Americans said they were "unaffiliated" with any religious group (G. Smith, "No Religion in U.S."; Pond, Smith, and Clement, "Religion among the Millennials"; Alper and Sandstrom, "If the U.S. Had 100 People"). Yet congregations don't die easily. In the United States, decline in the number of mainline Protestant congregations between 1980 and 2010 (7 percent to 18 percent) has not matched the rate of decline in affiliation (15 percent to 29 percent). (This data was collected by the Association of Statisticians of American Religious Bodies [ASARB], originally in *2010 U.S. Religion Census: Religious Congregations & Membership Study*.) Rather, congregations are simply getting older and smaller. See Chaves and Eagle, "Religious Congregations in the 21st Century," 6. Over half of Episcopal congregations are small, "family-sized" churches, meaning average worship attendance is seventy or less (Hadaway, "Episcopal Congregations Overview," 1).

Chapter 13. Closing Thoughts: And So We Sail On

1. Kimberly Lawson, "Why You Should Take Time to Mourn."
2. On pastoral stress and grief, see these English studies as well as Proeschold-Bell and Byassee, *Faithful and Fractured*; Ellison, et al., "Religious Resources, Spiritual Struggles, and Mental Health in a Nationwide Sample of PCUSA

Clergy"; Warren, *Cracked Pot*; Paveley, "When It Gets Too Much"; Peyton and Gatrell, *Managing Clergy Lives*.

3. See especially Hicks, *Dignity*; Cafferata, "Dignity for Pastors Who Close Churches"; Lawrence-Lightfoot, *Respect*; Cafferata, "Respect, Challenges, and Stress among Protestant Pastors"; M. Farley, "Feminist Version of Respect for Persons."

4. Kondrath, *Facing Feelings in Faith Communities*.

5. See, for example, Rendle and Bass, *Holy Conversations*.

References

Alper, Becka A., and Aleksandra Sandstrom. "If the U.S. Had 100 People: Charting Americans' Religious Affiliations." Pew Research Center, http://www.pewresearch.org/fact-tank/2016/11/14/if-the-u-s-had-100 -people-charting-americans-religious-affiliations/.

Ammerman, Nancy Tatom. *Congregation and Community.* New Brunswick, NJ: Rutgers University Press, 1997.

Armentrout, Donald Smith. "Chronology and Bibliography of Lutheran-Episcopal Dialogues." *Sewanee Theological Review* 40, no. 2 (1997): 228–31.

Ashforth, B. E., S. H. Harrison, and K. G. Corley. "Identification in Organizations: An Examination of Four Fundamental Questions." *Journal of Management* 34, no. 3 (2008): 325–74.

Ashforth, Blake E. *Role Transitions in Organizational Life: An Identity-Based Perspective.* Mahwah, NJ: Lawrence Erlbaum Associates, 2001.

Bandy, Thomas G., and Page M. Brooks. *Church Mergers: A Guidebook for Missional Change.* Lanham, MD: Rowman & Littlefield, 2016.

Bass, Diana Butler. *Christianity after Religion: The End of Church and the Birth of a New Spiritual Awakening.* New York: HarperOne, 2012.

———. *Christianity for the Rest of Us: How the Neighborhood Church Is Transforming the Faith.* New York: HarperOne, 2007.

Bass, Richard, ed. *www.congregationalresources.org: A Guide to Resources for Building Congregational Vitality.* Herndon, VA: Alban Institute, 2005.

Becker, Ernest. *The Denial of Death.* New York: Free Press, 1997.

Bendroth, Norman B. *Interim Ministry in Action: A Handbook for Churches in Transition.* Lanham, MD: Rowman & Littlefield, 2018.

Blount, Sally, and Shana Carroll. "Overcome Resistance to Change with Two Conversations." *Harvard Business Review,* May 16, 2017.

Bobbitt, Linda. "Competing Frameworks: How Theoretical and Theological Frameworks Influence Congregational Renewal Efforts and Color External Evaluations." Master's thesis, Luther Seminary, 2017.

———. "Congregational Vitality in the ELCA." Paper presented at the annual convention of the Religious Research Association, Atlanta, 2016.

———. "Creating Shorter Scales to Measure Congregational Vitality." *Review of Religious Research* 58, no. 1 (2016): 183.

Buber, Martin. *The Writings of Martin Buber.* Edited by Will Herberg. New York: Meridian Books, 1956.

Burke, Peter J. "Identity Processes and Social Stress." *American Sociological Review* 56, no. 6 (1991): 836–49.

Cafferata, Gail. "Dignity for Pastors Who Close Churches." *Vital Signs and Statistics*, 2015. https://carducc.wordpress.com/2015/03/30/dignity-for -pastors-who-close-churches/.

———. "Respect, Challenges, and Stress among Protestant Pastors Closing a Church: Structural and Identity Theory Perspectives." *Pastoral Psychology* 66, no. 3 (2017): 311–33.

Calhoun, Lawrence G., and Richard G. Tedeschi, eds. *Handbook of Posttraumatic Growth: Research and Practice.* Mahwah, NJ: Lawrence Erlbaum Associates, 2006.

"Called to Serve: A Study of Clergy Careers, Clergy Wellness, and Clergy Women." Executive Council's Committee on the Status of Women, the Church Pension Fund's Office of Research, the Episcopal Church Center's Office of Women's Ministry, and CREDO Institute Inc., 2009.

Carroll, Jackson W. *God's Potters: Pastoral Leadership and the Shaping of Congregations.* Edited by Becky R. McMillan. Grand Rapids, MI: Wm. B. Eerdmans, 2006.

Chaves, Mark, and Alison Eagle. "Religious Congregations in the 21st Century: A Report from the National Congregations Study Wave III." Duke University, 2016. http://www.soc.duke.edu/natcong/Docs/NCSIII _report_final.pdf.

Chimelis, Ron. "After Decision to Close Our Lady of the Rosary Church in Springfield, Diocese Faces Clash of Loyalty and Faith (Viewpoint)." https://www.masslive.com/opinion/2018/01/diocese_faces_clash_of _loyalty.html.

Clarke, Brian, and Stuart Macdonald. "How Are Canada's Five Largest Protestant Denominations Faring? A Look at the 2001 Census." *Studies in Religion/Sciences Religieuses* 40, no. 4 (2011): 511–34.

Cosgrove, Charles H., and Dennis D. Hatfield. *Church Conflict: The Hidden Systems behind the Fights.* Nashville: Abingdon Press, 1994.

De Wit, Frank R. C., Lindred L. Greer, and Karen A. Jehn. "The Paradox of Intragroup Conflict: A Meta-Analysis." *Journal of Applied Psychology* 97, no. 2 (2012): 360–90.

Doka, Kenneth J. *Disenfranchised Grief: Recognizing Hidden Sorrow.* Lexington, MA: Lexington Books, 1989.

Donne, John. "Now This Bell Tolling Softly for Another, Says to Me: Thou Must Die." In *Devotions Upon Emergent Occasions; and Death's Duel*, 102–4. New York: Random House, 1999.

Doolittle, Benjamin R. "The Impact of Behaviors upon Burnout among Parish-Based Clergy." *Journal of Religion and Health* 49, no. 1 (2010): 88–95.

Dyck, Arthur J. *On Human Care: An Introduction to Ethics.* Nashville: Abingdon Press, 1977.

Ebaugh, Helen Rose Fuchs. *Becoming an Ex: The Process of Role Exit.* Chicago: University of Chicago Press, 1988.

Edgell, Penny. *Congregations in Conflict: Cultural Models of Local Religious Life.* Cambridge: Cambridge University Press, 1999.

Ellison, Christopher G., Neal M. Krause, Bryan C. Shepherd, and Mark A. Chaves. "Size, Conflict, and Opportunities for Interaction: Congregational Effects on Members' Anticipated Support and Negative Interaction." *Journal for the Scientific Study of Religion* 48, no. 1 (2009): 1–15.

Ellison, Christopher G., Lori A. Roalson, Janelle M. Guillory, Kevin J. Flannelly, and John P. Marcum. "Religious Resources, Spiritual Struggles, and Mental Health in a Nationwide Sample of PCUSA Clergy." *Pastoral Psychology* 59, no. 3 (2010): 287–304.

Ellison, Christopher G., Wei Zhang, Neal Krause, and John P. Marcum. "Does Negative Interaction in the Church Increase Psychological Distress? Longitudinal Findings from the Presbyterian Panel Survey." *Sociology of Religion* 70, no. 4 (2009): 409–31.

Episcopal Church. *The Book of Common Prayer and Administration of the Sacraments and Other Rites and Ceremonies of the Church Together with the Psalter or Psalms of David: According to the Use of the Episcopal Church.* New York: Oxford University Press, 2005.

Episcopal News Service. "The Five Marks of Mission: A Checklist for Mission." https://www.episcopalchurch.org/library/article/five-marks-mission-checklist -mission.

Faith Communities Today. "2015 National Study of Congregations." Hartford Institute for Religion Research. http://www.faithcommunitiestoday.org /sites/default/files/Faith-Communities-Today-2015-Final-Survey-with -Frequencies.pdf.

Farley, Margaret A. "A Feminist Version of Respect for Persons." *Journal of Feminist Studies in Religion* 9, nos. 1/2 (Spring–Fall 1993): 183–98.

Farley, Wendy. *The Wounding and Healing of Desire: Weaving Heaven and Earth.* Louisville, KY: Westminster John Knox Press, 2005.

Fleming, David L. *What Is Ignatian Spirituality?* Chicago: Loyola Press, 2008.

Frank, Thomas Edward. "Leadership and Administration: An Emerging Field in Practical Theology." *International Journal of Practical Theology* 10, no. 1 (2006): 113–36.

Friedman, Edwin H. *A Failure of Nerve: Leadership in the Age of the Quick Fix.* New ed. Edited by Margaret M. Treadwell and Edward W. Beal. New York: Seabury Books, 2007.

———. *Generation to Generation: Family Process in Church and Synagogue.* New York: Guilford Press, 1985.

Gaede, Beth Ann, ed. *Ending with Hope: A Resource for Closing Congregations.* Bethesda, MD: Alban Institute, 2002.

General Board of Pension and Health Benefits of the United Methodist Church. "Annual Clergy Health Survey." May 15, 2013.

Gifford, Mary Louise. *The Turnaround Church: Inspiration and Tools for Life-Sustaining Change*. Bethesda, MD: Alban Institute, 2009.

Gilligan, C., R. Spencer, M. K. Weinberg, and T. Bertsch. "On the Listening Guide: A Voice-Centered Relational Method." In *Qualitative Research in Psychology: Expanding Perspectives in Methodology and Design*, edited by P. M. Camic, J. E. Rhodes, and L. Yardley, 157–72. Washington, DC: American Psychological Association Press, 2003.

Gooty, Janaki, Shane Connelly, Jennifer Griffith, and Alka Gupta. "Leadership, Affect, and Emotions: A State of the Science Review." *Leadership Quarterly* 21, no. 6 (2010): 979–1004.

Greene-McCreight, Kathryn. *Darkness Is My Only Companion: A Christian Response to Mental Illness*. Grand Rapids, MI: Brazos Press, 2006.

Guthrie, Julian. *The Grace of Everyday Saints: How a Band of Believers Lost Their Church and Found Their Faith*. Boston: Houghton Mifflin Harcourt, 2011.

Hadaway, C. Kirk. "Episcopal Congregations Overview: Findings from the 2010 Faith Communities Today Survey." Episcopal Church Domestic and Foreign Missionary Society. New York, 2011.

———. "Facts on Growth: 2010." Hartford Institute for Religion Research, Hartford Seminary, 2011.

———. "New Facts on Episcopal Church Growth and Decline." Foreign and Domestic Missionary Society. New York, 2015.

Heifetz, Ronald A. *Leadership without Easy Answers*. Cambridge, MA: Harvard University Press, 1994.

Heifetz, Ronald A., and Marty Linsky. "Leadership on the Line: Staying Alive through the Dangers of Leadership." Boston: Harvard Business School Press, 2002.

Helsel, Philip Browning. "Liminality in Death Care: The Grief-Work of Pastors. " *Journal of Pastoral Care and Counseling* 63, nos. 3–4 (2009).

Hicks, Donna. *Dignity: Its Essential Role in Resolving Conflict*. New Haven, CT: Yale University Press, 2013.

Hilliard, Linda M., and Gretchen J. Switzer. *Finishing with Grace: A Guide to Selling, Merging, or Closing Your Church*. Booklocker.com, 2010.

Hoffacker, Charles. *A Matter of Life and Death: Preaching at Funerals*. Cambridge, MA: Cowley Publications, 2002.

Hoge, Dean R., and Jacqueline E. Wenger. *Pastors in Transition: Why Clergy Leave Local Church Ministry*. Grand Rapids, MI: Wm. B. Eerdmans, 2005.

Illinois Great Rivers Conference of the United Methodist Church. "Creating a New Vision of Church Vitality for the 21st Century Church." http://congregationalvitalitysurvey.com/resources.html.

Irwin, Gail. *Toward the Better Country: Church Closure and Resurrection*. Eugene, OR: Resource Publications, 2014.

James, Molly. *With Joyful Acceptance, Maybe: Developing a Contemporary*

Theology of Suffering in Conversation with Five Christian Thinkers: Gregory the Great, Julian of Norwich, Jeremy Taylor, C. S. Lewis, and Ivone Gebara. Eugene, OR: Wipf and Stock, 2013.

Jones, Carol, William Kandel, and Timothy Parker. "Population Dynamics Are Changing the Profile of Rural Areas." *Amber Waves* 5, no. 2 (2007): 30–35.

Joyce, Adam. "Final Gifts: How Institutions Can Die Well." *Christian Century*, December 26, 2014. https://www.christiancentury.org/article/2014-12/final-gifts.

Kant, Immanuel. *The Metaphysics of Morals.* Cambridge: Cambridge University Press, 1991.

Kelley, Melissa M. *Grief: Contemporary Theory and the Practice of Ministry.* Minneapolis: Fortress Press, 2010.

Kondrath, William M. *Facing Feelings in Faith Communities.* Herndon, VA: Alban Institute, 2013.

Koopman, Nico. "Towards an Ecumenicity of Inclusivity in a Context of Exclusion and Alienation." *Ecumenical Review* 67, no. 4 (2015): 559–71.

Kotlyar, Igor, Leonard Karakowsky, and Peggy Ng. "Leader Behaviors, Conflict and Member Commitment to Team-Generated Decisions." *Leadership Quarterly* 22, no. 4 (2011): 666–79.

Kreiner, G. E., E. C. Hollensbe, and M. L. Sheep. "Where Is the 'Me' among the 'We'? Identity Work and the Search for Optimal Balance." *Academy of Management Journal* 49, no. 5 (2006): 1031–57.

Lawrence. *The Practice of the Presence of God.* Springdale, PA: Whitaker House, 1982.

Lawrence-Lightfoot, Sara. *Respect: An Exploration.* Cambridge, MA: Perseus Books, 2000.

Lawson, Kimberly. "Why You Should Take Time to Mourn during Career Transitions: Grief Is Common When You Leave a Job You Love." *New York Times*, August 23, 2018.

Leas, Speed. *Moving Your Church through Conflict.* Washington, DC: Alban Institute, 1985.

Lipka, Michael. "Which U.S. Religious Groups Are Oldest and Youngest?" In *FACTTANK: News in the Numbers.* Pew Research Center, 2016.

Living Legacy: Church Legacy and Closure Resource. Cleveland: United Church of Christ, 2015.

Lizardi-Hajbi, Kristina. "Gender Pay Gaps for UCC Clergy: Exploring the Numbers." 2016. https://carducc.wordpress.com/2016/01/17/gender-pay-gaps/?c=419#comment-419.

Long, Thomas G. *Accompany Them with Singing: The Christian Funeral.* Louisville, KY: Westminster John Knox Press, 2009.

Mann, Alice. *Can Our Church Live? Redeveloping Congregations in Decline.* Alban Institute, 1999.

McCarroll, Pamela R. *The End of Hope—the Beginning: Narratives of Hope in the Face of Death and Trauma*. Minneapolis: Fortress Press, 2014.

Merton, Thomas. *New Seeds of Contemplation*. Norfolk, CT: New Directions, 1972.

———. *Seasons of Celebration*. New York: Farrar, Straus and Giroux, 1965.

Miller-McLemore, Bonnie J., ed. *The Wiley-Blackwell Companion to Practical Theology*. West Sussex, UK: Wiley-Blackwell, 2012.

Mitchell, Kenneth R. *All Our Losses, All Our Griefs: Resources for Pastoral Care*. Edited by Herbert Anderson. Philadelphia: Westminster Press, 1983.

Moltmann, Jürgen. *In the End—the Beginning: The Life of Hope*. 1st Fortress Press ed. Minneapolis: Fortress Press, 2004.

Moore, Mary Elizabeth. "Purposes of Practical Theology: A Comparative Analysis between United States Practical Theologians and Johannes Van Der Ven." In *Hermeneutics and Empirical Research in Practical Theology: The Contribution of Empirical Theology by Johannes A. Van Der Ven*, edited by Chris A. M. Hermans and Mary Elizabeth Moore, 170–96. Leiden: Brill, 2005.

Olsen, Charles M. *The Wisdom of the Seasons: How the Church Year Helps Us Understand Our Congregational Stories*. Herndon, VA: Alban Institute, 2009.

Olson, Anna B. *Claiming Resurrection in the Dying Church: Freedom beyond Survival*. Louisville, KY: Westminster John Knox Press, 2016.

Owens, L. Roger, and Anthony B. Robinson. "Dark Night of the Church: Relearning the Essentials." *Christian Century* 129, no. 26 (2012): 28–30.

Pargament, K. I., H. G. Koenig, and L. M. Perez. "The Many Methods of Religious Coping: Development and Initial Validation of the RCOPE." *Journal of Clinical Psychology* 56, no. 4 (2000): 519–43.

Parsons, George. *Understanding Your Congregation as a System: The Manual*. Edited by Speed Leas. Bethesda, MD: Alban Institute, 1993.

Paveley, R. "When It Gets Too Much." *Church Times*, April 25, 2008.

Pennington, M. Basil. *Lectio Divina: Renewing the Ancient Practice of Praying the Scriptures*. New York: Crossroad, 1998.

Peterson, Eugene H. *Under the Unpredictable Plant: An Exploration in Vocational Holiness*. Grand Rapids, MI: Wm. B. Eerdmans, 1992.

Petriglieri, Jennifer Louise. "Under Threat: Responses to and the Consequences of Threats to Individuals' Identities." *Academy of Management Review* 36, no. 4 (2011): 641–62.

Peyton, Nigel, and Caroline Gatrell. *Managing Clergy Lives: Obedience, Sacrifice, Intimacy*. London: Bloomsbury, 2013.

———. "The Sacrificial Embrace: Exploring Contemporary English Parish Clergy Lives." *Expository Times* 126, no. 8 (May 1, 2015): 378–88.

Pfeffer, Jeffrey. *Dying for a Paycheck: How Modern Management Harms Employee Health and Company Performance—and What We Can Do about It*. New York: HarperCollins, 2018.

Poling, James N. *Rethinking Faith: A Constructive Practical Theology.* Minneapolis: Fortress Press, 2011.

Pond, Allison, Gregory Smith, and Scott Clement. "Religion among the Millennials." In *Pew Forum on Religion and Public Life*, edited by Louis Lugo. Washington, DC: Pew Research Center, 2010.

Price, Matthew, and Anne Hurst. "The 2014 Church Compensation Report: A National, Provincial, and Diocesan Analysis of Clergy Compensation." New York: Church Pension Group, June 2015.

Proeschold-Bell, Rae Jean, and Jason Byassee. *Faithful and Fractured: Responding to the Clergy Health Crisis.* Edited by Jason Byassee. Grand Rapids, MI: Baker Publishing Group, 2018.

Rambo, Shelly. *Resurrecting Wounds: Living in the Afterlife of Trauma.* Waco, TX: Baylor University Press, 2017.

———. *Spirit and Trauma: A Theology of Remaining.* Louisville, KY: Westminster John Knox Press, 2010.

Reformed Church in America. "Determining a Church's DNA." https://www .rca.org/news/determining-church's-dna.

Rendle, Gilbert R. *Leading Change in the Congregation: Spiritual and Organizational Tools for Leaders.* Lanham, MD: Rowman & Littlefield, 1998.

Rendle, Gilbert R., and Dorothy Bass. *Holy Conversations: Strategic Planning as a Spiritual Practice for Congregations.* Lanham, MD: Rowman & Littlefield, 2003.

Roozen, David. "American Congregations 2015: Thriving and Surviving." 2016. http://www.faithcommunitiestoday.org/sites/default/files/American -Congregations-2015.pdf.

———. "A Decade of Change in American Congregations, 2000–2010." 2010. https://faithcommunitiestoday.org/wp-content/uploads/2019/01/Decade -of-Change-in-American-Congregations.pdf

Rumsey, Andrew. *Parish: An Anglican Theology of Place.* London: SCM Press, 2017.

Schlafer, David J. *What Makes This Day Different? Preaching Grace on Special Occasions.* Cambridge, MA: Cowley Publications, 1998.

Schoen, David. *Facing Your Church's Uncertain Future: Helpful Practices for Courageous Conversations and Faithful Decisions.* Cleveland: United Church of Christ Church Building and Loan Fund, 2018.

Schwartz, Christian, and Christoph Schalk. *Natural Church Development.* St. Charles, IL: ChurchSmart Resources, 1998.

Seitz, John C. *No Closure: Catholic Practice and Boston's Parish Shutdowns.* Cambridge, MA: Harvard University Press, 2011.

Shimron, Yonat. "Legacy Ministries to Dying Churches Give Congregations a Way to End Well." In *Faith and Leadership*, September 5, 2017. https://www .faithandleadership.com/legacy-ministries-dying-churches-give-congregations -way-end-well.

Smith, Greg. "No Religion in U.S." Paper presented at the annual convention of the Religious Research Association, Atlanta, 2016.

Smith, Molly Dale. *Transitional Ministry: A Time of Opportunity*. New York: Church Publishing, 2009.

Society of St. John the Evangelist. "5 Marks of Love." http://www.5marksoflove .org.

Steinke, Peter L. *Congregational Leadership in Anxious Times: Being Calm and Courageous No Matter What*. Herndon, VA: Alban Institute, 2006.

———. *Healthy Congregations: A Systems Approach*. Bethesda, MD: Alban Institute, 2001.

———. *How Your Church Family Works: Understanding Congregations as Emotional Systems*. Lanham, MD: Rowman & Littlefield, 2006.

Stets, Jan E. "Identity Theory." In *Contemporary Social Psychological Theories*, edited by Peter J. Burke, 88–136. Stanford, CA: Stanford Social Sciences, 2006.

Tomberlin, Jim, and Warren Bird. *Better Together: Making Church Mergers Work*. San Francisco: Jossey-Bass, 2012.

Ury, William. *Getting Past No: Negotiating with Difficult People*. New York: Bantam Books, 1991.

U.S. Census Bureau. "U.S. Census Bureau Quickfacts Selected: United States." https://www.census.gov/quickfacts/fact/table/US/AGE275210#viewtop.

Van Quaquebeke, Niels, and Tilman Eckloff. "Defining Respectful Leadership: What It Is, How It Can Be Measured, and Another Glimpse at What It Is Related To." *Journal of Business Ethics* 91, no. 3 (February 2010): 343–58.

Vogel, Linda Jane. *Syncopated Grace: Times and Seasons with God*. Edited by Dwight Vogel. Nashville: Upper Room Books, 2002.

Warren, Yvonne. *The Cracked Pot: The State of Today's Anglican Parish Clergy*. Buxhall, England: Kevin Mayhew, 2002.

Webb-Mitchell, Brett. *Practicing Pilgrimage: On Being and Becoming God's Pilgrim People*. Eugene, OR: Cascade Books, 2016.

Weber, Max. *Economy and Society: An Outline of Interpretive Sociology*. Edited by Guenther Roth and Claus Wittich. Berkeley, CA: Berkeley University Press, 1978.

World Café Community Foundation. "The World Cafe." http://www .theworldcafe.com/.

World Council of Churches, Commission on Faith and Order. *Baptism, Eucharist and Ministry, 1982–1990: Report on the Process and Responses*. Geneva, Switzerland: WCC Publications, 1990.

Wright, Vinita Hampton. "The Inner Process of Letting Go." http://www .ignatianspirituality.com/24471/inner-process-of-letting-go.

Zscheile, Dwight J. *The Agile Church: Spirit-Led Innovation in an Uncertain Age*. New York: Morehouse Publishing, 2014.

CPSIA information can be obtained
at www.ICGtesting.com
Printed in the USA
FSHW020844220120
66320FS

9 780664 264987